{ GRAPHIC
DESIGN }

AUSTRALIAN**STYLE**MANUAL

To Lissa and Cayenne, to Australian designers past,
and to the sweat of those to come.

Andrew Barnum

To Haddocks x 3.

Suzie Haddock

To Bob, Megan, Knuckles and Dutch.
My heart, my brain and my wagging tails.

Astred Hicks

To my very patient family;
Kate, Stephanie and Eleanor.

Felix Oppen

{GRAPHIC}
DESIGN
AUSTRALIAN**STYLE**MANUAL

ANDREW **BARNUM**   SUZIE **HADDOCK**   ASTRED **HICKS**   FELIX **OPPEN**

The **McGraw·Hill** Companies

Sydney New York San Francisco Auckland
Bangkok Bogotá Caracas Hong Kong
Kuala Lumpur Lisbon London Madrid
Mexico City Milan New Delhi San Juan
Seoul Singapore Taipei Toronto

Reprinted 2012, 2015, 2021

National Library of Australia Cataloguing-in-Publication Data

Title:	Graphic design : Australian style manual / Andrew Townley Barnum ... [et al.].
ISBN:	9780071011051 (pbk.)
Notes:	Includes index.
Subjects:	Graphic arts--Australia--Handbooks, manuals, etc.
Other Authors/ Contributors:	Barnum, Andrew Townley.
Dewey Number:	760

Published in Australia by
McGraw-Hill Australia Pty Ltd
Level 33, 680 George Street, Sydney NSW 2000
Publisher: Norma Angeloni Tomaras
Editorial coordinator: Carolina Pomilio
Senior production editor: Yani Silvana
Permissions editor: Haidi Bernhardt
Copy editor: Laura Davies
Proofreader: Kathryn Fairfax
Indexer: Shelley Barons
Art direction and cover design: Astred Hicks
Cover illustrator: James Gulliver Hancock, The Jacky Winter Group
Internal design and typesetting: Em&Jon Design
Typeset in Karbon, Tiempos and Terital
Printed in Australia by SOS Print + Media

FOREWORD

{Graphic Design} Australian Style Manual is a proud labour of love in its diligent and steadfast pursuit of meaningful, relevant and contemporary resources from both the design and the Australian/New Zealand perspective. Not only does this textbook have sound educational content, but also it speaks with a distinctly Australian voice.

Australia embodies physical and historical characteristics that cannot be found anywhere else in the world, including the influence of its ancient Indigenous culture. These characteristics have impacted on how its inhabitants see and communicate among themselves and with other communities—and over time, a recognisable sense of Australian identity has evolved.

However, as markets become more global and information more accessible, cultural identity and practice within our societies are in danger of increasing homogenisation—the Ikea bookshelf looks just as comfortable in Shanghai as in Sydney!

In this converging landscape, Australia wants its voice to be clearly heard. *{Graphic Design}* does just that. It showcases Australian and New Zealand style—the range of attitudes and aspirations, the way design is created, viewed and experienced— and talent, both emerging and established. It also provides a platform for stimulating cultural discourse, confident in the knowledge of our design standing in relation to the rest of the world.

The chapters on the basic principles of graphic design—colour theory, typography, print and grids—are comprehensive and well documented, with supportive illustrations. Theories and fundamentals of design thinking, research processes, production techniques and professional relationships are discussed in a practical way, and key terms in each chapter—including tools for communicating with illustrators and printers—are collected in a glossary at the back of the book.

The designer or studio 'spotlight' case studies in each chapter provide a revealing window into the world of the design professional. These insights serve as inspiration and encouragement to aspiring designers, of whom there are now higher expectations than ever before.

As the book has rightly emphasised, 'ideas and innovation are where the currency lies now' for new young professionals in the 'creative age'. 'Clients are interested in innovation, adding value to their products and generating an edge or niche in a shifting marketplace. Designers must be prepared to produce ideas that respond to this need.'

I couldn't agree more.

Not only is the graphic designer expected to question, think, plan, do, make, collaborate, speak, manage and present ideas, but also she or he must walk the fine line between safety and risk in order to contribute and add value in an innovative, responsible way to a sustainable future for clients and the community. It's not enough to be just 'doing it'; it must also be about 'doing good'.

{Graphic Design} Australian Style Manual makes a huge contribution to teaching and stimulating graphic design students on this exciting and challenging journey. In the words of Kenneth Grange, co-founder of Pentagram, 'a life in design is to be constantly inquisitive and a love of the job is an absolute prerequisite'.

Congratulations to the team for initiating and delivering this invaluable resource, a uniquely Australian-focused graphic design textbook. The authors' love of their work will pay dividends for those who share in this journey.

Rita Siow
AGDA Executive Director

V

CONTENTS

01 : *design and its audience*

02 : *conceptualising and process*

03 : *colour, elements and illustration*

04 : *typography*

05: *print design*

06: *pre-press and print*

07: *digital design*

08: *three-dimensional design*

09: *studying and beyond*

ABOUT THE AUTHORS

RUTHLESS PHOTOS

ANDREW BARNUM

Andrew Barnum is a Sydney-based designer, design educator and artist (singer–songwriter, poet and painter) who holds an Associate Diploma Arts/Graphic Arts from Royal Melbourne Institute of Technology and a Master of Arts (Research) from the faculty of Arts and Social Sciences at University of Technology, Sydney (UTS). He has been a design educator since 1999, when he started lecturing for both Billy Blue and UTS Viscom.

Since 2006, he has been Head of College at the Billy Blue College of Design, responsible for Billy Blue's shift to delivering Bachelor of Applied Design degrees in the higher education sector.

With his wife Lissa, he is a partner of The Barnum Group, which has been communications designer for corporations (Macquarie Bank, Ord Minnett, HongKong Bank, Sydney Futures Exchange), community (Clean up the world, Clean up Australia) and the arts (Sydney Dance Company, Bloomers, Art Bank) in Sydney since 1981, when they relocated from Los Angeles.

The Barnum Group has won AGDA awards and Hollywood Reporter Foreign Press awards, and has been highly commended by the Australian Publishers Association Book Design Awards for the book *Girlosophy*. The Barnums had video-music hits as electropop duo Vitabeats in the 1980s, and since then Andrew has produced four original solo albums, the most recent being the double CD/book *Feed the Clouds—The Interactive Songbook*, featuring the work of 25 artists and illustrators.

Andrew is a member of AGDA and APRA/AMCOS.

SUZIE HADDOCK

RUTHLESS PHOTOS

After working in the graphic design and communications industry in Sydney, Melbourne, Perth and London for 20 years, specialising in tourism, conservation and packaging design, Suzie became an academic. Teaching and managing in both the vocational education and higher education sectors has allowed Suzie to gain a wealth of knowledge of the design industry, as well as management and teaching practice. To supplement this knowledge Suzie has a Master of Arts (print media), an Executive Masters of Business Administration and a Graduate Diploma of Vocational Education. Suzie has written on design practice for a number of Australian publications. She currently holds the position of Academic Manager at JMC Academy.

ASTRED HICKS

Astred Hicks is a Sydney-based graphic designer whose freelance business Design Cherry specialises in book design. Since being awarded an Advanced Diploma in Graphic Design from the Design Centre Enmore (Sydney Institute TAFE NSW) in 2001, Astred has worked with a number of publishers, most recently McGraw-Hill Education, where she was Art Director for three years. She was featured in *Curvy 4* and her work has appeared in the publications *Curvy* and *Curvy 2* and the magazines *Empty, Desktop, Desktop Graphics* and *Noise*.

In the Australian Publishers Association Book Design Awards Astred has been Commended and Highly Commended for her design and art direction for several years running. An active member of Australia's online design community, Astred is a vocal advocate for women in the industry and was the founder of Nest Collective, an online site created to promote and inspire female designers.

Astred strongly believes in passing on her knowledge, experience and love of design to early career designers, and she lectures in VET Design Fundamentals at Billy Blue College of Design.

RUTHLESS PHOTOS

FELIX OPPEN

Felix's family has historically been involved in forestry, arms sales, shipping, baking, civil engineering and printmaking (and other visual arts) on his father's side, and on his mother's side printing (newspapers and books). He himself has studied chemical engineering, inorganic chemistry, German, some French and Italian and economics before finally settling down to study graphic design at Billy Blue. During the mid-2000s he also completed a Masters of Design at UTS.

In addition to being involved with three graphic design businesses during his career, he has also worked as a barman, and as a clerk in a courthouse. Felix's first contact with design was seeing his grandmother's woodblock prints (mostly bookplates and some book illustrations) and later mucking about on an old Heidelberg platen press, printing hot metal linotype slugs in reflex blue (the only colour available). He has a growing interest in typography and letterpress.

RUTHLESS PHOTOS

ACKNOWLEDGMENTS

The authors would like to acknowledge the support from the Australian and New Zealand graphic design community, without which this book would not have been possible. Thank you to all the generous designers who have given us their work to display, time to be interviewed and ideas to explore.

In particular the authors would like to thank the following people:

Rita Siow, AGDA

Justin Fox and Damien Aistrope,
   Australian Infront

Lara Burke, frankie magazine

Dean Poole, Alt Group

James de Vries, de Luxe & Associates

Beci Orpin

Jeremy Wortsman,
   the Jacky Winter group

Kris Sowersby, Klim Type Foundry

Wayne Thompson,
   Australian Type Foundry

Rueben Crossman

Campbell Milligan, Monster Children

Rod Wade, Finsbury Green

Bronwen Black, Spicers Paper

Brad Eldridge, Soap Creative

Alister Coyne, Hairy Cow

Sophie Tatlow, Deuce Design

Neil Turner, Turner Design

Vince Frost, Frost* Design

3 Deep Design

Aldous Massie

Angus Jones

Andrew Ashton, Studio Pip and Co.

Billy Blue College of Design, academic
   leaders, educators and students

Canyon

Clinton Duncan

Daniel Elliot and Henry Luong,
   Organ Studio

Design Cherry

Eamo Donnelly

Eyesaw

Floating World

Iain Blair, AMCOR

Ian Chong, de Luxe & Associates

Image Mechanics

Ivana Martinovic

Jackson Dickie

Jadwiga Jarvis, Wayzgoose Press

Jens Hertzum, XYZ networks

Jeremy Saunders

Josh Logue, Mathematics

Kat Cameron, Team Kitten

Kevin Finn, Finn Creative

Lauren Carney

Linda Brainwood

Lissa Barnum, The Barnum Group Design

Louise Hawson, 52 Suburbs

Luci Everett

Lucy Feagins, The Design Files

Marc Martin

Marcela Restrepo

Matthew Remphre, Parallax Design

Megan Hicks

Michael Longton

Nathanael Jeanneret

Naughtyfish

Nick Hore, Animal Logic

Paul Mosig, Racket

Paul Tooth, Seeder House

Peter Campbell, CampbellBarnett

Pixel Fusion

Rena Jones

Rhett Dashwood

Simon Hipgrave, The Hungry Workshop

Something Splendid

Sonny Day and Biddy Maroney,
   We Buy Your Kids

Stephen Banham, Letterbox

Studio Round

Suzy Tuxen, A Friend of Mine

Tequilia

Toby Fraser, The Fox and King

Umeric

Zoe Walton, Random House Australia

Nic Cary, Studio Verse

Zann St Pierre

Thanks to the staff at McGraw-Hill Education: general manager PAVE Eiko Bron, publisher Norma Angeloni Tomaras, senior production editor Yani Silvana and permissions editor Haidi Bernhardt, as well as freelance designers Em & Jon Design.

We would also like to thank all the teachers who contributed to the development of this first edition text, assisted in its development by providing feedback on the original concept, and took the time to review the manuscript. They include:

Graphic Design Section, TAFE NSW, Campbelltown Campus

Jim Brodie, Southbank TAFE

Jane Connory, Holmesglen

Jen Webb, Grenadi School of Design

Lee Ingram, Curtin University of Technology

Lesley Redgate, TAFE SA

Jose Rodriguez, Gordon Institute of TAFE

Emma Fisher, RMIT University

Jeffrey Walter, Tasmanian Polytechnic

Mark Hilton, Charles Darwin University

Suzie Zezula, RMIT

The authors acknowledge the long line of design professionals who have contributed to the manifestation of Australian design culture that is now made evident through this book, and encourage the future designers it aims to spawn.

Lastly, we would like to acknowledge the critical support provided by our co-authors in the structure and intent of this book.

CONTRIBUTORS

Dylan Davis is a digital design lecturer at Swinburne University's Faculty of Design. He has worked in digital media for more than 15 years in Australia and the UK. Dylan has created a number multimedia artworks that have been exhibited around the world, most notably ACMI Melbourne, File Festival Sao Paulo, Brazil, and Soundtoys.net exhibition, London, UK.

Dr Zoë Sadokierski is a print designer and illustrator who lectures in the School of Design at the University of Technology, Sydney. Her favourite colours are red and stripes. Zoë authored the margin exercises on pages 81, 83, 85, 90, 94, 110 and the design brief on page 112.

E-STUDENT/E-INSTRUCTOR

E-STUDENT

OLC

The Online Learning Centre (OLC) that accompanies this text helps you get the most from your course. It provides a powerful learning experience beyond the printed page. Instructors have access to an additional instructor-specific resource area.

www.mhhe.com/au/graphicdesign

Teaching notes

Teaching notes provide further activities, examples, class discussion questions and reading for each chapter. These will assist instructors in creating valuable lessons.

Design brief templates

A series of design brief templates that students will find useful in completing practice assignments is provided.

E-INSTRUCTOR

Artwork library

In addition to the student resources, instructors have password-protected access to an online artwork library, where the illustrations from the text are available as digital image files. Instructors thus have the flexibility to use the illustrations in the format that best suits their needs.

INTRODUCTION

Inside this book you will find the tools you need to start your career as a graphic designer.

The content has been compiled and written as a starting point to introduce the principles of theoretical and practical graphic design. Our aim has been to give you a grounding in the world of design and provide a springboard for further research into areas of interest. This is by no means the only graphic design book you will ever need to own, but it should be one of the first.

As well as being a practical book, *{Graphic Design} Australian Style Manual* is also a showcase of the local talent currently exploding in Australia and New Zealand.

As design professionals, we realised there was a noticeable absence of practical textbooks with an Australian focus. While there are publications out there showcasing local talent, no other book examined Australian culture alongside the principles of graphic design. This book is unique in its outlook as we believe that Australians and New Zealanders have a different perspective in certain contexts, thanks to our culture and humour, and the remoteness that we once experienced. On the other hand, in many instances we respond to design just as people in other countries do.

One example of our uniqueness is that, on average, people in Australia spend more time social networking per month than in any other country. This is just one indicator of how digitally savvy we are. As a consequence we are hungry for innovation in digital design. It is important to recognise such differences—understanding them helps graphic designers create better work not only for local clients, but for international clients as well.

← Eamo Donnelly's personal style cheekily explores native flora, fauna and national icons, mixed with suburban characters of his childhood.

Illustrator **EAMO DONNELLY**
Client **THE JACKY WINTER GROUP**

'I think people are becoming more exposed and educated to design on a daily basis. We are a fast-growing consumer society, and people are becoming more aware of the power of branding and advertising. It is therefore making it even more challenging as a graphic designer to create a product that will catch your attention long enough for you to pick it up. Consumers ... are also expecting more from publishers so I think it will be an interesting time for physical book design in Australia, particularly with the emerging demand for media-rich digital publications.'

REUBEN CROSSMAN, BOOK DESIGNER

(SEE THE PROCESS SPOTLIGHT ON REUBEN CROSSMAN IN CHAPTER 5, PAGES 170–171)

No longer happy to stand on the shore and wait for the next big thing to arrive, Australian designers are shifting their perspective and looking inwards. This is particularly evident in the work currently being produced for the arts, entertainment and cultural industries. Theatre productions, movies, book covers, CD art, local music and culture festivals are all areas where a distinctive Australian graphic style is prevalent. It is a style that is characterised by a sense of place, cheeky wit and a relaxed sense of humour, often with darker undertones as well.

Graphic design is an international language born out of history, as you will learn in Chapter 1, 'Design and its audience'. Australian design has 'ripened' over recent years to the point where we are producing work that is naturally Australian. While the work still contains international traditions and constraints, it also filters international standards through our own lens. This book says to all students, educators and designers, 'You have inherited your own traditions as well as the world's'.

The last two decades have seen a meteoric rise in the formation of an Australian graphic identity. While that identity is young it is also determined and resilient. Its influences date to the 1970s and 1980s with designers like Ken Cato, Gary Emery and Barry Tucker, continuing with a number of Australian filmmakers, and with pioneers of Australian iconography like Jenny Kee, Ken Done, Mambo and Weiss. Some of these people's work may seem outdated now, but it was their exploration of an Australian cultural identity that forged the way for designers of today.

In 2001, after spending six months in Australia, Rick Poynor set about uncovering our design identity in a special issue of his *Eye Magazine*. The basis for that issue was, he says, 'disbelief that such a remarkable and fascinating country could be so quiet in a graphic sense and … a hunch that there was more going on than met the eye'. His hunch was right but he concluded that, to be successful in both the local and international markets, committed Australian designers will have to 'prise open [overlooked] spaces, negotiate relationships with sympathetic collaborators and offer alternative forms of culture'.

'Australians are more sophisticated than our mass media would have us believe, and they notice and appreciate when anything creative is done well.'

WAYNE THOMPSON, TYPOGRAPHER (SEE THE PROCESS SPOTLIGHT ON WAYNE THOMPSON IN CHAPTER 4, PAGES 122–123)

This textbook is in part a response to Poynor's observations. *{Graphic Design} Australian Style Manual* confidently showcases a range of original and world-worthy examples of illustration, corporate identity, publication, packaging, web, three-dimensional and interactive, photography and typography. Its intention is to give young designers the grounding they will need to meet new challenges as Australia's design identity evolves.

As the Australian graphic design community grows—and as you become a part of that swell—so too will the role of collaboration. Gone are the days of the 'rock star' designer working alone. Designers are joining together to create, learn and share. Collectives where freelance designers work together in one studio and collaborate on projects are being set up more frequently. With collaboration comes a growing sense of community and opportunities to experiment and brainstorm new trends and styles. This exciting development has a knock-on effect as graphic designers gain the confidence to form collaborations with their clients, building trust and better creative outcomes.

This is the changing face of the graphic design community, both in Australia and internationally. Thanks to new technologies, borders are broken down as people on opposite sides of the world become digital neighbours. As the world becomes smaller, trends are spreading more quickly than ever. And you will have the chance to influence what is happening.

CONTENT

Graphic design is always changing and evolving, so in this book we try to provide grounding in the principles of design and guidance on how to approach problem solving in a way that is sometimes referred to as 'design thinking'. These are the elements that form the foundations of graphic design. While trends may come and go, fundamentals such as colour and type theory have remained the same for quite some time.

The content has been developed so the book can be used as a stand-alone text or combined with other readings and information from lecturers. It is a learning tool for creative problem solving. Each chapter will help you understand the building blocks of one topic and introduce you to the associated vocabulary. You will use these building blocks, not only as the basis for creating designs, but also when you are explaining—or 'rationalising'—your designs. Rationalisation is a skill that you will need, both as a student and in your later professional life.

Topics covered include:

- understanding your audience and how to effectively reach them
- conceptualisation and problem solving
- the emotional power of colour
- the usefulness of clever typography
- appreciation of the grid and print layout
- developing relationships with printers and understanding print technique
- information structures and the new design principles of digital design
- issues in three-dimensional design, such as packaging and signage
- what to expect when you graduate and how to begin your life as a design professional.

Exercises

Margin exercises are scattered throughout each chapter. These quick exercises have been created to help students put theory into practice and to aid learning. At the end of each chapter there is a larger project in the form of a design brief that incorporates the learning from the chapter text and margin exercises. Your lecturer may choose to set these briefs as student assignments. But whether or not your lecturer specifically asks you to, it is a good idea to work through the exercises as a way of reinforcing what you have learnt and finding out which parts of the chapter you may need to revise.

Process and Profile features

Each chapter contains a Process spotlight and a Profile spotlight. These showcase a selection of the most talented and inspiring designers in Australia and New Zealand today. Profile spotlights explore the background and identity of a designer, looking at how they got their start and how their journey in the design industry has progressed. Process spotlights concentrate on the technique of a designer, exploring how they develop their projects. These features have been created to introduce students to real people in the Australian and New Zealand design community and provide an insight into their lives as designers.

References

Poynor, R 2001, 'Look inward: graphic design in Australia', *Eye Magazine*,
www.eyemagazine.com/feature.php?id=77&fid=440

'Australian audiences are extremely receptive to design in general. In this day and age of frequent international travel and exploration, with the incredible networking available through the internet, I feel the world as such has become smaller. Everything is accessible. Trends are spotted quickly and go nearly as fast as they come.'

LARA BURKE, *FRANKIE* MAGAZINE
(SEE THE PROCESS SPOTLIGHT ON
FRANKIE MAGAZINE IN CHAPTER 1,
PAGES 24–25)

chapter 7

DESIGN AND ITS AUDIENCE

INTRODUCTION

During graphic design's brief history as a widely respected and influential design discipline, its audience has expanded and evolved in response to social, commercial, environmental and technological change around the world.

The commercial conditions within which graphic designers work have radically shifted in recent times. This chapter seeks to illustrate key aspects of the designer's thinking and practice in relation to the audiences of design today.

Graphic design, now recognised as a specialisation of the broadly defined communication design field, is a profession bound in complex and creative problem-solving processes, combined with visual communication artistry and craft. To sustain a career in the design profession a practitioner is required to think (strategically, commercially, conceptually) and make (artistry, craft, materials, objects).

Designers need to have an insatiable hunger for what is going on in the world (in political, social and commercial contexts). They must be able to maintain a sociable, service-orientated, 'can-do' attitude throughout the conversation and negotiation that is the modern design process. A rigorous design process will generate meaningful, innovative design objects and materials.

CHAPTER OVERVIEW

The evolution of Australian graphic design

The role of the designer

Changed conditions: a quantum shift in consumer behaviour

The evolving designer

A closer look at the audience of design

Responding to the new designer/client/ audience conditions

Myself, my client, my profession

PROCESS:
frankie magazine

PROFILE:
Australian INfront

'Meere was one of a group of Sydney artists whose work modernised classical artistic traditions as a means of imaging national life during the inter-war period. The epitome of his vision by the late 1930s is *Australian Beach Pattern* ... Perennially popular, the painting has contributed more than any other in Australian art towards the myth of the healthy young nation as told through the metaphor of the tanned god-like body of the sunbather.'

THE EVOLUTION OF AUSTRALIAN GRAPHIC DESIGN

To understand the nature of graphic design and its many audiences, we should first turn to its humble beginnings as a discipline and its unique identity as an 'applied' art.

THE HISTORY OF GRAPHIC DESIGN

The term 'graphic design' as a descriptor for an objective-based form of visual communication was first used in 1922 by American William Addison Dwiggins (1880–1956). Dwiggins coined the term to describe his various activities in printed communications, such as book design, illustration, typography, lettering and calligraphy. The term did not achieve widespread usage until after World War II.

While the roots of graphic design were primarily print-based, today the discipline has been radically expanded into a range of digital extensions and expressions. The key elements of graphic design apply as much to animation, video games and numerous digital media applications as they do to the world of print.

During the rise of advertising in the 1950s, then primarily print-based, the creative who visualised ideas to appear as advertisements in newspapers or magazines was called a 'commercial artist'. This term described individuals with art-based training in drawing and

← Charles Meere,
Australian Beach Pattern, 1940
Oil on canvas, 91.5 x 122 cm
Purchased 1965

Collection **ART GALLERY OF NSW**
Copyright **CHARLES MEERE ESTATE**

→ *Australia Boomerang*. Gert Sellheim was born in Estonia and migrated to Australia in 1926. Sellheim designed the famous flying kangaroo symbol for Qantas, as well as the two-shilling 'Aboriginal Art' stamp in 1948.

Designer **GERT SELLHEIM**
(1901–1970)
Client **TOURISM AUSTRALIA**

← These posters reflect a surrealist approach to travel within Australia.

Designer **RONALD CLAYTON SKATE**
Client **ANA**

↙ It's November 1965: in the Australian magazine *Woman's Day*, surf's up, and these girls are 'walkin' the nose' at Bondi.

Client **BERLEI**

painting who could apply their skills in the commercial service of advertisers and their customers. The commercial artist's additional graphic design skills included an understanding of typography and lettering, technical print processes and image technologies such as illustration and photography.

It was during the 1950s that the term 'graphic designer' earned currency, as designers began to apply their skills to the new frontiers of 'corporate identity'. To build such an identity for their client, designers employed symbols and logotypes in a broadly distributed system of colour and typography; continued usage created a memorable signpost to a company's 'brand' values.

The audience of graphic design in the years after World War II was mainly in advertising, corporate identity and packaging. This equated to newspapers and magazines, corporate communications and supermarkets and neighbourhood stores. Companies were creating and marketing products for the growing 'mass market' that was a hallmark of advanced consumer societies in the 1950s and 1960s.

In Australia, the late 1970s and early 1980s was a breakthrough period for the recognition of 'local' graphic designers in Sydney and Melbourne. The use of symbols and marks to identify leading companies and events became a hallmark of commercial culture in the 1980s and placed Australian design within an international graphic design culture.

↓ The cover illustration of the book *Symbols of Australia*, an overview of iconic symbols and images of products from Australia's earliest history.

Designer **MIMMO COZZOLINO**
Client **PENGUIN BOOKS**

→ *Iconic Australian logos.*
Top to bottom

Designer **CATO DESIGN**
Client **COMMONWEALTH BANK**

Designer **BRYCE MINALE**
Client **TATTERSFIELD AUSTRALIAN BIENNALE 1988**

Designer **MAIN IMAGE HULSBOSCH; FROM TOP RIGHT: GERT SELLHEIM, LUNN DYER**
Client **QANTAS**

Designer **LUNN DYER**
Client **ROADS AND TRAFFIC AUTHORITY (RTA)**

Designer **BARNUM GROUP**
Client **SYDNEY FESTIVAL**

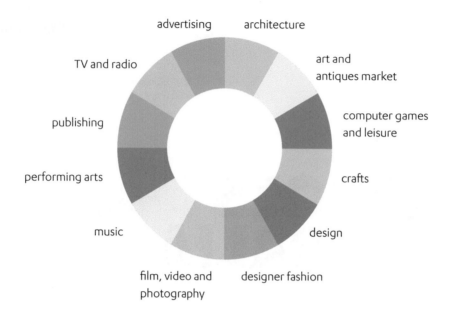

advertising

architecture

TV and radio

art and
antiques market

computer games
and leisure

publishing

crafts

performing arts

design

music

designer fashion

film, video and
photography

← The segments of the creative
industries sector

THE CREATIVE INDUSTRIES DISCOURSE: 'WHAT AM I NOW A PART OF?'

It is crucial to understand the historical shift that has occurred in graphic design through the formation of what is now called the 'creative industries'. This refers to a vast array of individuals working in one of 13 so-called 'creative' fields: advertising, architecture, arts and antiques market, crafts, design, designer fashion, film, interactive media software (computer games), music, performing arts, publishing, television and radio.

A professional shift has taken place in graphic design. With the growth of the creative industries, design practitioners need to broaden and diversify their practice: they are no longer the lone craftsperson working in a production line. Rather, theirs is a networked, collaborative process.

The creative industries 'idea' was developed in the late 1990s by the Blair Government in the UK and represented a policy shift where the above groups of practitioners were 'measured' as a vital economic force within the broad economy. The policy initiative was reflected the idea that:

'[creative industries] have their origin in individual creativity, skill and talent and ... have a potential for wealth and job creation through the generation and exploitation of intellectual property.'

UK Creative Industries Task Force, 1997

This policy initiative aimed to provide a greater degree of certainty for individuals seeking to sustain a meaningful and profitable livelihood from a personal and passionate ideas-driven vocation. It is important to understand that, for designers, this move towards working as an individual in a networked, collaborative way has generated new social and commercial conditions that require new understanding, flexibility and education.

The creative industries idea embodies a shift from a purely crafted, product-driven industry to a knowledge-based economy where the true currency and value is the idea, as well as the product. Ideas and innovation are where the currency lies today. New products and production will only flow out of these innovative approaches and their resulting breakthroughs. As a young designer, it is fundamentally crucial that you are able to respond to these fast-emerging conditions.

SUSTAINING THE FUTURE: THE COLLABORATIVE NETWORK APPROACH

Graphic design is a professional landscape where your resources and network of colleagues are a measure of your potential for innovation and output. As a designer, you must concentrate on building a collaborative enterprise to produce genuine sparks of innovation for the communication media industries. The myth of the lone practitioner is quickly becoming outmoded.

We are all still dependent on individual impulses and inspirations, but the real breakthroughs come through the combination of ideas. Today, generating ideas is very much a team effort: a rigorous, energetic dialogue between designer, client and audience is needed to produce a range of ideas for consideration. A tangible network of design all-rounders and specialists who can respond to the scale and scope of new design challenges is an essential part of the young designer's new toolkit.

The audiences of design exist in traditional markets like neighbourhood shops, supermarkets and shopping malls where people like to interact both socially and as consumers. Then there are community and political spheres, where communication of policy messages and initiatives are generated and distributed. These communication campaigns tend to be deeply personal and require specific sensitivity and appropriate media choices. Finally, there is the broad area of arts and entertainment, where design can bridge the gap between consumer audiences and the cultural work of artists.

All these audiences now interact with design work made for:

- print: advertising, newspapers, magazines, brochures, books, posters, flyers, stationery
- packaging: packages, labels, containers, display, point-of-sale
- branded environment: events, signage, way-finding, pop-up stores, retail, exhibition
- electronic media: radio, television, cable networks
- internet: websites, email, interactive animation, e-commerce
- interactive game design: PlayStation, Xbox, Wii.

→ Sydney Design is one of the world's longest running international design festivals. For two weeks, local and international designers showcase work and ideas across Sydney, opening up dialogue and inspiration for design across a range of disciplines.

Designer **BOCCALATTE**
Client **POWERHOUSE MUSEUM**

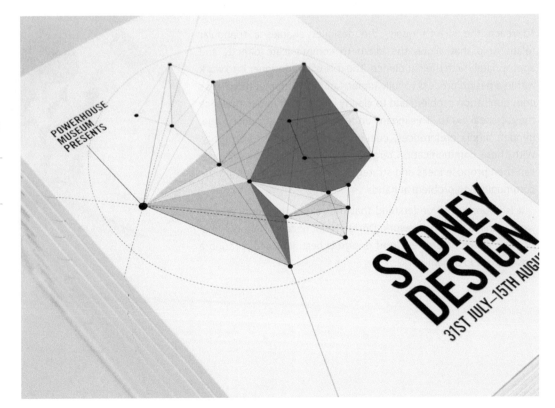

THE ROLE OF THE DESIGNER

The designer's role today is to act as a conduit of ideas and strategies to achieve the objectives of a client; to work closely with a client to *speak with imagination* to a clearly identified audience.

The client's audience might be:

❯ commercial (products or services for sale to the public)

❯ social (community service, religion, public or personal initiatives)

❯ political (government, public health, the environment)

❯ arts-related (promotion and awareness of artists and their communities).

DESIGNER, CLIENT, AUDIENCE: A TRIANGULAR RELATIONSHIP

To reach the client's goals, the designer enables a triangular relationship that allows the client to communicate directly and appropriately with their audience. The role of the designer is to work within a design process to fully understand the scope of the client's communication problem and to clearly identify the target audience they're speaking to. This means understanding the audience's age, gender, media preferences, culture, lifestyle habits and ethnicity. With these communication targets fully understood, the designer can then propose ideas and strategies to work towards solving the communication problem at hand.

It is important to understand that the role of the designer is to work within a team framework. Design is not necessarily about 'me' or what 'I' like or dislike. Good design is best achieved through a positive group dynamic.

↑ Wit, irony and Australian cultural sport referencing combine to create this 'alternative' program cover for a Brisbane music and arts festival.

Designer **CUTTS CREATIVE**
Client **LIVID FESTIVAL**

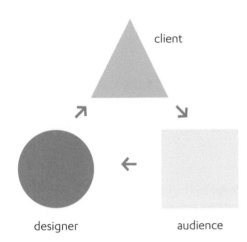

client

designer

audience

Tjukurrpa
Philosophy
Religion
Law

Ngura
Country
Place
Home

You
Body
Thought
Emotion
Spirit

Spirit
Soul
Psyche

Kurunpa

Walytja
Family
Kinship
Relationships

Kanyini Foundation

Kanyini is the Australian Indigenous principle of connectedness that underpins Aboriginal life. It represents an intimate relationship between Tjukurrpa, Ngura, Walytja and Kurunpa that is nurtured through caring and practising responsibility for all things.

↑ The designer's triangular relationship.

→ This Australian cultural initiative investigates languages and conversations within an Aboriginal context. The constraints of cultural understanding require restraint and sensitivity in translating the ideas alive in these cultures.

Designer **MARK GOWING DESIGN**
Client **THE KANYINI FOUNDATION**

Art versus design

To work as a graphic designer it is important to recognise the distinction between art and design. The clear difference between the process of design and the making of art lies in the objective.

A person does not give up their love of making art by becoming a designer; they just have to employ it in the service of communication with a client and their audience. The object is to make a beautifully designed communication object (print, packaging, web, interactive, illustration or animation) that is still brimming with individual expression and group effort.

Designers are not artists in the pure discipline sense. Designers might simultaneously engage in both art and design practices, but designing involves both the analysis and the validation of ideas (Martin, 2009, p. 55); its objective is certainly not art making. Design is a discipline where, through repeated stages of processing and gathering ideas, the creation of rough **prototypes** or **mock-ups** and the generation of feedback, we arrive at that rare object: a communication solution that contains aesthetic harmony, inspirational graphic techniques and a voice that's appropriate to the objective within the brief—something that looks good, sounds good and generates the right reaction.

A **prototype** is a 3-D, 'close-to-finished' version of a proposed design for research or user testing.

A **mock-up** is a print or screen-based 'rough' version of a proposed design, used when seeking approval for production.

→ Collider created a 'beautiful machine' as a central image and TV commercial spot for this promotional campaign for Qantas's Spirit of Youth Awards (SOYA). This image/real-life animation illustrated the creativity and imaginative possibilities for potential applicants and their submissions.

Designer **ANDREW VAN DER WESTHUYZEN, COLLIDER**
Client **QANTAS SPIRIT OF YOUTH AWARDS**

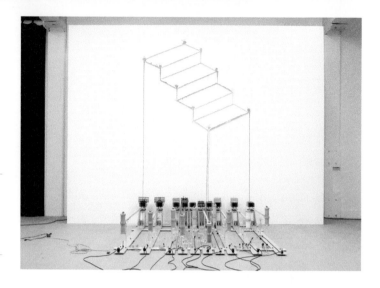

Working within constraints

The designer's aim is to combine a group of elements, content and research into a potent and memorable outcome within constraints set by the client and the audience. This is never easy, and the success rate is also inconsistent, depending on the working chemistry the designer has with the client.

A designer works within the following constraints:

- communication objective and strategy
- target audience
- media channels
- time frame
- budget.

Achieving great results within constraints almost defines the work of graphic designing. The design brief provides the constraints in which we generate ideas to solve a problem in an impactful and appropriate way.

Design incorporates both problem solving and the creation of an exciting, aesthetic object or use of media. A client comes to a designer with a complex web of personal, social and commercial problems. Clients also bring their likes, dislikes, prejudices, social conditioning and fear of the design process. This is a deeply human experience where people are in a state of confusion and change. Your client might be moving their business, starting a new one or producing a 'do-or-die' campaign to save a failing one. The energy created by these circumstances is very real. An understanding of people's reality is a serious part of the process of designing. One of the hallmarks of good designers is the ability to ease tensions in the circumstances surrounding a project in order to allow ideas and strategies to flow. Like a visual mechanic, we get under the bonnet of the design challenge and try to make that engine hum and produce a pleasing mix of graphic emissions.

TRADITIONAL TOOLS OF THE DESIGNER'S TRADE

In any role, especially a commercial design role where people are paying money for a product or service, there are certain tools of the trade. The designer needs to master these tools to create the communication solutions that the client and the audience are asking for.

From the outset, the designer requires the talent and ability to employ a set of skills within a design process involving curiosity, discovery, imagination, creation and presentation to solve a design problem.

The specific tools a designer needs are:

- skills to respond to an identified design problem with ideas and strategies
- an ability to confirm an idea's validity through a rigorous design research process
- visualisation/craft skills in drawing, typography, layout, photography, illustration and design prototyping
- computer and software skills for print, packaging, environmental, web, interactive and moving image
- interpersonal and public communication skills
- service-management skills
- time-management skills
- business skills around budgeting and pricing
- energy, passion, perseverance and attention to detail.

These images illustrate combinations of text, typography image and moving image. This highlights the idea options available to the contemporary designer. All must be specific to a communication's objective and audience.

↑ *Designer* **ANDREW VAN DER WESTHUYZEN, COLLIDER**
Client **IBM**

→ *Designer* **FINN CREATIVE**
Client **THE AUSTRALIA PROJECT: FEDERATION SQUARE EXHIBITION**

THE FUTURE
HAS PAST

→ This idea clearly responds to the desire for Sydney Film Festival to 'plug-in' to the world of local and international cinema. A well thought out brief will usually result in a strong idea that lends itself to innovative technical execution.

Designer **PRECINCT**
Client **SYDNEY FILM FESTIVAL**

THE DESIGN PROCESS AND THE AUDIENCE

In taking on a client's design project, designers employ a logical and systematic process to get to the root of the design problem and the audience they're trying to engage with. This process defines what is meant by the word 'creativity'. Creativity is both the defining of a problem and the application of talent, skill, expression and craft to solve that problem. Creativity is not just 'art making'.

To design a successful outcome for a client's audience, follow the steps of the design process:

- Define the design problem within a client's brief.
- Analyse the design problem (What does the client really need?) and clearly identify the target audience (Who are the specific people we are talking to?).
- Discuss ideas and brainstorm with your design team.
- Research the design problem by designing a set of research methods (prototypes, surveys, focus groups).
- Develop concepts by generating a set of visual responses (sketches, images, text, references, inspirations, examples, media).
- Select the best ideas and create an initial client presentation that addresses the design problem, audience, thoughts, inspirations, ideas, strategy).
- Evaluate your design work through all stages of the process: scrutinise your creative thinking and your approach to the design problem; review and revise your ideas; evaluate your client's reaction to the initial presentation and revise again.
- Implement the final design and deliver the finished product.

The brief is like a map. The job of the designer is to navigate the key points on the map: the most important points for the client, their audience and the designer. While there might be a lot of 'points of interest' on this map, it is the mission of the designer to identify and isolate the most fundamental objectives that they are trying to communicate.

Right here is your first step on the path to understanding what makes a successful designer: fully understanding and digesting what the brief requires—not missing a thing; reducing all the data provided to the most potent points. This initial contact with the brief only happens in your head: your only tools, at this point, are your brain and maybe something to scribble with. You'll need some paper to capture your first precious insights.

It's actually pretty simple: a client has a problem to solve and you can design an accurate and attractive solution. You can hit the communication nail on the head with an aesthetically pleasing hammer. As you read the brief, your brain and your intuition (or 'hunch mechanism') are sorting and prioritising layers of information. You start reading, re-reading, making little annotations in the margin, recording your initial responses—making little squiggles that represent your reactions and gut feelings. During this subtle and decisive time, you usually form a foggy picture in response to what you're reading. It's an intuitive step. You hatch an initial design thought. You have an idea. This process of recognition and response is your future currency as a designer.

PROJECT CHECKLIST

- ☐ Scope the project from start to finish: what is needed, how many, for whom, how much, by when?
- ☐ Sit down with the client. Be very clear about expectations. Take notes.
- ☐ Come back to your client with a written proposal of what the job entails and what you'll be producing. Produce a full breakdown of job phases, quantity, price breakdown (of design, presentations, artwork, printing, and so on), timeframe and clear terms of trade (deposit, payment or trade schedule).
- ☐ Get agreement or 'sign-off' on what you're creating—before you start drawing or thinking!

CHANGED CONDITIONS:
A QUANTUM SHIFT IN
CONSUMER BEHAVIOUR

For graphic designers, audiences are broad and varied. With the recent advent of a networked, borderless world of digital communication in the form of the internet, audiences are now both local and international, commercial and personal. The mass-market approach of commerce has been broken down and diversified by the immediacy and flexibility of digital communication and its access to new market opportunities. The new audiences of design have completely reinvented the way designers work.

A graphic designer must have a deeper and richer understanding of a client's 'design problem' before creating an effective and memorable set of communication strategies and materials. A designer needs to explore and investigate a client's objectives with passion and perseverance to generate truly valuable work. It is no longer commercially acceptable to provide 'surface solutions' that display only skill with software or graphic technique. Audiences of design today are far more sophisticated. They are driven by ideas and strategies as well as aesthetics and slick product finishes. A designer's work is now about an ability to generate meaningful communication that can honestly resonate with people's personal desires and aspirations. The audiences of design are now motivated by quality, innovation and originality.

Greater access to the tools of design has created new layers of communication between creators of products and the services and initiatives that now exist within a variety of growing communities and cultures. Companies, organisations and people of all ages and cultures are now capable of creating designed materials, with various levels of professionalism, to generate commerce, community, philanthropy or interpersonal communication. The audience of design has shifted from the purely professional, commerce-driven model to an exploding democracy of ideas and the desire to share and communicate across borders, ages, brands and cultures.

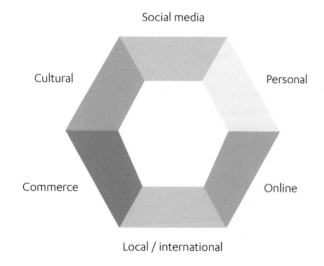

Social media

Cultural

Personal

Commerce

Online

Local / international

Audiences for design.

ACCESS AND AVAILABILITY TO EXPANDED MEDIA CHANNELS

Audiences of design now interact on more levels due to the availability of and access to more **media platforms**. Graphic designers now apply their expertise to print, digital and physical three-dimensional environments. Their text and image creations are both static and animated, and can be used in two-dimensional and three-dimensional, broadcast, interactive websites and video game interfaces. The audiences of design are now hungry for contact, interaction and communication. People spend a lot of their time interacting with screens, computers, hand-held devices, televisions and cinemas.

They also react to print media, packaging and product display. The audiences of design are now active participants, fully integrated in the life of brands. These brands can be products, services or social initiatives, and they compete for our attention now more than ever. Designers and their clients are at the heart of this wave of content creation and interaction. In the current era, digital media platforms, as well as traditional media, have increased the accessibility and flow of messaging and communication almost beyond recognition.

↑ This community project is all about interaction and motivation. Simple, clean and emotive messaging is reinforced by the restrained graphic style that is a hallmark of this highly credible international aid organisation.

Designer **DROGA5**
Client **UNICEF TAP PROJECT**

Audiences are no longer passive in their receipt of material. Feedback and communication is immediate and audiences are increasingly sophisticated in the way they react and interact with the flow of designed media. This landscape is both exhilarating and daunting for designers and their clients. To forge meaningful communication strategies, designers must be fully immersed in the objective of their communication. This requires strong research discipline and a rigorous process of generating ideas about strategy, visual communication, execution, production and delivery of communication materials.

Examples of **media platforms** include print, screen interactive, social media, games, apps, web, advertising, radio and TV.

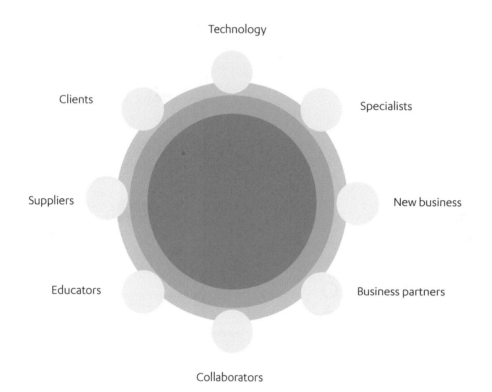

Technology

Clients

Specialists

Suppliers

New business

Educators

Business partners

Collaborators

← The people dynamic.

DESIGNERS AT THE SOURCE: LEADERSHIP, INNOVATION, IMAGINATION

Designers require the ability to listen and co-imagine with their clients. We no longer exist as purely 'craft people' who produce communication design objects in print or digital media. As a designer, you will have to step out from behind your studio table and enter into all aspects of the campaign production, whether it be in communication strategy, brand identity, advertising, publishing, environment or web-based media. The power and currency of design lies in the world of opportunity, ideas and imagination. The brands and initiatives that capture our aspiration and optimism and show innovation are now the true generators of commerce.

JOHN GOLLINGS

Designers increasingly need to be right at the source of the opportunity—'upstream', where the sparks of leadership, innovation and imagination are happening, not 'downstream' in a purely craft workshop mindset.

Designers need to understand teamwork and collaboration. We need both broad attributes and talents, and specific specialisation. With the amount of work that needs to be generated around brand campaigns or brand creation, designers need reliable resources to draw on. The lone 'crafts figure' in the design studio is no longer able to meet the demands of the increasingly social, networked world. Designers today require skills to create opportunities, generate ideas, manage design processes and conversations, delegate, craft and deliver quality materials around the clock, around the world.

THE SOCIAL DYNAMIC OF DESIGNING

As much as designers love the control and focus allowed by the tactile nature of design, we increasingly need broader skill sets. We need to get deep inside the minds of our clients and their audiences. This requires an ability to engage with the social dynamic of the design process: working with people, maintaining dialogue, and managing expectations and time frames. Designers need to take control of a project and work closely with all the individuals and groups in the supply chain who contribute to delivering a potent set of communication materials. We must cultivate an environment of trust and reliability.

frankie magazine

www.frankie.com.au

FIVE
CREATIVES
ON THE
MEANING
OF LIFE

BLOGGING
FROM A
WARZONE

BECOME A
VINTAGE FROCK
SPOTTER

30-SOMETHING
PRODIGIES

WHAT'S THE
BEST ROCK
MEMOIR
EVER?

Created by creative director Lara Burke and assistant publisher Louise Banister in 2004, *frankie* magazine provides a platform for intelligent editorial, talented photography and unique artists. Learning layout design during her diploma the old-school way (paste-up, paper and no computers), Lara worked in a collaborative design studio before moving on to design magazines for Morrison Media. It was there that Lara and Louise developed the idea for *frankie* magazine. Pitching it to publisher Peter Morrison, they were given the green light and started creating the first issue to launch in September of the same year.

Lara explains the vision for *frankie*: 'Louise and I were in our early 20s and very disillusioned by the mainstream women's magazines on offer. We wanted to create a magazine that was visually beautiful to look at, and editorially honest, smart and funny to read. One that celebrated and harnessed creative talents of fellow twenty-somethings in all fields of art, fashion, music, design and craft. We wanted to develop a magazine that held engagement with the reader—talk to them as a friend, someone in our social circle, someone we want to have a cuppa with. We wanted it filled with quirky, left-of-centre photography and nostalgic imagery, beautiful illustrations and simple, clean, timeless design. We think of *frankie* as a niche-style publication but with mainstream appeal.'

paper heart

ABOVE | Examples of frankie's consistent cover brand: clear and stylish, with an analogous colour scheme.

RIGHT | Playing with the idea of fashion editorial—this article uses cut-out illustrations to model scarves.

THE CUPCAKE SOCIAL

MY FAVOURITE THINGS WITH... AMELIA MEATH FROM MOUNTAIN MAN

PRIMOEZA

FAT QUARTER

Who you callin' a fat quarter?

MINNIE COOPER

BEARDS FOR ALL

A FANCY TEA CUP

OLA & OLEK

keep it simple, keep it sweet
SOFIA COPPOLA ON HER LATEST FLICK, *SOMEWHERE*.

WORDS ISABELLE VINCENT

Designed with the reader and content in mind, the layout for *frankie* is simple and calm. Approaching the design as visual interface for the content, the decision was made to let the design stand back and provide the content with the simplest of stages to perform on. 'The large use of white space mixed with the limited use of different typefaces never allows the reader to be distracted,' says Lara. 'This type of design can also be a risk because if your content isn't of high standard it'll show up loud and clear on the page—far more so than if the design was playing some sort of diversion role. Although *frankie*'s design may be disciplined and not follow trends as such, it still likes to frock up, it just doesn't lay the mascara on too thick. The ethos of *frankie* is to reflect in the design—aesthetics without substance doesn't endure.'

Design by its nature is changeable, but *frankie*'s layout is consistent, working to build trust and a steady voice for the readers. 'It's largely unadorned, pretty, but not loud or seeking attention, it's like a good friend. On another level, the decorative elements *frankie* uses feel wistful somehow, they seem to hark back to a more innocent time, a friendlier place, a place that isn't intimidating,' observes Lara. The most noticeable change in the design was the tweaking of the magazine's masthead on the cover of Issue 25. 'The tracking between the letters was condensed— this allowed the masthead to appear more prominent on the cover, larger and more confident.'

Sourcing content from all over the world, *frankie* has formed an international community of like-minded folk: '*frankie* has

grown and nurtured a solid family of writers and photographers whose contributions to the magazine form the guts of what *frankie* is', explains Lara. The team at *frankie* strive to encourage and promote local artists and designers through features in the magazine, as well as support Australian art events, design college alignments and design conferences.

THE EVOLVING DESIGNER

As technology, client expectations and audiences evolve, so too must the designer.

DESIGN EVOLUTION: THE EXPANDING PROFESSION

The access to digital applications now afforded to the public has caused complications for design professions. Digital applications enable individuals everywhere to generate their own design initiatives, shaking up the professional landscape. Historically, only trained professionals had access to the tools and processes of commercial design creation. We now find ourselves in a landscape where the '**produser**' can affect public interest and opinion and generate unexpected brand identities and media activity.

The previously existing lines drawn between design, advertising and communication are now blurred and open to re-invention. Advertising will always be about the 'selling' of products and services, but design-thinking and adherence to design processes are now the common denominators in successful communication with audiences. Alongside the design professionals, the audiences of design have become the co-creators of design. The distance between these usually distinctive groups has narrowed.

Brands need to be closely engaged with their audiences, in constant conversation, updating, posting news and developments, generating affection, loyalty, authenticity and credibility. Brands have to 'do things' not just 'stand for' certain values.

THE RISE OF TODAY'S DESIGNER

During the 1960s and 1970s, the working identity of the uniquely skilled practitioners of graphic design and art direction was one of mystery and misunderstanding. For a consumer of products or services in the general public, design and printing was a 'dark art', meaning most people had no clue about how this work was produced. It was a world of talented visual artists, designers, photographers and printers all working around the clock together to produce remarkable printed products for consumers and businesses.

These professionals all shared an understanding of a range of craft technologies and processes that were taught in tertiary trade schools, colleges and universities, where a combination of theory, technology and practice produced personnel for this mysterious industry.

The rise of today's graphic designer is the product of two key factors:

1. the commercial and personal 'take-up' of digital technology in design, printing, moving-image and interactive interfaces

2. the ability of designers to produce professional materials and content independently of an industrial scale of personnel and production.

The quantum shift from previous methods of design and print production, where people had individual tasks as part of a 'production line' approach, meant designers suddenly found their livelihood under threat if they weren't able to shift their skills into the digital mode. They had to transfer their physical desktops of pencil, ink and glue to a Mac desktop and all the peripherals a digital studio required.

This shift in technology created tremors in the design and print industry around the world. Within the space of a few years, designers had a whole new language of hardware, software and material output. Hand-drawn art and thinking skills were still essential, but the language and technology of product delivery had changed forever.

The shift to digital technology is a continuation of the relationship between technologies and human skills that has historically defined graphic design. From the invention of **moveable type** and the printing press up to today's networked world, we see how the needs of people, business and economics have produced technological invention that

A **produser** is a non-professional producer/end user who creates their own design, such as a mash-up animation for YouTube or social media.

Moveable type is individual letters within a language able to be combined to form words and sentences to be printed.

re-frames communication and its consequences. Graphic designers are always close to these changes, responding to and integrating change into rich and varied visual communication ideas.

With digital technology, the new breed of graphic designer can work in isolation from their desktop, networked with colleagues and suppliers to produce commercial design materials from any location. The proliferation of the personal computer has opened up a new set of opportunities for designers and their clients. However, this 'revealing' of the production methods and techniques associated with the previously 'dark' art of design has come with a price: the secret language of design materials—typography, colour, photography and illustration—is now available to all.

Graphic designers now find themselves in a situation where they have to prove their unique talent in creating commercially measureable outcomes for their clients.

This is where we, as a profession, find ourselves today: we must rely on our ability to generate ideas that capture the imagination of our target audience *and* our clients. This demands commercial rigour and reliable, streamlined delivery of high-quality products. This expands the brief for designer education from a traditional practical, 'art-making' focus to one that also emphasises thinking and ideas.

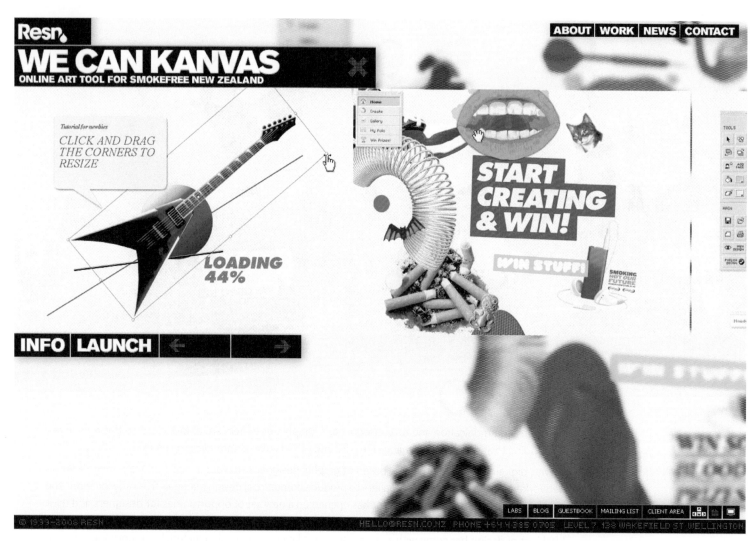

↑ This initiative was created to give a young audience a way to interact with anti-smoking messages. They were invited to create, post images and win prizes through a unique screen-based interface and gallery.

Designer **RESN**
Client **SMOKEFREE NZ**

A CLOSER LOOK AT THE AUDIENCE OF DESIGN

ANDREW CURTIS

↑ This website was commissioned by property developers in response to the buying behaviour of the property market in Melbourne. The designers avoided clichéd marketing, creating a truthful tongue-in-cheek brand personality, with designs placed uniquely to drive buyers to display suites.

Designer **CORNWELL BRAND AND COMMUNICATIONS**
Client **SALTA PROPERTIES**

Designers today are facing a marketplace of increased competition and activity. Both clients and audiences have developed more awareness of, and dependence on, design's potential to provide innovation for products, services, arts and community/political projects. Designers need every edge available to engage their clients and provide additional value beyond the traditional skills-base of designing. By allowing designers to engage deeply with a target audience, design research can provide that edge.

DESIGN RESEARCH: DEFINING THE PROBLEM AND THE AUDIENCE

Designers need to make informed choices about potential design outcomes rather than just relying on aesthetic considerations. Design research helps designers to create solutions that are supported by data and interaction with design prototypes. Design research methods add value to the design outcome for the audience, the client and the profile of the designer and their profession.

We will now look in detail at some useful design research methods. To fully identify your audience, use both *quantitative* and *qualitative* methods of data collecting.

Quantitative research

This approach is all about measuring hard facts and figures. If we're considering a target audience we need to collect a range of defining data to paint an exact picture of our audience. Below are some example answers to questions in a quantitative survey of a target group:

- Age range—35 years old
- Gender—female
- Height and weight—H 160 cm, W 60 kg
- Ethnic origins—Australian immigrant
- Languages—bi-lingual
- Education—university
- Religion—Christian
- Sexual orientation—heterosexual
- Occupation—tertiary educator
- Employment—employee
- Full-time or part-time income—$60 000 to $80 000
- Saving and investment habits—3 per cent of annual $AU income in savings
- Lifestyle behaviour—surfing, shopping, reading
- Media habits and locations—TV, radio, newspaper, magazine, web
- Colour preferences—primary colours
- Clothing—General Pants, Myer
- Foods and flavours—ethnic tastes, home cooking

This set of measured data findings will deliver a focused view of exactly who we're speaking to both at an individual and group level. By cross-referencing all the group responses for 'matches' there will be some key data emerging to define our audience.

Qualitative research

To contrast the 'hard data' of quantitative data, we collect qualitative information, which is more about defining certain 'qualities' in our categories. This information helps to flesh out the facts and figures we've already collected. It provides the nuance and subtlety designers need to create innovation and difference in their outcomes.

For example:

- Age range: youthful 35 year olds
- Gender: 'tomboy'
- Height and weight across a sample of the audience: 'curvy, not skinny'
- Ethnic origins: blonde and blue-eyed, but not English/Anglo-Saxon; certain 'Aussie' characteristics
- Languages: sounds 'European' with some 'Aussie' speech inflections
- Education: smart, bookish but not strictly academic or nerdy
- Religious persuasion: doesn't believe in a Christian god, but still deeply spiritual
- Sexual orientation: bisexual
- Occupation: ambitious, energetic educator with leadership potential
- Employment: full-time employee of 4 years at current workplace
- Full-time or part-time income: full-time with leave accrual and super benefits
- Saving and investment habits: has an investment property, is engaged to be married
- Lifestyle behaviour: likes restaurants, night-clubs and parties; part-time musician and cyclist
- Media habits and locations: print, magazine, street press, television, interactive web, games interfaces
- Colour preferences: some bright primaries, fluro, black and white
- Foods and flavours: Thai, Japanese, Italian, Middle Eastern

Primary research is original research undertaken by an organisation or individual.

More design research methodology

With the audience well defined we can now look in detail at what this audience responds to. This is important in the crafting of ideas that can connect with our audience. Both primary and secondary research are used to collect further data.

Primary research is original research generated specifically by a company or organisation for its own ends. This can be in the form of a focus group that comprises our target audience. It could also be the commissioning of a market research company to collect specific data according to a unique formula. It can be observational research, interviews, questionnaires, **photo-ethnographic studies** or evaluating responses to design prototypes or mock-ups.

Secondary research is the collection and review of existing data or findings. This can be sourced from magazines, newspapers, journals, the internet, podcasts, radio or television. This research can also be in the form of a literature review from academic journals or papers delivered at conferences.

As designers, we are interested in formulating a set of research methods that help us see deeply into the habits, aspirations and motivations of our target audience. Any unique lead or insight can be useful to add nuance, flavour and relevance to our design outcomes. Without this rigorous exploration our design solutions may not reach our audience at an inspirational level. The design might go only part of the way in delivering a meaningful communication result. It's important to try to gather a series of research strategies. In their book *A Designer's Research Manual*, Jennifer and Kenneth Visocky O'Grady outlined a number of useful tactics (Visocky O'Grady, 2006, p. 21).

↑ This is The Company We Keep, a rag tag bunch of misfits with a passion for transforming ideas into bespoke, tangible realities. They have combined forces to deliver a range of talents and specialty skills because two heads are better than one, and seven heads are unstoppable.

Designer **THE COMPANY WE KEEP**
Client: **SELF-PROMOTION**

Photo-ethnographic studies involve the scientific description of individual cultures, in this case through photography.

Secondary research is the collection and review of existing data or findings from sources such as magazines, newspapers, journals, the internet, podcasts, radio or television.

GEORGES ANTONI

32

Anthropology is the science that deals with the origins, physical and cultural development, social customs and beliefs of humankind.

Visual anthropology is a subfield of cultural anthropology. It is the study of visual representation, which includes performance, museums, art and mass media.

Web analytics refers to the measurement of number of hits for a website, traffic through web pages, user habits or web locations.

Competitor analysis

- Literature review
- Surveys, questionnaires
- Focus groups

Ethnographic research

- Photo-ethnography (the scientific description of individual cultures, in this case through photography)
- **Visual anthropology** (the science that deals with the origins, physical and cultural development, biological characteristics, and social customs and beliefs of humankind)

Marketing research

- Demographics (a section of the population sharing common characteristics, such as age, sex, class)
- **Web analytics** (e.g. Google)
- **Colour theory and forecasting**

User testing

- **Iterative** design process
- Observational research
- Evaluation of design protoypes and mock-ups

To finally confirm our research findings we employ a process of **triangulation**. This is defined as 'the process of combining several different research methods to illuminate one area of study' (Visocky O'Grady, 2006 p. 76). By combining and overlapping various research findings we are able to discover 'key truths' within our design problem.

In addition to quantitative, qualitative, primary and secondary research, other terminology for discussing design research includes *background research, empirical research, theoretical research* and *fieldwork*. We will look at these further in Chapter 2.

It is important to understand that graphic design is an intellectual and social pursuit, transforming ideas and communication strategies into visual communication materials and media on behalf of your client's objectives. A designer's worth lies in their ability to generate these ideas and approaches within a group context.

← This image captures the unique quality of Australian light, positioning Westfield Sydney as 'the leading light' in fashion and lifestyle in a brochure and online film created by Eskimo Design to promote leasing space to Westfield's potential business clients.

Designer **ESKIMO DESIGN**
Client **WESTFIELD, SYDNEY**

Colour theory and forecasting relates to trends and factors that influence the choice of specific colours for mood, voice and the intention of a design. It applies

specifically to fashion, but can also be applied to consumer behaviour.

An **iterative** design process involves repeating a set of instructions a set number of times or until a desired result is achieved.

Triangulation is the cross-examination of a particular subject using two or more research methods.

Australian INfront

www.australianinfront.com.au

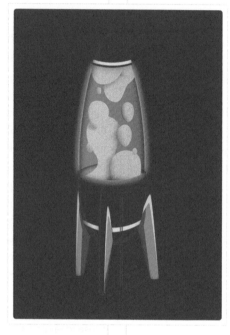

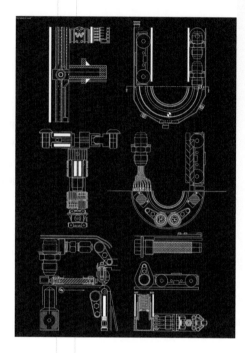

Australian INfront was founded in 1999 by a small group of like-minded individuals, all of whom where under 25 and working in interactive media. They used a simple email group and ICQ chats to discuss and develop the idea that would ultimately become one of the most influential website portals for Australian design.

Their mission? To elevate international perception of Australian design. It was this ambitious manifesto that they presented at Sydney Design 99. Founder Justin Fox explains: 'At the time it was a common thought that you had to work overseas to "make it". As a group, we were against this idea. We were keen to explore our own Australian surroundings and look locally for inspiration as opposed to being inspired by design movements overseas. We wanted to fight the backwards image Australian creatives saw in the mirror. "INfront" is the opposite of "OUTback", we were calling out to other creatives on the edges of our country (Perth, Melbourne, Sydney); in front of everyone else, we were yelling out to the rest of the world that Australian INfront exists and our work rocks. A lot of attitude, sure, but we were grass roots, driven and doing it for the love and recognition.'

With the growth of the internet leading to the creation of a global community, Australian design is largely respected worldwide. Justin concedes the mission may have been accomplished and is no longer relevant. 'But by continuing to promote local talent we're hopefully continuing to inspire both local and international designers', enthuses Justin. 'As long as there's graduating design students and international designers looking to come to Australia to work, INfront will have a purpose.'

With a motto of 'Get Involved, get INfront', the Australian INfront team has worked hard over the years to inspire their community of designers. 'We have collaborative visual projects, [the] most successful of them is *Visual Response* where our visitors are invited to create a piece inspired by a single word. We also have a forum, which encourages design-related discussion.'

Along with web-based projects, INfront has had the opportunity to present at Sydney Design 99, DiGiT Conference 2002 and Semi-Permanent 2003. They have also represented for AGDA at the 2002 ICOGRADA regional meeting and continue to support numerous offline events.

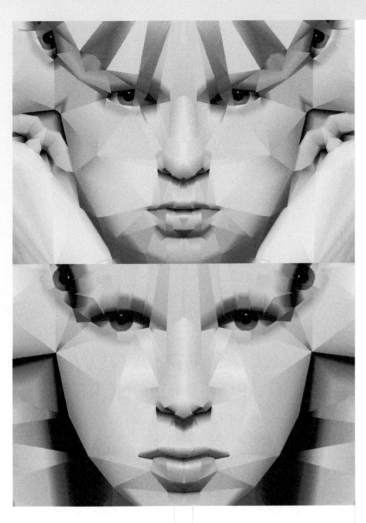

Running an Australian-focused website could have created a backlash over exclusivity; however Justin insists there has been none, with Australian-only content being something they are proud of.

This is not to say that only Australians visit the site. 'Early on, many of the large design portal/community sites linked to each other via a logo bar on their home pages and INfront was one of the few linked sites,' explains Justin. 'We've had a few T-shirt designs over the years and half of the runs go out to overseas customers. We've also met a lot of designers who come from overseas and a lot of them have let us know that they visited INfront's directory in order to locate studios to approach for work.'

Today, Australian INfront continues to promote and inspire Australian design as well as nurture the next generation of designers. 'Our directory lists local studios that students can send CVs to and we're always listing events students can get involved in,' says Justin. 'We've also visited (and continue to do so) local design schools to do talks as well as live *Visual Response* projects.'

This spread shows a selection of submissions for the Visual Response project 'Future'.

OPPOSITE PAGE
L-R | Marc Martin; Toby Fraser, The Fox and King; Daniel Elliott and Henry Luong, Organ Studio

THIS PAGE CLOCKWISE | Rhett Dashwood; Paul Mosig, Racket; Paul Tooth, Seeder House

RESPONDING TO THE NEW DESIGNER/CLIENT/ AUDIENCE CONDITIONS

As we've discussed, times have really changed for the creators and receivers of communication design. The idea of regimented contact and formal interaction has been replaced by a more fluid and constant communication flow between clients, designers and audiences.

Designers are now engaged at an organisational, strategic level as much as an aesthetic or craft level. Clients are in search of ideas, resources and the ability to provide a reliable, innovative service with measurable outcomes. Clients and audiences are seeking more than the 'idea, artwork, product-delivery' cycle. They're interested in innovation, adding value to their products and generating an edge in a shifting marketplace. Designers must be prepared to investigate this volatile marketplace to produce ideas that respond to this need.

This is design-thinking from a business perspective. It's about creating rigorous, integrated ideas that can produce more communication, activity and brand awareness. Branding today, as an example, is no longer about passive repetition of symbols and colour. Brands must be seen as 'doing' things, as being active and engaged in the world of their audiences. Brands must deliver a philosophy and reality that's honest, believable and consistent.

This credo should then be something to live by for all the people working within that brand. The audiences of design are becoming increasingly educated in the truth and lies within brand language. The winners in design today fully understand this fact and work to help companies, individuals and organisations to extract their genuine working essence and present it in a compelling and creative way. This is a risky business: the winners in our media-rich world must take big chances with crazy and sometimes illogical ideas.

BUILDING ASSETS: A NEW TOOLKIT FOR DESIGNERS

Earlier in the chapter, we looked at the traditional tools of the design trade. The challenge for young designers today is to understand the true nature of design practice as it evolves; what it's really about; the true needs and desires of clients and their audiences.

Designers must search for powerful ideas using every possible resource at their disposal: this means people, technologies, opportunities and energy.

Today, designers facing these realities need to focus on a new toolkit. This toolkit will contain **tangible** technologies like colours, typography, software, craft-skills, digital-media, interactive formats and physical environments. The innovative leap and measurable creativity expected also requires a set of seemingly **intangible** tools like qualitative research, methods of prototyping, feedback and response mechanisms and the luck and insight generated by sheer energy and the force of will towards discovery and breakthrough. This toolkit should contain an appreciation of philosophy, personal and collective values and a sense of camaraderie and collegiality. This toolkit is a self-sustaining professional resource hub.

Tangible means finite, quantifiable and measurable.

Intangible means less defined, or immeasurable. Intangible qualities can be combined to give a fuller understanding of that which is being designed or examined.

↓ This Sydney-based group created a bold identity highlighting what made the Moonlight Cinema unique: the beautiful natural setting in which it screens its movies, and the experience that it offers its audience. The result was a whimsical, illustrative identity that utilised the moon and nature as devices to set the Moonlight Cinema apart.

Designer **PAUL GARBETT, NAUGHTYFISH**
Client **FORD FIESTA MOONLIGHT CINEMA**

→ Hand-drawn typography and a historic poster approach combine to form a down-to-earth communication vehicle for a community direct mail campaign.

Designer **BOHEEM**
Client **UNITING WORLD**

← The design duo Something Splendid (James Yencken and Jonathon Bellew) envisioned a city made from the creative output of its residents as the key image for the Melbourne Fringe Festival. They constructed a replica of Melbourne's CBD from 512 pieces of treated pine; that's just over a tonne of timber. The photo shoot was constructed on the main stage of The Lithuanian Club in North Melbourne, which is one of the festival's main venues.

Designer **SOMETHING SPLENDID**
Client **MELBOURNE FRINGE FESTIVAL**

DESIGNER: NOT JUST A SERVICE PROVIDER, A COMMUNICATION PROFESSIONAL

In accord with the new conditions in which designers must work, an updated professional approach is called for. Young designers need to embrace higher standards of professionalism and organisation to back up their expressive artistry. To work with innovative clients, designers must rise to the challenge of providing deeper meaning, improved management and content depth to their work. The expectation that designers will successfully create breakthroughs is becoming more commonplace. Professionalism, innovation and value are now the hallmarks of this so-called 'creative age'.

MYSELF, MY CLIENT, MY PROFESSION

The galvanising nature of change that has swept through our communication design landscape today continues to be digested by the broader global profession. Despite the growth and diversity of our industry, there are a few rules of thumb that still hold true. Yes, we are moving in new collaborative circles and yes, we are being required to maintain lifelong learning. However, as designers our natural impulses and inspirations remain true.

We work within trusted processes and frameworks that still produce powerful, meaningful materials that can affect people's lives and aspirations. For all designers of all ages, great work will always contain a tangible 'personal humanity' that is responsive and generous towards a client's grand or humble ambition. Great design appears transparent and invisible, fully in service of a problem posed and solved with nerve, daring and meaning. Our profession is a thoughtful, responsible population of thinkers and makers. We straddle the divide of objectives and risky ideas in the service of our higher selves, our clients' ambitions and our collective imagination.

→ This image is from Studio Pip and Co's 'Posters for pleasure' series. It was also a submission to The Australia Project (www.australiaproject.com). The legend of colonial anti-hero Ned Kelly is called upon in this poster. Kelly stoically peers out of a crude and barren world of 'the sale' and invites the viewer to discover and materialise Australian culture and identity.

Designer **ANDREW ASHTON**

DESIGN BRIEF: CREATE A CORPORATE IDENTITY BRIEF

 Design a corporate identity 'system' that contains:

1. a logotype (name of company in chosen font/typeface)
2. a symbol (e.g. Nike 'swoosh' or McDonald's 'golden arches')
3. a colour palette (use only two colours, plus white)
4. typographic design (set of fonts)
5. application of identity elements to key print and digital communication materials (e.g. interactive website, blog, social media, business cards, letterhead, print materials/brochures, etc.).

Client

Greenfield Perpetual is a financial services division of a leading consumer bank (Bankwest) that is specifically concerned with 'investment and infrastructure products' that support environmental sustainability (e.g. alternative energy, farmed forests, recycling, environmentally-friendly materials).

Audience

- 30- to 50-year-old men and women
- Individuals with existing investment portfolios
- Existing patrons of Bankwest as well as new customers
- People with an interest in climate change and its consequences
- Conservative, insightful, successful professionals (dual or single income)

Design process

Research the Bankwest brand and the bank's customers to identify an approach that fits with their current communication strategy and materials. The object of the brief is to use the existing Bankwest brand attributes (sound, character, tone-of-voice, colour, visual language, comedic flavour) and bring them alive in the context of a range of products that are engaged in environmental sustainability, sympathetic materials and strategies that would be within the mindset of the target audience.

Presentation format

You are required to produce:

- three key identity system 'marks' for consideration (combined name, logotype, symbol or typography as listed above)
- application of logo to key business communication materials (business cards, letterheads, etc)
- website strategy and visualisation
- digital presentation templates
- advertising/communication launch event materials in print, digital media and branded environment.

SUMMARY

The audiences of design have shifted and grown with rapid technological and social change within a newly networked matrix of communication channels and platforms. Graphic designers have been encouraged to expand their vision, skills and attributes to respond to the new conditions working as communication designers.

An ability to think and make within a personal and commercial context is now the entry point for young designers with professional ambitions. Personal inspiration and artistry is always required, but an additional curiosity, knowledge and responsibility towards uncovering innovation is now the profession's pressing challenge. Our aim should always be to move our worth 'upstream' to where the first flashes of ideas and possibility are being discussed and strategised by our clients and patrons. It is here that our long-term value and contribution lies.

KEY TERMS

REFERENCES / WEBSITES

Ambrose, G & Harris, P 2006, *Basics design 05: colour*, Ava Publishing.

Florida, R 2003, *The rise of the creative class*, Pluto Press, Melbourne.

Heller, S 1997, 'Design is hell', in *Looking closer 2*, Allworth Press, New York.

Martin, R 2009, *The design of business: why design thinking is the next competitive advantage*, Harvard Business School Press, Watertown.

Roberts, L 2006, *Drip dry shirts: the evolution of the graphic designer*, AVA Publishing, London.

Saville, P 2006, 'Thinkers and doers', *Open manifesto*, No. 4, Brisbane.

Visocky O'Grady, J & Visocky O'Grady, K 2006, *A designer's research manual*, Rockport Publishers, Minneapolis, MN.

Australian INfront (www.australianinfront.com.au)

Design is Kinky (www.designiskinky.com)

agideas (www.agideas.net)

Australian Creative (www.australiancreative.com.au)

frankie (www.frankie.com.au)

Two Thousand (www.twothousand.com.au)

http://en.wikipedia.org/wiki/William_Addison_Dwiggins

British Council Arts (www.britishcouncil.org/arts-creative-economy.htm)

chapter 2

CONCEPTUALISING AND PROCESS

INTRODUCTION

Everything starts with an idea. Some people believe that great ideas happen when creativity and relevance meet and this is evident when you come across a really well designed object. Sometimes the object functions so well that you are oblivious to the cleverness of the design. Other times it is the design that draws attention to an otherwise nondescript object.

Call it the big idea, concept or theme, designers work hard to contextualise their designs in the social fabric of the society in which we live. There are three key stages in the design process: research and analysis; conceptualising; and the design phase—a continual evaluation linked to the use of typography, design elements and principles, colour, layout, refinement (post-design evaluation) and finish. This chapter provides a framework with which designers can work through the process of creativity relevant to a client's problem or brief. Specifically it will enable creative, but ordered, thinking as well as provide a process for interpreting the brief and testing the designer's approach to the client's problem.

THE DESIGN PROCESS

THE BRIEF

MARKET PARAMETERS

Client's needs
Purpose
Deadline date

COSTS

- Quote
- Timetable

1. Define

2. Analyse

The problem —what does the client need?

3. Discuss ideas

Notes, preliminary roughs

4. Research

Brief requirements:

- Feasibility of client's needs
- Alternatives
- Market niche/needs
- How is the competition promoting itself and why?
- Are they on the right track?

5. Develop concept

Develop lots of ideas and concepts
looking at everything that is possible
(as many as 50—see mind map on page 55)

6. Select

Select the best three concepts to refine and
present to the client

7. Implement

Once the client has agreed, complete the
finished artwork and send it to the printer

8. Evaluate

BRAINSTORM MINDMAP

- What else do you need to know?
- Where will you find the information?
- Will you require specialist services?

DEFINE

- Compliance with
  brief specifications
- Check, proofread copy

ANALYSE

- Relevance of concept
  to client's needs
- Results

DISCUSS

Thumbnails
↓
Selection process
↓
Rough visuals
↓
Final selection process
↓
Client approval
↓
Process finished
artwork

REVIEW
finished product

REFLECT
on outcomes,
alternatives

LEARN
through experience,
problem solving

THE DESIGN PROCESS

So you've been given a brief from a client (in reality clients don't generally give briefs, unless they have had experience working with graphic designers; they just tell you what they think they need). Now you have to turn it into a well-designed printed or digital object that meets their expectations and increases their sales.

Graphic design is creative communication. It can be achieved through type and image or just one of these. Your approach to the design process will include aesthetic choices, media and material alternatives, and appropriate design solutions. These should all be focused on the parameters of the brief. Your ability to overcome obstacles, select ideas and make decisions involving critical analysis skills will be highly valued by your client and your design team. Table 2.1 overleaf outlines the key points of the design process.

↑ A spark of an idea led Timba Smits to create free magazines. *Wooden Toy* became so popular that now it is produced regularly at a cost to its readers.

Designer **TIMBA SMITS**
Client **WOODEN TOY**

← There are many variations in the design process but this flow chart gives an idea of the sequence of events and things you may need to consider.

47

TABLE 2.1   KEY POINTS OF THE DESIGN PROCESS

Design stages	Process choice 1	Process choice 2	Process choice 3
Research	Product	Client/company	Competitors/market place
Mood board	Five areas: theme, type, colour, texture, shape	Montage of ideas	Current branding context
Inspiration	Design books	Galleries and exhibitions	Analysis of materials and manufacture
Ideas/concepts/ brainwork	Word association	Brainstorming	Mind mapping
Refinement	Layout options	Concept map	Refine 3 ideas into viable concepts
Presentation	PDF or PowerPoint®	Mock-up or test sample	Communicate solution with multimedia presentation
Digital file management	Choose software wisely	Create document accurately	Get client signoff before uploading to the internet or sending off to print

All the above process choices give the designer options that are interchangeable within each phase of the process.

Fully consider all relevant information from the outset of the design process. The next stage involves applying different conceptual approaches to the ideas that you have selected and weighing these against the production and technical considerations relevant to the project. A fabulous design concept for a brochure can be a real disappointment if the only material that can be used from a technical viewpoint can't be printed on or folded.

Be prepared for client changes and alterations to the original brief: this is where negotiation skills will be an advantage. Clients often like to use the latest stylistic trends; however, it will be your job to convince them that while it may be trendy today, the design will look very dated in a year's time.

Montage is the process and result of making a composite image by collating and joining a number of other images either digitally or by hand.

Multimedia refers to a combination of different media (often including digital and interactive media) and can include video, still images, audio and text.

An unusual approach to two-dimensional design using a three-dimensional image.

Designer **PAUL GARBETT, NAUGHTYFISH**
Client **ARJO WIGGINS**

↑ A poster design using only typography as imagery.

Designer **LANDOR ASSOCIATES**
Client **AGDA**

DESIGNER DO'S

Innovative (conceptual) thinking, first-rate executions, a great eye for type and a genuine passion for design are all attributes that senior designers want in more junior staff. Design studios do not need another geek who is really good at Photoshop®, Illustrator® or Flash® and not much else—they also need you to have good communication skills. After all, that's what design is: communicating an idea. Listening, speaking and writing are all important in all stages of the design process, from presenting your design to a client to briefing the printer. You need to communicate your passion for design, your knowledge on the subject, your ability to frame and answer the question and your ability to produce a fabulous end result.

THE IDEAS START HERE

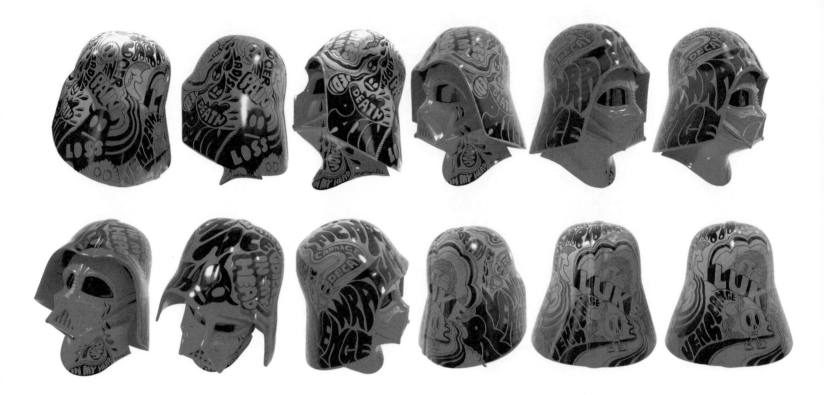

Ideas can be intelligent, stimulating, challenging and conceptually rigorous. They can encourage us to think beyond our experience and perspective to hold the attention of viewers. Graphic designers often use concepts to centre the theme of their designs and layouts. Concepts then become the frame that holds the content or elements of the communication together. Mass civilisation and the inherent culture in which we live compel the design challenges, or problems, that broadcasting, interactive digital media, magazine design and advertising provide. The pursuit of cleverness, novelty and innovation drives many graphic designers and other creatives to produce a new format to communicate an idea or promote a product.

↑ Artistic representations have been made of cultural icons since Andy Warhol painted Marilyn Monroe and Elvis. Now there are new materials and new images, and mass production is much cheaper.

Designer **JEREMYVILLE**
Client **THE VADER PROJECT**

Culture is the set of shared attitudes, values, goals and practices that characterise the society in which we live.

Interactive digital media are electronic media in which the user participates. Examples include websites, interactive

television, social media and advertising kiosks.

Although design is essentially communication between people, there are two types of focus for graphic designers: Business to Consumer (B2C) and Business to Business (B2B) solutions to problems. Graphics have long played a powerful role as a social tool by raising awareness, providing critical debate and ultimately provoking change. These are the issues often raised in a B2C graphic design problem and are inherently more risky in relation to concepts used to determine the end result. Graphic design communication that leaves the viewer wondering where the (wacky, way-out, and often bizarre) idea originated often uses risky concepts.

B2B problems, on the other hand, are often solved through different techniques that are more conservative and less socially confronting but require a similar process to solve. In fact, the design process is now utilised by people in many different sectors to solve all kinds of business problems. The way designers portray the solution to a client's problem has changed as our culture, knowledge and the viewer's ideas and perspective change. The nature and manner of people's understanding of our culture has an impact on how we as designers decide to communicate. This is why research and analysis form such an important part of the design process.

Although those new to the design profession think that the design process is linear and straightforward—read the brief, look out the window, have an idea, turn on the computer, make something—it is usually anything but. This kind of approach to the process would ultimately be unsustainable and often won't deliver the quality product that today's savvy clients demand. To do justice to the problem, the client and ultimately the audience, designers need to take time to fully digest the brief, identify the true design problem and set a process of discovery in motion.

→ Cows, psychedelic writing and rainbows seem to have no relationship to light fixtures and globes as seen on the right of this sticker sheet from Globe.

Designer **DE LUXE & ASSOCIATES**
Client **GLOBE**

Perspective is a person's particular attitude and point of view.

57

DEFINING THE SCOPE OF THE PROJECT

The first step to understanding what sort of research you need to complete is to be aware of the scope of the project. The project scope helps the designer identify the work that must be done to deliver the solution to the client's problem. The project scope can help the designer, and the client, identify the required functions and features of the desired solution. Often, the scope cannot be completely identified until the designer's research is finalised. This way all the constraints and assumptions and the desired result can be itemised for the client in a return brief that serves as a formal acceptance of the project terms.

The graphic design work may be a banner ad, invitation, book design, flyer or brochure, business card, logo, poster, packaging, signage, exhibit design, annual report, advertising, corporate stationery, web design, animation or interactive graphic. The client may request a flyer because that's what they think they need, but the designer may find, through scoping the project and completing the research, that in fact the client needs a website.

↑ What reflects the face of Melbourne? Or is it many faces?

Designer **LANDOR ASSOCIATES**
Client **CITY OF MELBOURNE**

← Business to Business design tends to be a lot more serious. In this example a paper company is promoting itself to designers.

designer **LANDOR ASSOCIATES**
Client **SPICERS PAPER/ MACDONALD & MASTERSON**

Project scope is the work that needs to be accomplished to deliver a product, service or result with the specified features and functions.

IDENTIFY THE
CLIENT'S PROBLEM

Thinking involves processing the information as we engage in problem solving, form concepts, reason and make decisions. Employers are looking for young designers who portray originality, ingenuity, unusualness, usefulness and appropriateness. These five traits enable final designs that are: (1) ingenious solutions that solve problems in a surprising way or that reflect a new and different perspective and creatively link remote ideas; and (2) solutions that are practical and appropriate to the brief, the client, the budget and the target audience, and therefore are more creative because they have met the often tight constraints of the problem while still producing original solutions.

To be useful and appropriate, designers need to have sufficient information on the background of the product or service, the target market, the competitors and the social and environmental impact of the product. As well as background information, there may be legal, contractual, ethical and copyright considerations, technological impacts and material constraints that will heavily affect the final design but often aren't evident until the design research is completed. By looking into all these areas designers will be able to build a client profile and a user profile. There are a range of research methods that graphic designers use to analyse, prioritise, summarise and draw conclusions from relevant material. It is important that designers are able to identify, select and apply a range of research methodologies to support a specific design enquiry.

By taking time to explore client and user profiles at the beginning of the project, designers gain a better understanding of the overall design environment. This also gives them a better understanding of the context of the problem. Sometimes designers immerse themselves in the client's business environment to gain real understanding of the 'customer experience'. The client's satisfaction with the end result will be determined by a number of things, including the value perceived to have been gained by their company from the designer's outcomes. An improved level of customer experience should result in increased sales.

Beware of unrealistic expectations by the client. The formulation of a client profile should provide the opportunity to educate the client about their design task. It will also serve as a reality check on what they can or cannot expect from the design they are commissioning. For example, a small budget that does not allow for purpose made photography can limit the look of the end result. A poor end result, rather than increasing sales for the client, can result in a negative impact on the client's brand.

→ A mind map analysing the different issues associated with a product. Drawing up such a map can be helpful in understanding the context of a design problem.

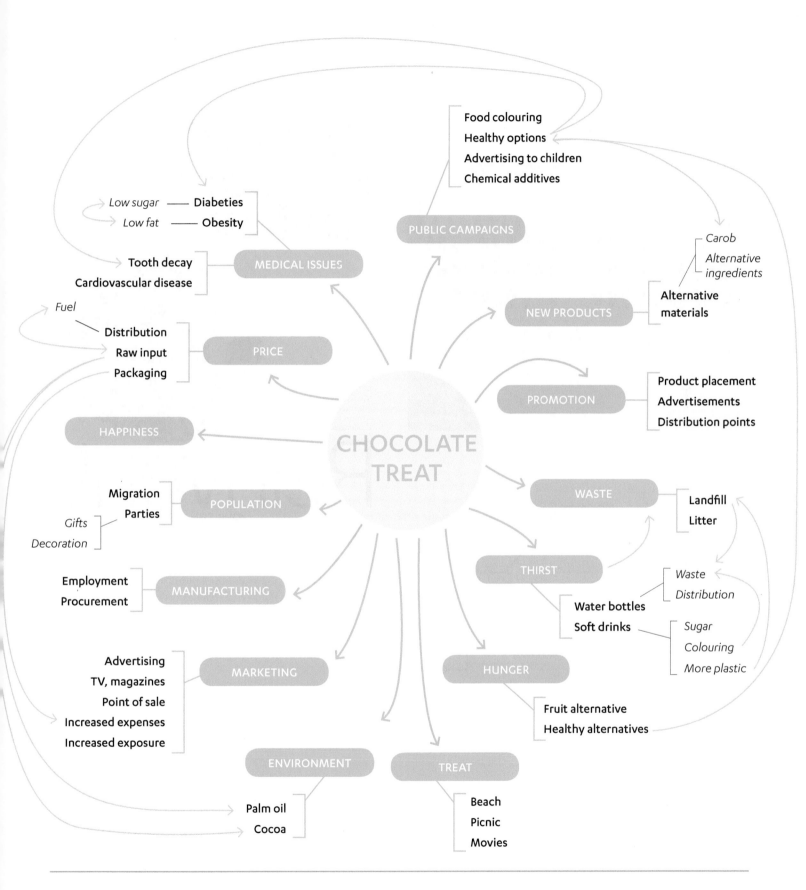

CHOCOLATE TREAT

Food colouring
Healthy options
Advertising to children
Chemical additives

PUBLIC CAMPAIGNS

Carob
Alternative ingredients

NEW PRODUCTS

Alternative materials

Low sugar —— Diabeties
Low fat —— Obesity

Tooth decay
Cardiovascular disease

MEDICAL ISSUES

PROMOTION

Product placement
Advertisements
Distribution points

Fuel

Distribution
Raw input
Packaging

PRICE

WASTE

Landfill
Litter

HAPPINESS

THIRST

Waste
Distribution

Migration
Parties

POPULATION

Gifts
Decoration

Water bottles
Soft drinks

Sugar
Colouring
More plastic

Employment
Procurement

MANUFACTURING

HUNGER

Fruit alternative
Healthy alternatives

Advertising
TV, magazines
Point of sale
Increased expenses
Increased exposure

MARKETING

ENVIRONMENT

TREAT

Palm oil
Cocoa

Beach
Picnic
Movies

de Luxe & Associates

www.de-luxe.com.au

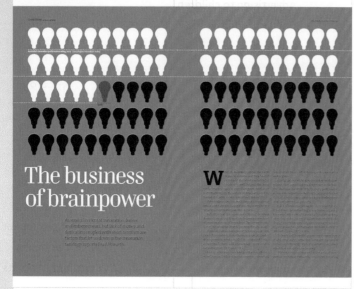

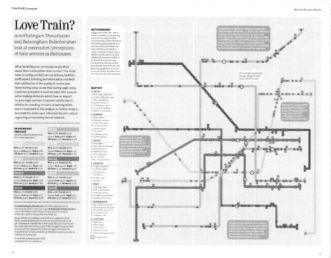

ABOVE | Spreads from Monash Business Review.
ABOVE RIGHT | Harvard Business Review cover

OPPOSITE | A mock-up design for South China Morning Post business section.
FAR RIGHT | Spread from Harvard Business Review.

With roots in prestigious Australian publications like *POL* and *FollowMe* it is little wonder that James de Vries has continued to explore and develop editorial communication through his company de Luxe & Associates.

'I always enjoyed the story-telling nature of editorial design,' he says.

After graduating from Sydney College of the Arts, James had the opportunity to work with Gary Fletcher at POL Publications.

'[Gary] taught me some of the attention to detail and personal discipline that is necessary for good magazine design,' explains James.

From *POL*, his journey took him from freelance work to art director of *FollowMe* magazine. 'It was an independent and inspiring magazine group, and provided me with many learning experiences, good and bad. I still keep in touch with friends I made at that magazine.'

He continued to work freelance for corporate design firms, producing annual reports as well as working for his own clients. 'I remember being in the office of a client the morning Sydney found it had won the Olympic Games, and seeing people dancing around in the streets while I was hunkered down on a Mac. So I realised I really needed to get myself one of these newfangled things called a computer.'

So along with his co-director/wife, an office space in Oxford Street Darlinghurst and a new 230 megabyte Macintosh, James launched de Luxe & Associates in 1993. 'Pretty soon it became clear that my passions of understanding the corporate imperative and magazine design were a strong point, and I found de Luxe began to build a reputation in this area. We kept a wide range of projects, but our competitive advantage was magazine design.'

James continues, 'de Luxe & Associates has continued to grow through publication design. This has taken us in a few directions. Early on, it led us into projects to comprehensively redesign many of Australia's newspapers and magazines. We created the first of the big colour inserted magazines in Australia,

for the *Australian Financial Review*. It was an amazing editorial and commercial success; this led to a long-term relationship with Fairfax Media that included redesigning all their major metropolitan newspapers and a number of their magazines.'

'Our experience at "deep and complex" typography grew and we have worked on numerous international magazine and newspaper designs, too. Typically we would work on large and complex projects that would involve significant culture and organisational change for our clients. We'd do a lot of development work in our studio and some weeks or months of implementing our designs embedded in our client's office.

A newspaper or magazine design project is a curious mix of designing for designers, where you have to take into account the talent and potential of the day-to-day designers, as well as the brand ideals and the business goals of the clients. Early on, we also realised that the investment in a redesign was wasted unless the organisation was able to transform its culture to make the most of their new "toy". So we have also developed a long-term relationship with a culture change consultancy called PRIMED, as a way of trying to tie the design project more closely to the organisation's culture.'

'So, over the years, our experiences have made us more interested in the abstract communication of ideas that editorial design achieves so well: connecting with an audience, making meaning and providing a designed product that is a true team effort. In turn this has led us into the field of Strategic Design and Design Thinking.'

In all their complex work, James and de Luxe feel that collaboration is one of the most powerful aspects of their design process. 'The nature of our projects means that it is impossible to take the position of "designer god". We love to engage the strengths of those we're working with. In an environment of mutual respect and effort, it can lead to a vastly better, more bullet-proof solution for our clients.'

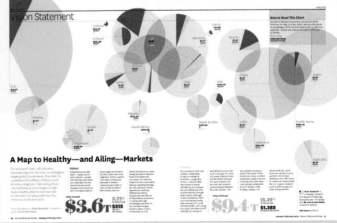

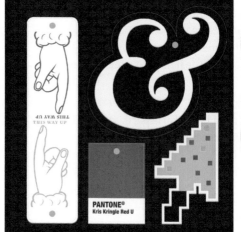

↑ Pumphouse Logomark.

Designer **FINN CREATIVE**
Client **PUMPHOUSE
RESTAURANT AND BAR**

← Research can provoke different,
even unexpected, imagery.

Designer **DE LUXE & ASSOCIATES**
Client **RALEIGH PAPER
COMPANY**

'From the beginning of the project until the end there was
always somebody who was visually impaired testing
the shapes and textures of the design proposals.'

JADE ALOOF, 2002

RESEARCH AND ANALYSIS

You may have to ask the client a lot of questions to find out the real task of your design. You will also need to determine the client's needs in terms of timing (speed), quality (physical characteristics that meet the desired result) and cost (budget) as these three factors will have a large impact on the determination of the components of the end product. Then you will have to undertake some independent research and analysis. This stage can be really important, not only because it gives you an understanding of the environment in which the client's product or service operates, but because research is the start of the design process. You can do most of your research on the internet, but you may also need to visit the competition to look at the way they promote themselves; visit newsagents to see other magazines in your client's category or market segment; or go to art galleries, shopping centres and communities to get a feel for the type of imagery, themes and concepts that are in the marketplace. These choices will depend on the nature of the brief and the relevant product or service.

RESEARCH METHODS

The range of research methods includes background research, empirical research, theoretical research and field work. The sources used to acquire the research include:

- information systems (databases, the internet)
- library services (books, journals, newspapers, CD-ROMs, online services)
- public and private archives (National Film Archives, company files)
- museums and galleries (permanent, temporary or travelling exhibitions)
- industry sources for expert knowledge and professional experience (including up-to-date information on materials, processes, production and manufacturing)
- promotion and marketing material
- research and development information
- the community for user knowledge and local consumer needs, perceptions and preferences.

Essentially, background research is based on historical records that include photographic, film and sound archives; books, newspapers and journals; and official registers of information. Empirical research is based on controlled observation or experiments including surveys, focus groups, case studies and data searches. Theoretical research is based on ideas including investigations using theoretical papers or texts to analyse particular issues. Fieldwork is based on methodical collation and interpretation of firsthand experience including interviews, oral histories and recorded observations.

A young designer was asked to set up a clothing labelling system for people who are visually impaired, and formed a focus group consisting of people with varying degrees of visual impairment. This enabled the designer to understand their vision requirements and their perception of colour.

'Great (meaningful) design ensures
that the message is well-targeted
at the audience the client seeks.'

ANDREW LAM-PO-TANG, AUSTRALIAN GRAPHIC DESIGNER, 2003

RESEARCH TYPES

As discussed in Chapter 1, two main types of research are qualitative
research and quantitative research. Quantitative research is about
measuring hard facts and figures, whereas qualitative research
focuses on defining certain 'qualities' to flesh out those facts and
figures. Table 2.2 outlines the different features of these types of
research.

TABLE 2.2   FEATURES OF QUALITATIVE AND QUANTITATIVE RESEARCH

Qualitative research	Quantitative research
Exploratory	Based on testing or hypothesis
Loosely organised	Conclusive
Descriptive	Structured
Anecdotal	Systematic
Flexible	Statistical
Versatile	Scientific (based on disciplined experiments)
Casual/informal	Formal
Random/selective sampling	Representative sampling
Opinion or observation based	Considered more objective and impartial
Prone to subjectivity and partiality	

↑ Logos come in many forms.
Some may be spontaneous and
organic; others, like this logo,
hard-edged and precise.

Designer **JUSTIN FOX**
Client **MODERNPET.COM.AU**

Perception and observation skills, as well as curiosity and an inquisitive approach to problem solving, are important attributes for a graphic designer. A willingness to question and challenge issues, and compare and contrast how the competitors in your client's industry are managing their design and promotion, is essential. It's not about copying what other people are doing; it's about finding a voice for your client's product or service that is in tune with its unique environment of competitors, buyers and potential rivals. It's about finding the difference or, as marketers would argue, the 'unique selling point' that sets your client's product or service aside from its competitors. So what is the client requesting and what are their needs? Your research methods will help you decipher some of the challenges your client faces in gaining successful recognition, and in turn increased sales, for their product or service.

Once you have gathered the information from your research it will need to be assessed for relevance and collated in a client-ready format, and prioritised for presentation and implementation. Support documentation is essential and this may include photographs, sketches, graphs, annotations and other evidence. Your research will be assessed on the methodology used, the quality of the execution and documentation, the interpretation of research results and its relevance to the target market and the client's brief.

RESEARCH AS INSPIRATION

Research needn't be a dry information-seeking exercise. It can also be a means to explore the design environment and become inspired. Design inspiration can come in the form of colours, textures, shapes, fonts and themes. Research encourages curiosity, exploration and cross-fertilisation of ideas. It also enables development of an individual interpretation of experience and exposure to outside sources. This leads to more informed decisions in the design process.

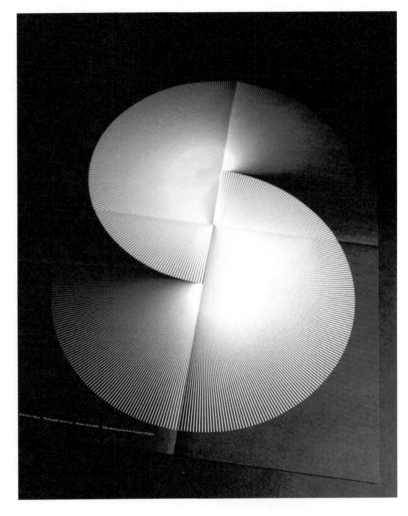

↑ Graphic design is everywhere— it is believed that most people see thousands of graphic images every day as they go to work. Some designs are memorable due to their uniqueness and beauty.

Designer **LANDOR ASSOCIATES**
Client **SPICERS PAPER/ MACDONALD & MASTERSON**

→ To express their client's unique approach to winemaking, these designers had their illustrations dimensionally embroidered—a fitting metaphor for the care and attention to detail Logan crafts into their wine.

Designers **IVANA MARTINOVIC AND CLINTON DUNCAN**
Client **LOGAN WINES**

MICHAEL HALL

CONCEPTS AND STRATEGIES

As a graphic designer, 50 per cent of your task is working with the client to understand their needs, communicating your needs in terms of information (written and visual), and working with suppliers to make sure that the client gets what you have agreed on. The other 50 per cent is concepting, designing, evaluating (and constantly re-evaluating), refining, implementing, and overseeing the production of the final product. These tasks can be divided among a number of individuals depending on the size of your design studio. As a student, most of the time the 'design studio' means only you—unless you work on a group project when the tasks can be shared.

There is a lot of emphasis on evaluation. This is because the design process can take months (and sometimes years) and it's easy to lose track of the original plan unless you keep evaluating whether the design is still relevant. Consider the original criteria and whether they need to be reassessed.

Aids to thinking:

❯ use of models, symbols, diagrams and pictures

❯ use of abstraction to simplify the effort of thinking

❯ use of mind mapping to focus on a concept

❯ talking with like-minded people

❯ idea generation

❯ desire for learning.

→ These three logos are very different from each other but have all been created by Kevin Finn.

Designer **FINN CREATIVE**

EXERCISE How do you design a promotional campaign that stops people from wanting something?
As a group exercise, brainstorm how you might dissuade people from wanting a particular commodity.

63

COMING UP WITH THE DESIGN

The first steps in coming up with your design involve 'thinking big'. You can then develop your creative ideas using visual techniques such as concept maps, mood boards and thumbnails.

Thinking big

Once you have researched and analysed the environment it's time to think big. Brainstorm the concepts, using written words, mind maps or images to come up with the 'big idea'. It doesn't matter what process you use as long as you come up with a wide spectrum of ideas relevant to the needs of the brief. The cultural context needs to be identified. In addition to brainstorming and mind mapping, the best way to do this is by using word and image association, idioms, metaphors, linkages or lateral thinking. These techniques can help designers to identify solutions to challenges as part of the creative process.

Lateral thinking

It is important to be clear about the design process by bringing lateral thinking into the open as a means of shared problem solving. 'Lateral thinking' means shifting thinking patterns away from predictable thinking to new or unexpected ideas. By using a lateral thinking methodology, designers avoid looking too narrowly at the problem; instead, they are open to every possible idea and perspective. Some ideas generated this way may not be the ideal solution in themselves but they move thinking forward to a new place where different ideas can be produced.

Although unrefined ideas may appear to be silly and impractical, they can often be a step towards finding a workable idea that fits the brief well.

Brainstorming techniques

Usually considered a group activity, brainstorming involves a list of lead questions that are used to provoke ideas, which are then evaluated. Participants are encouraged to elaborate on all ideas. Anyone who inhibits idea generation, and possibly reduces the effect of the creative process, is discouraged from participating.

Brainstorming is an organised approach for producing ideas because it lets the mind think without interruption. The group should agree on a way to stay on track and to measure success. The solution should not require skills or resources that the group does not have. Recognising and cultivating ideas in a group situation and in response to a design brief is a skill worth developing. The greater the number of ideas generated, the higher the chance of producing a radically effective solution.

Mind mapping

A mind map is a diagram used to represent words, ideas or objects that are linked to a central key word or idea. Mind maps are more ordered than brainstorming in that the ideas are segmented along branches. Mind maps are an effective method of note-taking that capture every idea and represent associated thoughts or concepts. Associated concepts can be words, images or symbols. If the conceptualiser is having trouble getting started the best way to get going can be to use the '5 Ws' approach: consider the 'what', 'why', 'where', 'who' and 'when' of the problem (you can also add 'how').

When all possibilities have been exhausted, circle the four or five words or images that appear to be the strongest. Develop these into visual images that fit the brief. Keep refining until you come up with images that convey the intended message.

Word association

Using a creative connection, conceptualisers freely associate words until they come up with a predetermined number, for example 250 words. The idea is to start with one word and then list any other words that come to mind when thinking of the first word. Then by circling the words that stimulate further ideas, or are most relevant, a series of concepts can be created.

It's important to refer back to your research and analysis at this point—are you still on track?

Select the most appropriate concepts and try to develop them further. If they don't seem to lead anywhere, that's OK: you've got more ideas to work with. Keep exploring and refining until you have three solid ideas to develop into full designs for presentation to the client.

→ Mind mapping can help to develop alternative ideas and explore how seemingly unrelated things actually do affect each other, as demonstrated in this environmental design

Designer **TURNER DESIGN**
Client **TAYLOR ROBINSON ARCHITECTS**

↓ Concept drawings are made en masse until all possible ideas have been put down on paper.

↘ Sometimes designers start with hundreds of sketches hoping that that they will find the best idea to solve the client's problem.

Designer **TURNER DESIGN**
Client **LIMONCELLO**

Idea engineering

The next step involves using the conceptual thinking skills to develop interesting and productive strategies. Although idea engineering may initially be a challenge, it is important for all designers to be imaginative and innovative and to develop their own individual approach to generating ideas into visuals or images. Eventually, with practice, visual images, language and interrelating ideas will easily link to visual concepts or themes that can be communicated through design into a layout. The goal is to end up with at least five viable words from whichever of the above concept strategies are used. By applying the following techniques the words can become interesting images or themes for further development:

- repetition and accumulation
- exaggeration
- turning it right around
- omission and suggestion
- paradoxes and optical illusions
- provocation and shock tactics
- change of perspective
- spoof and parody
- symbols, icons and signs
- telling stories
- absurd, bizarre, surreal
- taking it literally
- changing the product
- double meaning
- play with words
- metaphor, idioms and analogy
- breaking out of the frame.

Concept maps

A concept map, or visual essay, can be a helpful tool in revealing the design progress to date and enabling a designer to stay focused. A concept map entails placing appropriate research findings with mind mapping or brainstorming examples, mood board and concept ideas on the one large image. Thumbnails can also be added and this will display the design journey of the brief and act as a catalyst for the final phase of the process: the synthesis and production of the final designs.

Mood boards

Mood boards are a great way to visualise a theme or concept before putting pen to Wacom tablet or paper to create sketches or thumbnails. By creating a visual feast of colours, textures, shapes, fonts and theme choices, a designer can communicate their proposed ideas to a client. Many designers present three different strategies to a client, explaining the reasoning behind each one and how the design strategy will be applied in the finished projects.

Used to help establish a theme or direction for the design, mood boards often consist of found objects like paint swatches for colours, printouts for type, fabric or other material for textures, and magazine tear outs or digital imagery for shapes. There are no hard and fast rules and the content can be anything that inspires the general look. For designers who are averse to sketching first, the mood board can be a great first step and a way of getting a client on board with the theme. Mood boards are an asset in providing the opportunity to think broadly initially.

Texts on 'graphic agitation' (graphic art and design that addresses social and political issues) often display some of the most creative ideas in graphic design. Social issues are often subject to change and mirror current cultural concerns. When commercial companies get involved (sometimes in the guise of sponsorship) designers and educators may question whether it is right to use socially controversial campaigns to sell products.

A **theme** can be used to determine symbolic relationships, the premise of a story or the use of a visual metaphor.

↑ Original concept

→ Amended concept after client consultation

↑ Final t-shirt design

It is often interesting to look back at the design process once you have finished a project. Here, Kat Cameron from Team Kitten has hand-drawn concepts to present to the client. This has allowed her to easily take in the client's changes or corrections. The final t-shirt design was then created in Adobe Illustrator.

Designer **TEAM KITTEN**
Client **FRENCH KITTY**

Thumbnails

Further development of ideas for alternative design solutions needs to be completed by producing thumbnails. Thumbnails are roughly drawn visuals that are small in size. Initially, drawing thumbnails can be difficult as students concentrate on the way drawings look rather than their content. However, with practice, production of thumbnails becomes easier.

Thumbnails can be done in pencil or fineliner, or on a Wacom tablet straight to the computer. It is important to use whichever method is fastest, so that every visual idea is recorded. But don't compromise your creativity by jumping on the computer if your skills aren't amazingly good—you'll be restricted by your ability. Because digitally produced thumbnails look more finished than hand-drawn thumbnails, there is the trap of settling for a visual just because it looks finished rather than because it has real substance. Avoid this.

EXERCISE

Create a mood board for raising awareness of the need for more live music venues: produce a montage of images that give an idea of the theme of your piece, highlighting colours, shapes, textures, type and theme on an A3 board.

→ Mood boards help to clarify initial thoughts and obtain the client's approval to continue before spending hours on layouts. They also help to keep focus.

Designer **LANDOR ASSOCIATES**
Client **CITY OF MELBOURNE**

Thumbnail sketches do not need complex detail. At this stage, body text is represented by lines and squiggles but large print is more realistically executed. A variety of layouts can be explored by concentrating on the special relationships of foreground and background elements. Thumbnails also help the designer explore white or negative space, which will be instrumental to the success of the design.

A variety of images and perspectives could be used to communicate your theme. Try to aim for about 60 thumbnails and perspectives, then edit them down to four or five. The first 20 drawings will be influenced by everything sitting in your subconscious—the poster you saw on the street last week, the magazine you glimpsed in a shop, the ad you saw on TV or online, or a recently viewed YouTube, animation, or movie. Pull those sketches out and dispose of them—they are somebody else's vision. The next 20 drawings could be innovative, getting to the real answer to the client's problem; however, they will more than likely still be influenced by someone else's vision. The final 20 'ways of looking' should be yours—unique to you, your experiences, exposure to the world, and heritage—but also heavily impacted by the research and analysis you have completed.

Constantly ask 'why' at every stage of the conceptualisation process to challenge your assumptions, beliefs and conclusions. One of the hardest tasks for some new designers is being critical of their own creative thinking. The ability to choose between ideas to select the best solution is seen by many senior designers as a required skill in itself. Sometimes it's a good idea to give your ideas some space and evaluate them the next day to see how valid they really are.

The expression of ideas are a designer's intellectual property so always sign your name at the bottom of a page of thumbnails with the date and a copyright sign (©) to establish your ownership. Copyright is free and automatically safeguards your original work. Note that it is not the concept or idea but the way it is expressed that is copyrighted.

EXERCISE Keep a journal to record and refine ideas no matter where you are. Use the journal to record visual or verbal information that acts as a stimulant for the creative thinking process. Feel confident drawing in a book that no one else has to see.

COMPOSITION IN DESIGN DEVELOPMENT

Composition involves everything that goes into making the image and the page design and is specifically relevant to the way the viewer's eyes move around the page. Designers utilise compositional characteristics to align images and text but composition is also about how colours, shapes and the page format relate to each other. The same elements can be composed in an infinite variety of ways and this is often the difference between successful and unsuccessful graphic design.

Tension between colours or shapes can create unease in the viewer. How the elements relate to each other will determine whether the design comes together as a whole or the elements look like disparate objects. It is important to look at the overall shape of different objects within the composition and not just the individual items.

Creating dynamism and impact

CROPPING By deleting (and therefore selecting) specific areas of an image, the attention of the viewer can be focused. Cropping can improve the composition of the image and enables removal of distracting or intrusive elements. It also enables relocation of the focal point. Text can also be cropped but doing this can reduce readability.

ANGLE Changed viewpoints can make a huge difference to otherwise dull imagery. Because we usually view objects at our eye level, when we change the angle, we change the viewpoint and this captures the viewer's attention.

INTERACTIVE TYPE Designing type at different angles as text on a page forces the viewer to interact with it in order to read it. Angled type works best when it is perpendicular to the page diagonal or at less of an angle.

LIGHTING AND SHADOWS Dynamic layouts are created with light and shadow because they cause interaction with the viewer. Intrigue can be created with shadowed areas because there is ambiguity in shadow. Diffuse lighting techniques use scattered, spread out light, which doesn't concentrate on one object.

SYMBOLIC IMAGERY Our world is made of symbols that represent other things. Symbols allow designers to communicate by reducing ideas to their essence. All designs depend on what isn't in the composition as much as what is. Understanding of symbolic references changes depending on culture, religion and language.

PERSPECTIVE As objects get further from the viewer, they look smaller. They also become foreshortened. Colours weaken as they recede into the distance, which makes objects more difficult to distinguish as they lose contrast with their surroundings. Designers can use these natural occurrences to create illusion or focus.

DISTORTIONS Distortion is an expressive technique and can take many forms including making an image unfocused; distorting type shapes, position, general characteristics and sizes of everyday objects; and distorting facial characteristics (caricatures).

Legibility

Your designs may need to be legible at a range of different sizes. For example, a logo appearing on a business card and on a truck requires flexibility in its use of line and type. Designs that work well at one size may be too spacious and have too much white space when enlarged. On the other hand, when the designs are reduced the white space may shrink to the point where the lines run into one another and the result is a nondescript black shape.

Consider whether your logo or image can be reduced and enlarged proportionally and still maintain the integrity of the design. When working with logos, this entails presenting the logo in the various applications required by your client, as well as demonstrating how it will work in co-branding situations. For example, Tim Tam as a brand has a high profile but its initial appeal was that it was a product of Arnott's— a company that has substantial brand and corporate equity. Therefore, the two logos are always positioned on the product's packaging.

Equity The various qualities of a product or service and the total experience that is communicated to the customer adds equity (real value) to the company logo. This is often referred to as brand equity.

Dean Poole/Alt Group
www.altgroup.net

Germinating from a conversation between art school colleagues, Alt Group has grown into a multidisciplinary design studio based in New Zealand, producing some of the most prolific design solutions around today. Working across brand strategy, communication design, interactive design and new product development, their clients range from furniture companies, arts and culture organisations, fashion brands, restaurateurs, energy providers and large professional services companies.

Creative director Dean Poole explains the beginnings: 'We were in London at the time and the conversation was around where the art world was going. It was at the time in the 90s when Brit art had shaken up the whole art world and all sorts of things were being done that hadn't been done before. Our real interest was art, but what really drives art are ideas—ideas are the guts of any kind of communication. So our interest was in taking our art training and thinking outside of the white box, and putting it within a commercial context. The idea was to start a company that sells ideas.'

Alt Group has taken this initial concept and built their processes around it. 'To have a good idea is one thing, but to innovate one must also develop the ability to understand how an idea can spread. This is at the heart of the creative process—developing an idea within a social context,' says Dean.

When approaching a brief, Alt Group realises that each job is different and with that in mind each process is slightly different. 'The design process is often explained as a series of sequential steps in which you move from one phase to the next. However the process of designing is not as tidy and rational as it seems on paper,' explains Dean. 'We usually start the process with asking the big question, what do we want the "design" to do. This is the "discovery" stage in which we try and understand the business

THIS PAGE | Poster designs for Auckland Museum events using neon light sculptures.

OPPOSITE | Examples of the I AM campaign created for the Auckland Museum.

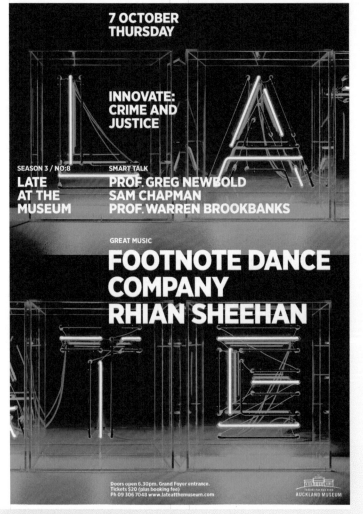

and establish the context in which it operates. For a period of time we become the company's external ambition. We ask a series of questions, to give us a sense of what ambitions the company has. What sort of idea are we? What part do we play in people's lives? What problem or issue do we solve? What is the everyday life lived around our product? Where do we fit in to daily habits? What are the underlying dynamics of the brand? We use this inquiry to set up a framework for the ideation process.'

One project that benefited from this approach was the Auckland Museum branding. Dean explains the conceptual challenge: 'We were faced with the challenge to develop a campaign identity and communications platform that reconnected the museum with its audiences.

'The solution came from questioning what a museum is. A museum is about identity—it defines who you are, where you have been, it hints that you belong, as well as connects the past with the present. Museums are about what it is to be human. Rather than a place for dusty objects, we wanted to create a brand that behaved more like a social hub.

'This highlighted the need to rethink the role of the organisation and how it connected with people—both within its building and beyond it. AM was developed as the campaign mark in conjunction with a brand voice that could operate in different modes. AM is an acronym for Auckland Museum. I AM is an introduction. I AM is an affirmation. It could make statements—
I AM not what you think. This created a voice, which could modulate and represent the multiple audiences. It could pose questions—Who AM I? What AM I? Where AM I? It also described the role of the institution—I AM yesterday, I AM today, I AM tomorrow.'

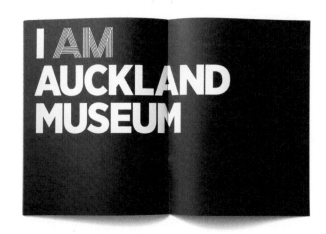

CORPORATE IDENTITY

A graphic designer needs to understand brand strategy, consumer research and name generation requirements to work with companies on their logo design or corporate identity. To create a successful corporate identity you have to investigate the essence of the brand. A business's corporate identity is more than just a symbol: it incorporates everything from how the logo looks, to what it appears on and what it appears with.

The main difference between the terms 'branding' and 'corporate identity' relates to the consumer. The business market, or consumer, determines whether the company has any brand profile and, if so, how the brand is perceived. If no one has ever heard of the company, it has no brand profile. The corporate identity is the visualisation of a company's goals, values and personalities and contributes to the brand profile.

Few Australians would not have been exposed to the flying kangaroo of the Qantas logo. Designed as a one-colour (red) logo, the first version appeared in 1944 and it has since been redesigned five times. The latest reworking of the Qantas corporate identity was undertaken by a Sydney design firm in 2007. The Qantas logo is applied to websites, brochures, advertisements, aeroplanes, trucks, cutlery, staff uniforms, luggage tags and so on. It is the combination of these applications of the logo that communicates the company's corporate identity. In other words, the corporate identity is reflected not just by one item, but in how the logo appears in all its variations. To be so flexible in many situations the design has to have a clear and logical structure that communicates to the end user the corporate philosophy of the company.

Logo design is a prime example of a brief that needs to be pared down, clean and slick. Workable in many contexts and sizes, it can communicate the attitude of the company to its business. A good logo design applied appropriately across a well-planned corporate identity can stimulate, and even revive, a failing business. The logo, or mark, can be used extensively by marketing and management and it is now widely recognised that marks often become a symbol of pride for employees. Logos have become a major component of the corporate culture.

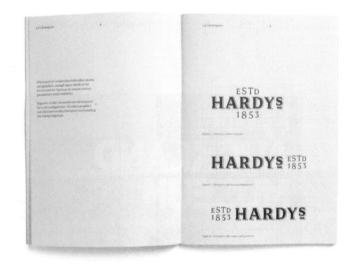

A **logo** is a design or symbol that forms the visual focus for a company's corporate identity. Most commonly a logo is either symbolic (using shapes, figures or abstract forms) or type based, in which case it is referred to as logotype or wordmark.

'We create brands that leave a lasting impression. Every aspect of a brand is an opportunity to resonate with an audience. Colours, typography, imagery and words are tools that reinforce what a brand stands for and make it stand out.'

HOYNE DESIGN, 2011

Trademarks

A trademark can be a logo, picture, word, phrase, packaging design, sound, scent, shape, letter or even a number. A trademark is considered an integral part of a company's marketing strategy. The different components of a trademark make up the company's corporate identity. A trademark can be registered forever as long as the registration is renewed every 10 years.

The logo in context

Whether a corporate identity is based on initials, typography, enclosures, display type, calligraphy, crests, people, animals or symbols it is imperative that the corporate identity sends the right message to the customer. It would be unusual for an identity to only have imagery, although this has been done successfully by Nike with their swish. Most corporate identities consist of typography (the name of the company or at least the initials) and a symbol or image. When the image becomes well-known, the name becomes less important as Nike, Qantas and fast-food chain McDonald's have proved.

Some logotypes (a logo that is constructed with typography) use a symbol inserted into the type to give the identity an individual and unique image. Logotypes can be produced using a typeface that is crafted by a designer or typographer specifically for that purpose.

Whichever type of corporate identity is being designed, there are a number of points to consider.

1. THE CORPORATE IDENTITY SHOULD PORTRAY THE ESSENCE OF THE COMPANY, USING THE RIGHT TONE OF VOICE.

If the company requiring a corporate identity is an airline or a bank, customers want to know it can be trusted. Therefore, a solid image may be more appropriate than a transparent scribble. If the company creates children's toys, then a fun but caring corporate identity is the solution.

2. ALL THE DESIGN ELEMENTS NEED TO WORK TOGETHER IN TERMS OF LINE WEIGHT AND SHAPES USED.

The components of the design need to have equal strength to give the identity credibility. One line shouldn't be thicker or thinner than another, or the design will look less credible.

3. IF THE IDENTITY HAS BEEN DESIGNED IN COLOUR IT WILL ALSO NEED TO WORK IN BLACK AND WHITE.

There are various mediums that only print in black and white or don't provide specific logo colours for printing. Even some situations on the web may call for a black and white logo.

4. CONSIDER THE LIFE OF THE IDENTITY.

To build equity in a company logo, it needs to become familiar to customers over a period of time. Updating to meet short-term trends can be short-sighted in terms of building trust with customers. However, not changing a logo design when it looks 'out of touch' with current thinking communicates that the business is also out of touch. A logo should be designed to have a life of five to ten years, but the best logo designs are those that are timeless.

5. THERE NEEDS TO BE FRAMEWORK OF CONSISTENCY IN THE USE OF THE LOGO ACROSS THE COMPANY'S VARIETY OF PRODUCTS.

A corporate style manual is often designed at the same time as the logo so that all users understand how the logo, as a part of the corporate identity, should be applied in a variety of situations and on all the company's products.

Checklist for logo design

- Be objective, visionary and a problem solver.
- Always brainstorm a range of ideas to ensure you hit the mark selected by the client.
- Make the final design accurate and producible.
- Search the trademarks database to ensure you are not infringing on someone else's existing logo design. Go to TM Headstart at www.ipaustralia.gov.au (accessed 7 March 2011) for further help.
- Always add value—graphic design is a creative business exchange.

THE END PRODUCT

The end result of your design work shouldn't be a surprise to the client. Work with your client to create the best solution. The majority of your clients will be non-creative people and therefore the rough drafts for a concept may have to look 'real' for them to understand how the designs will work in practice. The production of proofs and realistic mock-ups of material, such as T-shirts or bus stop ads, are key stages in the design process. You may need to have many meetings with the client to make sure that the end result is a true solution to the design problem. In a design studio you should be privileged to work with a senior designer who will guide you through the process. Use their expertise, knowledge and experience to develop the process and obtain a great end product.

← The concept behind this identity, for a web designer and developer, was to reflect the depth of work that goes into coding and developing websites. Starting with a monogram of the client's first name, the designer created a figurative logo that resembles the infinity symbol.

Designer **NIC CARY/STUDIO VERSE**
Printer **TAYLOR'D PRESS**
Client **ZANN ST PIERRE**

↓ A concept for Miller light globe identity and packaging. The designer has created a figurative logo that echoes the spiral shape of the globe. However, when the logo is turned on its side, it cleverly becomes a stylised 'M'.

Designer **JACKSON DICKIE**
Client **MILLER LIGHT GLOBES**

DESIGN BRIEF: DEVELOP A NEW CORPORATE IDENTITY

 Develop a new corporate identity for Creative Mix Clothing Company.

Logotype dimensions

Maximum width 70 mm (with legibility at 30 mm)

Step 1

Undertake research of the target market, the range applications of the logo (business card, website, clothing labels), the competition (collect logos of your main client's competitors), other places and spaces for inspiration.

Step 2

Using word association, brainstorm or mind map to select three themes for your mood boards. Think about what the words 'creative mix' mean to you.

Step 3

Create three mood boards, suggesting colour, texture, shape, theme and type.

Step 4

Based on the information you have gathered, the mood boards created and the themes selected, sketch different logotypes using a Wacom pencil and tablet, or a fineliner and sketch pad. The words 'creative mix' should be larger and more prominent than the words 'clothing company' but all four words should be part of the logotype.

Step 5

Select three sketches that you think have the most potential to be final designs. Draw them up to the dimensions listed either by hand or use a vector software program like Adobe Illustrator. Present each selected design twice—one version in black and white and one version in colour—mounted on board so that the client can compare which design works best and suits their business needs.

SUMMARY

To be able to design for clients, a graphic designer needs to be able to identify problems, have research and analysis skills and develop multiple concepts based on parameters set by the client. As well as excelling in the visual communication of ideas and concepts, a designer needs to be able to communicate well to their client and design team members. Being receptive to the opinions and attitudes of others is an important component, as much of a designer's career in a design studio will be team-based. Also, client opinions can vary from yours so it is important to be able to communicate your ideas well and negotiate changes and alternatives.

Emphasis has been placed on the process of designing, creative and alternate thinking and the process of evaluation. Evaluation of the chosen designs throughout the process is essential to producing a final product that solves the client's problem. Once the design criteria have been established, tools including mood boards and concept maps can help to maintain focus. The design process has many variations and each designer will eventually use the best one for them, but the information in this chapter provides a useful starting point.

KEY TERMS

REFERENCES

Austin, T 2007, *New media design*, Laurence King Publishing, London.

Barnard, M 2005, *Graphic design as communication*, Routledge, New York.

Cole, S 2005, *Dialogue: relationships in graphic design*, V&A Publications, London.

Fiell, CJ & Fiell, PM 2003, *Design for the 21st Century: 100 of the world's best graphic designers*, Taschen.

Gardener, B 2003, *LogoLounge*, Rockport Publishers, Minneapolis, MN.

Heller, S 2004, *Design literacy: understanding graphic design*, Allworth Press, New York.

Heller, S & Fernandes, T 2006, *Becoming a graphic designer: a guide to careers in design*, 3rd edn, John Wiley and Sons, Hoboken.

Hembree, R 2006, *The complete graphic designer: a guide to understanding graphics and visual communication*, Rockport Publishers, Minneapolis, MN.

Igarashi, T 1987, *World trademarks and logotypes II*, Graphic-sha Publishing Company Ltd, Japan.

Zappaterra, Y 2007, *Editorial design*, Laurence King Publishing, London.

chapter 3

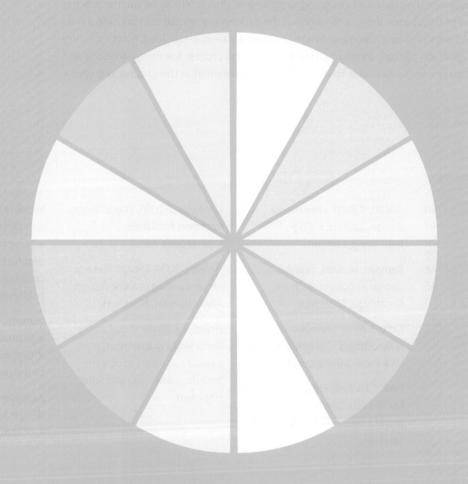

COLOUR, ELEMENTS AND ILLUSTRATION

INTRODUCTION

There are certain basic principles that form the foundation of all graphic design. It is necessary to understand and master these before moving on. In this chapter, we will look at colour—the most subjective component of graphic design.

The influence of colour is enormous and its power to convey a message can never be underestimated. Understanding how your audience perceives and responds to colour is key to creating successful design. Colour is one of the essential elements of graphic design along with line, shape, space, texture, value and scale. These are the basic tools of the graphic designer and when utilised they can create balance, unity and rhythm.

We will also look at illustration in this chapter. Illustrations incorporated into graphic design can include photographs or hand- and computer-rendered drawings and paintings. The use of illustration involves colour and the other elements of design. Appreciating scale and dimension in order to quickly communicate comprehensive concepts is a valuable skill. Understanding the collaboration between graphic designer and illustrator is essential.

THE ROLE OF COLOUR

Colour is an emotional language that communicates both attitude and meaning. By selecting the right palette we are able to influence the audience and generate an instant reaction and a lasting impression. It is therefore important that designers understand colour theory so that they can create a product that effectively conveys the client's message.

As a graphic designer you will be required to create a unique palette for each project, and while the client's or your own personal preferences will often influence this palette, the end result will always need to be tailored to engage the audience.

Working with colour is a practised skill that you will always be testing and revising by dealing with clients and audiences and by understanding the effect your work has. Fashion and popular trends also influence some colour palettes. It is your job to understand the effect of colour and tailor it to meet your client's brief.

Engaging the viewer can be as quick as grabbing their eye in order to get them to pick up your client's product or read your poster when bored on the bus. Clever use of colour is invisible; it is seamless and assails the audience without their knowledge. Dynamic colour combinations can excite the viewer and convey a feeling, while harmonious colours can sooth and allow information to be absorbed. A good palette can introduce an idea and, with repetition, remind and comfort; it can brand ideas and aid in recognition and brand loyalty. An effective palette doesn't always need to use multiple hues and tones either; sometimes the simplest selection can be powerful.

Some companies can base their entire brand on one colour. For example, the successful tea traders T2 have used orange as their signature. Combined with particular typography, they have chosen this colour to take into account the product and services they sell and the demographics of the customers they wish to attract.

Another company that relies on a single colour to create a particular attitude to their product is Cadbury. So important is this colour to the chocolate company that it has been the subject of ongoing trademark litigation.

Colours are also used to convey more general identities. Walk into a bookshop, for example, and without reading the signs you can tell what kind of books are in each section by the palette of colours there. The same goes for magazines and websites.

Colour can be used to provoke an automatic reaction, stir emotions or create excitement, particularly when it taps into social conditioning. The most obvious examples include using green for 'environmentally friendly', green and gold for Australian national loyalty, or pink for girls and blue for boys. But there are subtle examples as well, like yellow for sunny happiness and blue for calmness. Sometimes graphic designers use spot colours in a monochromatic setting to intensify an audience's response. In fact, lack of colour is also an effective form of colour use. Sometimes colour can even generate a physical reaction: for instance, when red is predominant in a physical location it can increase blood pressure, while blue can decrease blood pressure and have a calming effect. Even clever use of some colours in restaurants can make people salivate.

→ The simple but striking use of sky blue highlighted with a touch of yellow creates a strong brand for this annual festival. Repetition in all uses helps to create recognition. Hand-drawn illustrations and stylish typography make the design come alive.

Designer **SAATCHI & SAATCHI**
Illustrator **MARCELA RESTREPO**
Client **SYDNEY FESTIVAL**

Hue is used as another word for colour.

Tone is the particular quality of brightness or depth of a tint or shade of a colour.

EXERCISE Collect 10 squares of coloured paper, cut to 100 mm. Find a spectrum of colours (black, white, yellow, orange, red, purple, blue, green, pink, brown). Use specialty paper or paper sourced from printed matter, but each square should be predominantly one colour. Hardware stores are a great place to source free colour swatches. Form groups of four. Cut each square in quarters, and give three pieces of each square to the other students (each student should end up with 40 different squares).

COLOUR THEORY:
HUES, HARMONIES AND DISCORD

Before we can discuss harmonies and discord it is necessary to have an understanding of how colours (or hues) are applied by various technologies and how the different colours relate to each other.

PRIMARY COLOURS

There are two kinds of primary colours: additive and subtractive. The additive primary colours are red, green and blue, and these combine to form white. The subtractive colours—or printer's primaries—are cyan, magenta and yellow, which combine to produce black. Designers use both colour models: additive or RGB for digital design, subtractive or CMY primarily for the offset printing process.

RGB

RGB is the additive primary colour model. The zero or natural state of RGB is black, which is the absence of light. Once red, green or blue are introduced and overlaid they produce other colours. Varying the amount of each colour creates the RGB gamut, which contains a huge range of colours. When all three primary colours are combined they produce white light. RGB is used for all digital and electronic based displays including television, computer monitors, cameras and colour scanners.

RGB can be thought of as having the properties of light, like a rainbow, prism or computer/TV screen.

CMYK

CMY is called subtractive because the process starts with white or a blank area, parts of which are obscured (or 'subtracted') as colour is overlaid. When the full combination of colours is applied the result is a black area. Adding or subtracting these colours in different proportions and intensities can also create a full gamut of colours.

This colour model with the addition of black is used for offset printing. The colours are printed separately using colour plates, one over the top of the other, and are always printed in the order cyan, magenta, yellow and black—or CMYK. The K stands for 'key' and comes from the printer's method of 'keying' or aligning the colour plates to the black plate for perfect alignment.

CMYK can be thought of as having the properties of pigment, like ink, paint and the printing process.

Spot colours

A spot, or special colour, is ink that is used in offset printing to produce a solid non-CMYK colour using one plate. Multiple spot colours can be used in any project but each colour requires a single plate as opposed to the CMYK process of overlaying each colour to produce other combinations. These inks are special because they come in a wide range of vibrant colours that cannot be produced by the CMYK process. Printers generally refer to any non-standard CMYK ink as a spot colour, however the most dominant spot colour inks are the Pantone® Matching System®. The Pantone library includes individually numbered inks (referred to as PMS), swatch books and digital colour control devices, all of which help designers to specify, match and control colours. Another advantage of the Pantone Matching System is that the printer doesn't have to try to match a CMYK colour sample. They can simply mix the ink formula for the specific Pantone colour correctly. This saves lots of time and money. Other spot systems include TOYO (Japan), ANPA (USA) and Dai Nippon Ink Colours (Japan).

A **colour model** is an orderly system for creating a whole range of colours from a small set of primary colours.

Gamut is a subset of colours that can be accurately represented in a given circumstance, such as within a given colour space or by a certain output device.

Subtractive primary colour model

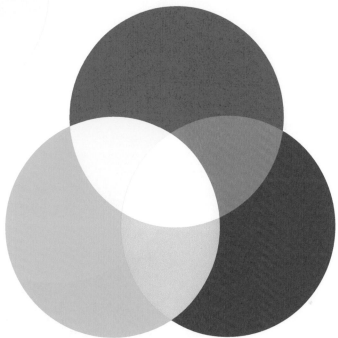

Additive primary colour model

The Pantone® Matching System® provides a wide range of options to help designers choose the right colour for the right job, from Pantone markers to colour swatch books and tint books (to show how each colour will look at incremental percentages).

EXERCISE

COLOUR ASSOCIATIONS 1. Write five words you associate with each colour: red, blue, yellow, green, black and white. **2.** Find a hue among the colour squares you collected in the previous margin exercise that matches most closely each word from your list. For example, for red you may list: love, blood, danger, hot, anger. Of your red squares, which one best represents love? Why? **3.** Discuss—were there differences in opinion of what some colours represent? Were some colours easier than others to identify?

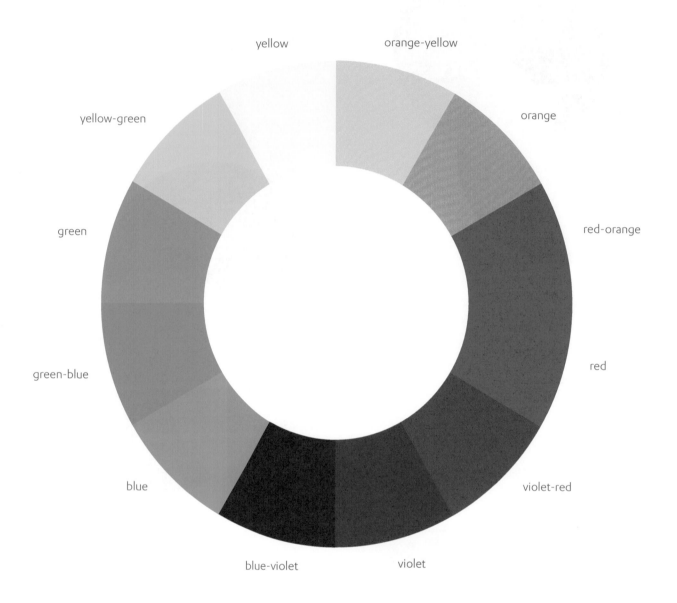

yellow   orange-yellow

yellow-green   orange

green   red-orange

green-blue   red

blue   violet-red

blue-violet   violet

COLOUR WHEEL

The colour wheel is an essential tool in colour theory. Understanding how colours relate to one another and where they sit on the colour wheel will help you to select colours and create colour schemes. Colour wheels can vary from the simple 12-step primary/secondary/tertiary version above to complex versions showing **tints** and **shades** as well (opposite).

↖ Simple 12-step colour wheel showing primary, secondary and tertiary colours.

Tints are created by adding various amounts of white to any colour.

Shades are created by adding various amounts of black to any colour.

Colour wheel schemes

ANALOGOUS COMBINATIONS use two or more adjacent hues on the colour wheel. They are harmonious and sit well together; however, they often lack the impact that complementary combinations provide.

COMPLEMENTARY PAIRS use two colours on opposing sides of the colour wheel. They offer high contrast and produce vibrant designs.

SPLIT COMPLEMENTARY SCHEMES use three-colour combinations of a colour and the two colours adjacent to its complementary. This produces a well-rounded contrasting palette.

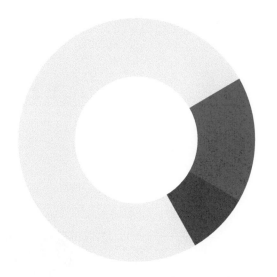

Analogous combinations

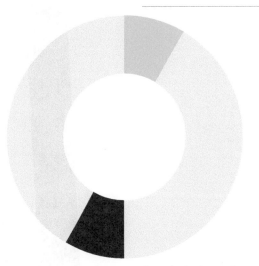

Complementary pairs

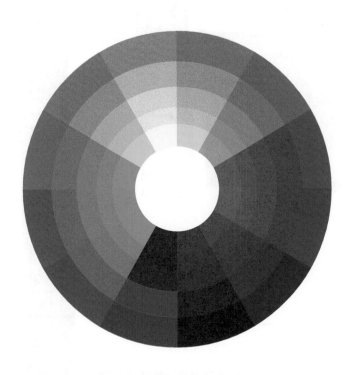

↗ A more complex colour wheel combining shades with the original 12-step colours.

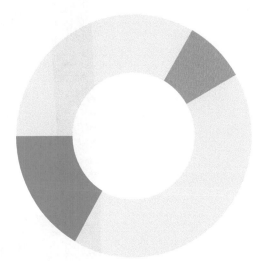

Split complementary

EXERCISE

COLOUR WHEEL 1. Following the colour wheel on page 84, arrange your set of squares (see the exercise on page 81) into a colour wheel. Identify primary, secondary and tertiary colours. There may be gaps in your colour wheel—that's fine. **2.** Create four different colour schemes by pulling out complementary and contrasting colours. Paste your favourite schemes on a sheet of paper. Use these as a guide for the design brief on page 112.

85

→ This website design combines
three previously separate sites:
music, motion and noise. The
designer has colour-coded each
section blue, red or green for easy
navigation.

Designer **ONE TONNE GRAPHIC**
Client **CREATE DIGITAL MUSIC**

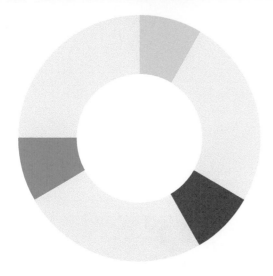

Triadic colours

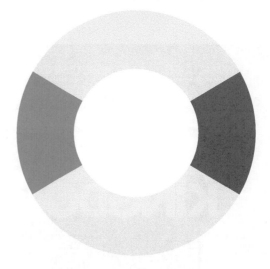

Double complementary

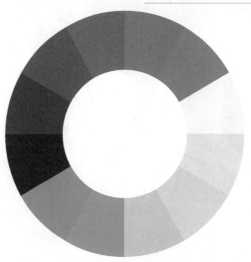

Monochromatic

TRIADIC COLOUR SCHEMES have three colours equally spaced from each other, using an isosceles triangle (even-sided triangle) to locate their positions. These combinations can often seem jarring but, used well, can be vivid and eye-catching.

DOUBLE COMPLEMENTARY SCHEMES use two pairs of complementary colours. Since four colours are used this can look unbalanced but can be effective if one of the colours is chosen to be dominant.

MONOCHROMATIC SCHEMES use one colour in multiple tones, shades or tints.

MUTUAL COMPLEMENTARY SCHEMES use a four-colour combination consisting of a primary colour and a trio of colours adjacent to their complementary.

ACHROMATIC COLOUR SCHEMES use neutrals that lack strong hue content. They are unsaturated.

SECONDARY COLOURS are made by combining two primary colours. It is through this mixing that the colour gamut is increased. Secondary colours slightly differ between the two colour models, as the original primaries are not the same.

TERTIARY COLOURS are made by combining one additive primary colour and one additive secondary colour. Tertiary colours are not created this way with the subtractive colour model, as adding more and more colours will create black.

Mutual complementary

unsaturated colours are dull
and muted.

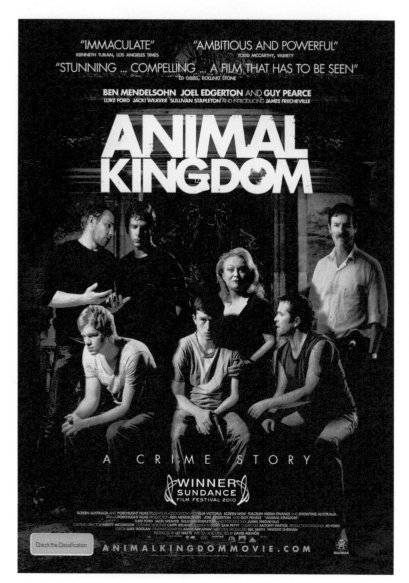

COLOUR VOCABULARY

With something as complex as colour there needs to be a vocabulary. Learning this complex but vital set of terms will help you describe and discuss design with senior designers, creative directors and ultimately the client. Below is a short glossary of colour terms.

HUES are the pure colours that form the 12-step colour wheel. Tonal variations of the same hue are often described using an added adjective, for example, 'dark-red'. Hue is also used as another word for colour.

WARM COLOURS are in the yellow, orange and red spectrum of the colour wheel. They advance, or come towards the viewer, and are called warm, as they are reminiscent of the sun, fire and heat.

COOL COLOURS are in the purple, blue and green spectrum. They recede, or move away from the viewer, and are termed cool as they are reminiscent of water, ice and the cold.

NEUTRAL COLOURS are greys, whites and blacks.

TINTS are created by adding various amounts of white to any colour.

SHADES are created by adding various amounts of black to any colour.

SATURATION refers to the purity of a hue or colour. It signifies the absence of neutral colours like black, white or grey. Saturated colours are rich and vivid. If a colour is unsaturated it is dull and muted, containing higher percentages of neutral colours.

BRIGHTNESS measures the lightness or darkness in a colour. Whether a colour is bright or not will depend of the amount of white, black or complementary colour it contains.

CREATING HARMONY AND DISCORD

There are no set rules for creating harmonious or discordant colour schemes. Generally a discordant colour scheme is one that 'hurts the eyes', creates a jarring effect and repels the viewer. Although there may be some situations in which you want to deliberately use a discordant design to produce a particular response, more often you will be aiming for a harmonious design.

The colour wheel schemes mentioned above provide a guide. Understanding the relationship between colours and how they respond to each other helps to create a strong palette on which you can base a successful design. This is often something you will need to experiment with and can rarely decide on without running through several options first.

Harmonious designs do not rule out high contrast and high impact schemes altogether. You can still produce a punchy design using high contrast that does not 'hurt the eye'.

↑ Having trouble distinguishing between red and green is one of the most prevalent kinds of colour blindness, or colour vision deficiency. Can you read what is written in this simple test for colour blindness?

EXERCISE

1. Select colour squares (see the exercise on page 81) that reflect 'Australia'. Discuss your choices in groups of four. Are there common selections or combinations—for example, burnt orange and sky blue to represent the desert, or green and yellow to represent wattle or sporting teams? Where do these colour associations come from—the landscape, the media, cultural stereotypes?
2. Lay your selections out on a table. Compare them to other groups' selections.

COLOUR AND ITS AUDIENCE

Putting colour theory into practice means using colour to create a response in the intended audience. This is a complex business and involves dealing with how people perceive colours and colour combinations physically (how their eyes work and what technologies they are using) and how they perceive them emotionally, which depends on their innate responses as well as their social and cultural conditioning.

COLOUR PERCEPTION

People's perception of colour is highly subjective. It depends not only on the physical characteristic of individuals' eyes and brains, but also people's conditioning and preconceptions, and the context in which a colour is presented.

Our eyes can interpret three kinds of colour: the additive primaries red, green and blue. So all the colours we perceive are combinations of these. The human eye can recognise approximately 10 million colours, however this visible spectrum is interpreted by the brain differently in every human being thanks to the sensitivity of the cone-receptors in our retina that receive the light waves that carry colour.

This means that no two people see the same exact colour. Instead they see slight variations and because of this you will no doubt find in your career as a graphic designer that you may have disagreements with clients over the minutiae of a certain hue.

Colour blindness comes in different forms but generally it is caused by lack of sensitivity in the cone-receptors. For many people, colour blindness does not have an overly detrimental effect on their lives. However, if you are colour blind, you may be unable to work as a graphic designer, a pilot, an electrician or in certain other fields.

Computer screens are unreliable indicators of colour as each one displays colour differently, particularly if they are not colour calibrated. They are also affected by different lighting conditions and environments. Most people do not routinely colour calibrate their monitors. Calibration is a method of adjusting colour to a specified colour setting such as the Pantone Matching System. Designers should regularly calibrate their computer monitors to ensure the colours they are seeing are true. Importantly, it will also guarantee that the work they produce matches the final outcome on printed products.

COLOUR MEANINGS

Colour often has strong emotional and cultural associations and these play an important part in the way people react to a design and the kind of impact it will have.

Colour is also a contentious issue, and no matter how skilled you are at colour palette selection there is always one variable within the project that can create problems if not handled carefully: the client. Therefore it is important to be able to talk about your colour choices and explain the rationale behind them, while at the same time respecting the brief and trying to gain an understanding of the client's needs and prejudices. Your ability to negotiate might make the difference between an effective design and one based on the favourite colour of your client's spouse.

Colour can be a character portrayed within the design, influencing the feelings of the viewer. It can be the darkness that lurks under the surface of a theatre poster, or the shock of an intense red splash to enrage us on a political website.

A person's culture and background play a large and important role in how they interpret signs, symbols and colours. For example white in Western culture is associated with weddings while in some Asian cultures it is associated with funerals. However, some reactions to colour between cultures are more similar. Yellow, for instance, tends to create happy feelings no matter which culture a person is from.

Table 3.1 overleaf shows colour associations that people generally have across Australian and international contexts.

TABLE 3.1   COLOUR ASSOCIATIONS AND CULTURAL MEANINGS

Colour	Association	Cultural meaning
Red	Blood, danger, warning, passion, lust, stop, femininity, love, excitement, revolution	Chinese good luck and celebration; Communism; colour of mourning in South Africa
Blue	Freedom, medicine, masculinity, corporate, sea, sky, calmness, intelligence, cool, refreshing	Iranian colour of mourning; Virgin Mary; a traditional colour for little girls in China
Green	Naturalness, heritage, tradition, substance, environmental, growth, jealousy, fresh, poison	Colour of Islam; colour of Ireland
Yellow	Sunshine, happiness, prosperity, energy, cowardice, spirited	Colour symbolic of Hindu culture; colour of mourning in Egypt
Purple	Royalty, modernity, luxury, romance, spirituality	Thai colour of mourning for widows
Orange	Modernity, citrus, fresh, vibrancy, Autumn	National colour of the Netherlands, robes of Buddhist monks
Grey	Industry, security, conservativeness	Helpfulness in some Asian cultures
Black	Premium, masculine, confident, authoritative, death, seriousness, darkness, mourning, evil, formal, classic	A traditional colour for little boys in China
White	Cleanliness, virtue	Chinese, Japanese and New Guinea funerals

EXERCISE

What colour is Australia to you? Create a mood board that reflects colours that you feel represent the essence of Australia. Then create a mood board of colours that represent your own lifestyle.

COLOUR OF AUSTRALIA

There are some colours that are readily associated with Australia, such as the red, white and blue of the national flag; the green and yellow sporting colours; and the red, black and yellow of the Aboriginal flag. None of these colours were chosen arbitrarily and all have meaning.

Other colours that have been associated with physical characteristics of Australia include the yellows, blues and whites of sky, sand and surf; the red of the outback and Uluru; the blue and greeny grey of gum trees; the golden sandstone of the public buildings that give Sydney its look; the bluestone of Melbourne and Adelaide; the red of tile roofs in sprawling suburbia.

There are other less tangible values associated with Australia as well. What colour schemes do you think might represent Australia as an ancient land? A young country? A multicultural country? A clever country?

COLOUR MOOD-BOARDS

Because colour is open to misinterpretation it is good practice to create a mood board when submitting an idea or concept to the client, and before completed artwork is available. Using reference material to explain your proposed colour combination allows the client to experience the reaction intended for their audience.

Graphic designers often build asset libraries to draw from to create and customise mood boards. Image aggregator websites such as www.tumblr.com or http://ffffound.com, along with magazines, books, promotional material, postcards, photographs, paint swatches and found objects are all valuable sources to help build your design asset library.

Your library is not only a useful resource when you are preparing something visual to show to a client, you can also find inspiration from it yourself. When you are creating a concept, browsing through your library can help produce ideas and feelings that you can transfer to your mood board or final design.

USING COLOUR

Colour is important in everyday life and colours are important to all design. Whether the brief calls for an annual report, corporate website, business card, signage or bus shelter poster, you will use colour along with all the other elements of design to produce the desired result.

Your choice of colour will impact on the success of the intended message and your ability to choose the right colour for the right application is integral. For example, an annual report will need to portray quite a different message to, say, packaging on a crowded retail shelf. In both instances you need to assess your target so that you know what they want from your product.

When designing products for large retail environments you need to evoke strong reactions from shoppers in order for them to pick your product off the shelf and consider it for themselves. Market research has shown that the colour plays a significant part in a person's initial, emotional response to the pack, when they might make assessments such as 'How does this make me *feel*?' and 'Is this a product/brand *for me*?'.

↑ This simple packaging helps build a desirable brand. It is instantly recognisable, even as you pass someone holding a T2 bag on the street.

Client **T2**

← The many uses of Cadbury's now trademarked purple.

Client **CADBURY**

→ When designing wayfinding for the Faculty of Pharmacy and Pharmaceutical Sciences at Monash University in Melbourne, design studio Hofstede used striking colours against neutral backdrops to create high impact and instantly recognisable areas

Designer **HOFSTEDE DESIGN**
Client **MONASH UNIVERSITY**

94

EXERCISE

COLOUR BRANDING 1. Collect a range of logos (e.g. Woolworths, Channel 10, Telstra, Google, Qantas, Breast Cancer Foundation). Have a class discussion about how colour is used: What associations do you have with the colours? What do you think the design is communicating through colour? How would the communication of the logo shift if you changed the colour of the logo? **2.** Have a class discussion about Pantone Matching System colours, and making colour swatches in InDesign, Photoshop and Illustrator.

In their *Colour Design Workbook*, Terry Stone, Sean Adams and Noreen Morioka state: 'Psychologists have suggested that colour impression can account for as much as 60 per cent of the acceptance or rejection of a product or service.'

Australian tea retailer T2's warm, inviting signature orange, combined with simple yet stylish typography, gives an edge of modernity. It is vibrant enough to attract a youthful market, while the monochromatic scheme has a simplicity that doesn't offend older audiences. The orange is reminiscent of brewing tea without being murky and brown; it promises a refreshing and enlivening product. The flavours of tea are then colour-coded into categories with large, easily identifiable labels. Clever use of colour, a strong palette and repetition have helped build instant brand recognition for T2 in their stores, and in cafés and supermarkets.

Educational textbooks (like this one) often use colour to emphasise particular pedagogy (that means bits of information that teach you something specific), because if you are reading a book and cramming for an exam you will only want to read the bits of information most important to you. Colour-coding along with good layout design can help you by delineating the features. A soothing colour palette can also help calm you down while you're reading particularly dense or difficult text, while a vibrant, high-contrast palette can distract you and give you a headache, which is not the ideal outcome.

Colour can be used to define areas and aid memory in environmental design. For example, car parks use bold, notable colours on each level along with the level number because, for most people, colour recognition is more memorable then a number alone.

Colours are so powerful that companies can create product recognition using only signature colours—no logos. It comes as no surprise, then, that many brands are starting to trademark specific hues. Australia Post has successfully trademarked the yellow associated with their mail delivery services; Telstra has trademarked the yellow of their *Yellow Pages* phone directories. Other examples include BP's use of Pantone 348C green, and Nestlé's use of purple in the packaging of their cat food line 'Whiskas'.

Perhaps the best known case of trademarking a colour involved Cadbury's iconic purple. Cadbury Schweppes Pty Ltd attempted to register a number of shades of purple in relation to packaging from 1996–2006; Australian confectionary company Darrell Lea and Nestlé opposed the petitions. In 2006, a judge agreed with them, stating that Cadbury did not own the colour purple. However, in 2009 Cadbury reached an out-of-court settlement with Darrell Lea and has now registered five shades of Pantone purples as the dominant colours of the packaging for their chocolate products. It is interesting to reflect on why the colour purple has been so important to at least three confectionery brands: Cadbury, Darrell Lea and Nestlé. What is it about purple that makes people want to eat chocolate?

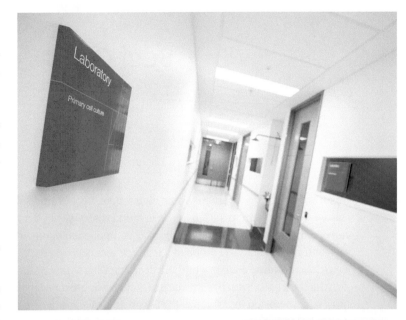

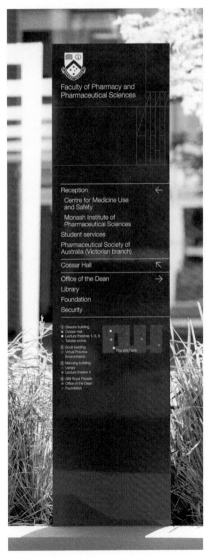

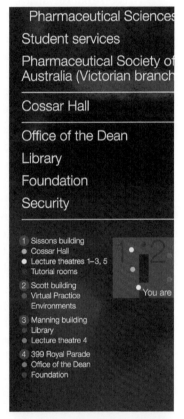

Beci Orpin

www.beciorpin.com

Unsure of what career path to take in high school, Beci Orpin started to study fashion design but soon found that it wasn't her cup of tea. 'There weren't enough drawing components for me, it was far too technical. So I dropped out after a semester and did a portfolio building course, while still deciding what I wanted to do. And then I discovered textile design, which was great because I was still interested in fashion … it was still quite a graphic course but very heavily drawing-orientated, which is what I wanted to do,' Beci explains.

'When I graduated I kind of assumed I would get a job with a company, but on the opening night of my graduate show I got offered my first freelance job and it happened like that.' The 'it' Beci refers to is her successful career as a freelance designer, clothing designer and highly desirable artist.

Beci started her own clothing label 'Princess Tina' in 2000 when she was asked to create a product to accompany an exhibition at Sydney fashion week. She printed 20 hankies (handkerchiefs), which were spotted by the buyer for renowned Parisian store Colette, who immediately commissioned her to print another line of hankies to sell in Paris. From there Beci produced T-shirts and tote bags and by the time she retired 'Princess Tina' in 2008, the label had produced full clothing collections that were sold in stores around the world.

Along with her clothing line 'Princess Tina' and kids clothing line 'Tiny Mammoth' (launched in 2009) Beci has created designs for both Australian and international clients. Some of her projects include editorial work, book and instructional illustrations, café rebranding, product design, snowboards and vehicle graphics design. She has also participated in solo and group exhibitions in Sydney, Melbourne and New York. Recently Beci art-directed children's entertainer Justine Clarke's video *Great Big World*; she describes this as her biggest project to date.

TOP | 'Bird Portrait' gouche/paper collage for Outré Gallery display at Melbourne Art Fair

RIGHT | Textile pattern design of Little Red Riding Hood for Jethro Jackson night wear.

When designing for such a variety of media, finding inspiration for colour is vital. 'Colour is a really important part of what I do. At university they taught us a lot of colour skills. It was a really important part of textile design.' Beci continues, 'Finding inspiration for colour is a lot like finding inspiration for anything really, it can come from anywhere. I am always looking for it. I never use **trend forecasting** or anything like that. I look at a lot of blogs and I have lots of books. I am always putting things into my inspiration folder. But generally I find that I am working within the same colour palette. I tend to favour one colour palette at a time and it then becomes relevant to what I am working on. Obviously with things like the Justine Clarke video, it's for kids so it has to be clear and bright. So that was fairly obvious what colour palette [to use].'

'I look at blogs all the time and I stick things on my wall all the time, so I guess that's like a inspiration wall and that tends to incidentally form a colour palette. I will stick things up on the wall and be "Oh look, there's the same blue being used all the time and there's a fluorescent orange being used all the time." So then that will be my colour palette, it just happens.'

ABOVE | Laser-cut wooden tree from 'Folklore' solo show at xgirl, New York
LEFT | Medal print

Trend forecasting refers to the concept of collecting information and attempting to spot a pattern, or trend, in the information. This is often used in fashion to assist in creating new looks many seasons in advance.

ELEMENTS OF DESIGN

In graphic design there are a number of basic elements that combine to create the final piece. All design will consist of at least one of these elements and by understanding this visual language you will have the tools to communicate the client's message while creating an integrated design.

The basic elements are:

- line
- shape
- space
- texture
- value and contrast
- size and scale
- colour

← This eye-catching billboard uses multiple design elements to create a successful design. Negative space is highlighted by the use of a black background. Layered shapes are created through transparent fruit. Bold use of colour enlivens the sign.

Creative **DDB, MELBOURNE**
Illustrator **STUART MCLACHLAN**
Client **ORIGINAL JUICE CO.**

BASIC DESIGN ELEMENTS

Line

Line is the element of length as a mark connecting any two points. Lines can organise, direct, separate, enclose, be expressive, suggest an emotion or create rhythm. They can join elements or divide them (a line that separates one element of a design from another is called a rule). A line marks movement from one point to another, like the trail left by a pencil on a surface. It is also the outer edge of any shape. A line can go in any direction, can be any thickness and does not have to be straight. It can be curved, wavy, zigzag, dotted—the list goes on.

Shape

Shape refers to the external outline of a form or anything that has height and width. It can be either geometric or an organic self-contained form. It is a defined space that stands out from the area around it. Examples would be the three basic shapes—circle, square and triangle—considered to be the fundamental shapes found in all design.

Space

Space refers to the distance between shapes and forms, but it is best understood in design as white space and negative space—terms used to refer to the empty but often active areas that are devoid of visual elements. The Chinese yin and yang symbol is a great example of integrated positive and negative space.

Negative space refers to the form created by the space between and around other shapes

← The use of multiple lines to create a pattern in turn creates negative space in which the client's brand is displayed.

Designer **A FRIEND OF MINE**
Client **CARLA GRBAC**

→ The designer uses scanned and photographed pieces of textured paper to add depth and whimsy to this gig poster.

Designer **LUCI EVERETT**
Client **THE ELK**

Texture

Texture is the appearance of an object and it can be both visual and tactile. It adds detail to a form by reflecting light differently. Texture allows us to understand the essence of the object, for example: furry often means animal, shiny can mean metal.

Value

Value is the relative lightness or darkness of an area or object. It can also be called brightness and tone. Value adds dimension by creating the illusion of depth in a design. With the addition of colour, you can create and convey a mood to enhance a strong concept.

Size and scale

Size is how big or small something is in relation to other objects. Scale refers to the process of making size relationships. Unless there is a scale of reference within a design, it is impossible to discern the relative size of objects and the meaning they represent. Good use of scale can produce a sense of movement, a quality of depth or feelings of tension. 'Scale' can also be a verb, used to describe changing the dimensions of an object. You can transform the scale of an object using graphic design software. Scaling an object disproportionally leads to distortion.

Colour

As you have seen in the early parts of this chapter, colour is an important element of design and can be used with any of the other elements to produce different effects.

our djs don't play big clubs

elk

LIVE ENTERTAINMENT AND DJs TIL LATE
THE FINEST LIVE ACTS FEATURING ON ROTATION:

EVERY FRIDAY + SATURDAY NIGHT

MR WILSON, RAY MANN, GLEN CUNNINGHAM, DARRYL BEATON, DJ DISCO KID + DJ CHE JOSE

FOR ALL FUNCTION ENQUIRIES
PLEASE EMAIL
SARAP@PALACEGROUP.COM.AU

WWW.THEELK.COM.AU
THEELK@PALACEGROUP.COM.AU

PH. 8354 0164
23 DARLINGHURST RD
KINGS CROSS

ASTRED HICKS

↑ A spread from *The Arrival* by
Shaun Tan shows his detailed
hand-drawn illustrations.

Illustrator **SHAUN TAN**
Client **HACHETTE AUSTRALIA**

→ Loose, energetic and youthful,
Rebecca Welzer's watercolour
illustrations are a great match for
this book on beauty.

Illustrator **REBECCA WELZER**
Client **ALLEN & UNWIN
AUSTRALIA**

ASTRED HICKS

DESIGN PRINCIPLES

Designers use combinations of the design elements on pages 99–100 to compose designs that are based on the following principles:

- balance
- rhythm
- pattern
- unity
- proportion
- emphasis
- contrast.

Balance

Visual balance occurs when elements are distributed evenly through the design space. There are two kinds of balance within design: symmetrical and asymmetrical. Symmetrical designs tend to be stable yet static. They are evenly weighted with an obvious structure. Asymmetrical designs can be more organic and active. They can create an imbalance, which implies dynamic movement. However, asymmetry does not always mean lopsided; it also can provide a type of balance. If a design has text on one side, say, and shapes on the other, even though the elements are dissimilar they can be satisfyingly balanced and stable.

Rhythm

Repeating elements creates rhythm. Rhythm denotes movement in the way that elements direct our gaze to scan the message for understanding or information. The term 'sequence' is used to refer to the viewing order of the elements and to determine the flow of a multipage publication such as a magazine or book.

Pattern

Pattern is the unbroken repetition of an object. Patterns can include grids, geometric shapes, hand-drawn elements or even computer code. Repetition can offer contrast and recognition.

Unity

Unity is achieved when all the design elements relate to one another and project a sense of completeness. A viewer will always seek unity in a message. Without it, the viewer will lose interest.

Proportion

Proportion is the relationship between sizes in different elements. It can also relate to the surface area of different colours. Proportion within design can enhance the functionality by giving elements size comparison and adding depth.

Emphasis

Emphasis helps guide the eye around the design area using various levels of focal points. These levels form a hierarchy that gives direction and organisation to the design. For example, the element that is most important in the design should be dominant.

Contrast

Contrast stresses the visual difference in size, shape and colour between the elements to enhance the perception of an intended message. Contrast also draws and directs the viewer's attention to specific areas of information.

Symmetrical balance is a mirror image balance, with the same or very similar parts facing each other on either side of an axis.

Asymmetrical balance is typically off-centre and created with mismatched elements.

103

ILLUSTRATION

Illustration is an important skill to have as a designer. You don't have to produce masterpieces but being able to understand scale, proportion and balance enables you to quickly sketch concepts that are easily understood by your creative director or client. This aids communication and allows ideas to be freely discussed.

However, whether you are a proficient illustrator or not, you will sometimes need to commission an illustrator to complete a design. This may be because a different illustration style is needed or because you simply don't have time to create a bespoke image yourself.

You only have to look through the web pages of some of Australia's illustration agents to see that in the 21st century there are no limits to the style, format, technique or tools that can be used to create illustrations. Book illustrators like Shaun Tan excel in the use of newspaper and other typed pages for background texture, while other illustrators mix photographs and illustration in many effective ways. Digital imagery has opened the possibilities even further with many illustrators using both handmade and computer-made media to produce dramatic post-digital mixes.

If you would like to study illustration techniques further, we recommend you look at these resources:

Magazines
◉ *Digital Artist*
◉ *Wooden Toy*
◉ *Adbusters*
◉ *Computer Arts Projects*

Websites
◉ Deviant Art (www.deviantart.com)

← ↓ Using a combination of pencil and watercolour these illustrations have an elegant, ethereal feel.

Illustrator **BETH-EMILY**
Client **SELF-PROMOTION**

← Eamo explores the Australian cultural identity through his illustration. He weaves eskies, thongs, zinc and man-made icons like the big banana and the big Merino with native fauna like the jellyfish into his work. Intricate detail and an Australian sense of humour are trademarks of this illustrator.

Illustrator **EAMO DONNELLY**
Client **OWL MOVEMENT**

Bespoke means that an object is made to order. The term is often used to describe unique, highly customised pieces that have a great deal of direction from the client. It can refer to 2-D or 3-D pieces.

105

The Jacky Winter Group

www.jackywinter.com

The Jacky Winter Group is an illustration agency with a difference. Describing themselves as more of a talent agency that represents illustrators, founder Jeremy Wortsman started the group in 2006, representing 12 Australian illustrators. It has since grown to over 100 different artists, with five staff in dedicated offices in Melbourne with an associated gallery, Lamington Drive.

What really sets Jacky Winter apart from the crowd is their large cross-section of talent, from seasoned veterans to recent graduates, alongside some of Australia's premier illustration talent. Illustrators from the agency have made their mark across a number of fields both locally and internationally. 'We've worked on everything from national ad campaigns to artwork wrapping trains in New York. We've done editorial work for *Readers Digest* and *Playboy*. Storyboards for pitch work and fully animated TVCs. Everything, really!' says Jeremy.

The agency works as a conduit between the illustrator and the client. Jeremy explains, 'Mostly it's about managing expectations between all parties involved. Once the fundamentals are there, like number of revisions, when sketches are due, etc, then we can really set up a base to go from.' Briefs and expectations differ from editorial work to advertising. And it is during the process of revisions and communicating with the client that the agency sees themselves as most valuable to the illustrators, aiding them to navigate difficult requests or tackling unexpected issues. Jacky Winter's experience in taking hundreds of jobs from concept to completion helps them take the right path.

However, the agency does manage the interests of their clients, alongside that of their illustrators. 'At the end of the day though, each job is unique and we try to identify problems early on and try to help get the most accurate information out of the creatives so they can get the best result from our talent.'

WHO IS JACKY WINTER?

Jacky Winter (*Microeca fascinans*) is a native Australian Robin. It also happens to share Jeremy's initials. The name for the agency was chosen as a wink to the founder but still made sure the focus was on the talent they represented. It is also a metaphor for the agency's desire to give Australian illustrators 'flight' in terms of getting their work out in the world.

ABOVE | *A Field Guide to the Birds of The Jacky Winter Group*, a quirky promotional book to display the illustrators represented.

TOP RIGHT | The work of James Gulliver Hancock
BOTTOM RIGHT | The work of Edwina White

At a time when stock photography and digital illustration is a cheaper option, illustrators can struggle if clients' budgets are tight. It's a challenge that Jacky Winter is willing to take on. 'If you asked someone whether a bespoke suit has more value than something purchased off the rack, there would be no question. Some people get it and some don't. We find that with many advertising clients, they will come to us with a small job and the client will love it, and then it rolls out into a national campaign. In that regard, part of our job is as educators to both our clients and illustrators.' The reward for the client, when commissioning an illustration, is having a piece that is unique and tailored to fit their needs.

For aspiring illustrators, Jeremy warns 'Any sort of freelance career in any creative area is going to be a challenge no matter where you are. Especially at the current time where so many people are skilled in so many areas. I think supplementary income is a must at first, but the potential for a more enriching career in the arts has never been more of a reality for those with the drive and passion to make it a reality.'

COMMUNICATING WITH ILLUSTRATORS

When you commission services from other creative trades, collaboration is the key. It is valuable to understand the process of illustration in order to brief and direct an illustrator properly and save frustration, time and money.

Compiling the brief

A good rule of thumb for all briefs for illustrators is to think about what information you would need if you yourself were receiving this brief from a client. The information could include, for example, size of illustration, colour specifications, materials used and deadline. Relevant background on the job, as well as a mood board to give a visual idea of the result you are after, are also important.

If you cannot be specific in your brief requirements (for example, 'a yellow bird in a cage'), you will need to give the illustrator an open brief. In such cases it is best to have a meeting to discuss your brief and ask them to present their ideas as rough sketches before they present their first round of concepts. This helps to narrow down ideas and focus the illustrator's skill.

The next step is to work out how the illustrator will present you with illustration concepts and how many they will do. Your budget can be affected by the number of concepts and the degree of finish you require.

Negotiate the number of revisions allowed in the brief. Make sure all parties understand that any changes requested after the approved illustration has been supplied may incur extra charges.

Getting approval, or sign off, can be tricky as the illustrator must fulfil your brief and you must fulfil your client's brief. You should consider whether you need to integrate the illustration into your design, or whether you can present it to the client separately. Hiring creative help does add an extra degree of difficulty to a job! However, in most cases the benefits of collaboration far outweigh the stresses of the ping-pong match that getting client approval can turn out to be.

↑ Mixed media adds texture to this poster by renowned gig poster illustrator duo We Buy Your Kids.

Illustrator **WE BUY YOUR KIDS**
Client **DUNGOG FILM FESTIVAL**

The Design Files and The Jacky Winter Group collaborated on this neighbourhood calendar, which showcases 12 Australian illustrators, to celebrate their local neighbourhoods.

→ *Illustrator* **KAT CHADWICK**
Client **THE DESIGN FILES AND THE JACKY WINTER GROUP**

↑ *Illustrator* **RIK LEE**
Client **THE DESIGN FILES AND THE JACKY WINTER GROUP**

↓ *Illustrator* **KAT MACLEOD**
Client **THE DESIGN FILES AND THE JACKY WINTER GROUP**

EXERCISE

ILLUSTRATION BRIEFS - Look at three illustrated book covers. Discuss: **1.** How does the cover reflect the book's content and its genre? **2.** What kind of instructions do you think the illustrator was given (e.g. a fresh, contemporary look; a handmade quality; non-figurative; leave space for the title and author name; colour palette should be bold/desaturated/young/retro)? **3.** Write a brief for each book—this is an exercise in working backwards from the finished product to understand the design process.

← Illustrations can be incorporated in a number of ways. Here, the illustrator was commissioned to create silhouetted people and their fashionable bookshelves to serve as an elegant backdrop for luxury brand Hermès's Melbourne boutique window.

Illustrator **ALDOUS MASSIE**
Client **HERMES**

→ This whimsical illustration shows there is an adventure for everyone at these markets.

Illustrator **LAUREN CARNEY**
Client **THE FINDERS KEEPERS**

SPRING/SUMMER MELBOURNE
INDIE DESIGN & ART MARKETS
9TH & 10TH OCTOBER 2010
10AM - 5PM
LIVE MUSIC & CAFE/BAR

ARTWORK BY LAUREN CARNEY
WWW.LAURENCARNEYART.COM

SHED4 - VICTORIA HARBOUR
NORTH WHARF RD, DOCKLANDS
FOR MORE INFO VISIT:
WWW.THEFINDERSKEEPERS.COM

PUBLISSIMO:
pr+events
frankie magazine

Leeloo
made590

Another important factor in commissioning an illustration is usage and rights. How will the illustration be used and for what duration? Is this a commercial project, such as a magazine or book cover? Is it for multiple mediums (print and TVC, for example)? Or maybe it is to be a company brand. All these things will affect the price, as there may be a sliding sale of fees for different uses. The rights of the image need to be negotiated in the original brief. Rights refer to copyright and ownership of the work (the illustration). Australian copyright law states that the illustrator will own copyright of the commissioned work, unless they have agreed otherwise. In these cases, the client will have the right (licence) to use the work only for those uses for which it was commissioned. So it is important to have a clear agreement in the brief, stating exactly what rights the client and the illustrator will each have.

TVC stands for television commercial.

DESIGN BRIEF: CREATE A POSTER

 Design a poster for a travelling exhibition called 'Vibrant Antipodes'.

The exhibition celebrates innovative use of colour in Australian design, featuring work by a range of practitioners from diverse disciplines (graphic design, interior design, industrial design, fashion design). Considering the diversity of the content, we do not want to use the work of a single practitioner or discipline. Instead, we would like an original illustration to use on the poster and other promotional material. This illustration may be any media you choose that best suits your concept: photographic, illustrated, collaged, digital image.

Starting at The Powerhouse Museum during the annual Sydney Design Festival, the exhibition will tour the nation, so the venue and date information need to be alterable (i.e. do not integrate the typography of these details into the artwork).

Style/look

We want the poster to look 'Australian', without resorting to stereotypical icons like the Opera House or Uluru. It should be vibrant and dynamic. It should communicate 'design' and 'innovation' and 'colour'. There should be a strong relationship between the title of the exhibition and the illustration.

The name of the festival should be prominent, and the website should be easily read. As mentioned, the venue and date need to be altered for different cities.

Audience

We are appealing to a design-savvy audience: practitioners and students. Consider how your poster could be playful or witty in a way this niche audience would appreciate.

Format

A2, CMYK, no budget for further embellishments

Text

Vibrant Antipodes: a celebration of colour in Australian design

www.vibrantantipodes.com.au

31 July – 15 August (year)

The Powerhouse Museum, 500 Harris Street, Ultimo

Extension

To expand this brief, design a range of promotional material for this speculative exhibition, including postcards, invites, a webpage and an iPhone app.

SUMMARY

As a graphic designer you will need to put your thorough knowledge of the elements of design into practice until they become intuitive. With this foundation you will have the skills and confidence to produce successful designs and inspire the trust of your clients.

Colour is a powerful element and a good designer is not afraid of experimenting with colour to get the right result. However, clients who are unfamiliar with colour concepts may feel intimidated and opt for conservative choices. It is the role of the designer to guide the client into an understanding of how their message can be put across with the use of colour.

When illustrations are required in a design, the designer must not only choose the right illustrator but know how to work with that person in a collaborative and respectful way.

KEY TERMS

REFERENCES / WEBSITES

Ambrose, G & Harris, P 2006, *Basics design 05: colour*, Ava Publishing, London.

Australian Copyright Council, Information sheet G75 *Graphic designers*, www.copyright.org.au

Hayse, R, Vivid research, interview.

Krause, J 2004, *Design basics index*, How Design Books, Cincinnati.

Lupton, E & Phillips, J 2008, *Graphic design: the new basics* Princeton Architectural Press, New York.

Morioka, A & Stone, T 2006, *Colour design workbook*, Rockport Publishers, Minneapolis, MN.

Resnick, E 2003, *Design for communication*, John Wiley & Sons, Hoboken.

Australian Copyright Council (www.copyright.org.au)

Beci Orpin (www.beciorpin.com)

Colour Lovers (www.colourlovers.com)

The Design Files (www.thedesignfiles.net)

Henry David York Lawyers (www.hdy.com.au/attachments/IPInsight_Nov2009.pdf)

IP Australia media centre (www.ipaustralia.gov.au/media/pages/lead/cadbury_purple.htm)

The Jacky Winter Group (www.jackywinter.com)

Pantone (www.pantone.com)

chapter 4

TYPOGRAPHY

04

INTRODUCTION

In the middle of the fifteenth century a man named Johannes Gutenberg (ca. 1398–1468) invented a system for the quick preparation of the letters of the alphabet for printing. Gutenberg's invention was moveable type: a collection of metal letters that could be arranged into words, sentences, paragraphs and pages. Today, more than 500 years later and with very different technology, the system we use is essentially the same. In this chapter, you will discover how the system came about and learn a little about the history of our alphabet. Most importantly, you will learn about type: how it is described and organised, and finally how to use it. You will also learn how to organise type on a page and explore some of the issues involved when it is printed, viewed on screen and used in the wider environment.

WHO USES TYPE?

Almost from the day we are born we are interacting with text that has been set in **type**. Type surrounds us: it informs us, directs us and warns us. Unless you happen to be out in the wilderness away from all civilisation, if you look around right now you will most likely see many examples of type.

Type helped you learn to read and write. In fact, before you learned to read and write your brain had already learned to recognise the shape of the letterforms that make up type and typefaces.

Virtually everyone uses type on a daily basis. Whenever they write a letter on a computer, create a 'Lost Pet' notice or party invitation, send an email, or contribute to a blog or social media website they make typographic decisions. True, the options that are available may be limited and the results may be poor, but the fact is that they have made choices about type, such as how to lay out the text and which **fonts** to use.

So many aspects of our modern lives involve text-based information that it is more important than ever to understand type. Graphic design is about communication, and as text is vitally important in the communication process, an understanding of type and how to use it is essential for graphic designers. This goes for print communication as well as screen-based communication.

ONE DOLL SALEWK2
SAT& SUN ...SALE NO2
BARGAINs START FROM
$1 - $2 - $5 ....
EVERYONE WELCOME ,
55 VOYAGER CRES
BAWLEY POINT
9AM START..
ps please come down drive
to house

Page 1

FELIX OPPEN

← A found handbill promoting a private sale of dolls. As this example shows, many people use type but they do not necessarily have the means to use it effectively to communicate—that's where the skill of the graphic designer comes in.

Designer **UNKNOWN**

Type or **typeface** refers to a particular design of the letterforms of a character set.

A **font** (or fount) is the character set of a typeface at a particular point size. These days, 'font' is often also used to mean 'typeface'.

TYPE PROFESSIONALS

As a graphic designer you will be expected to know about type and how to set it well. There are also other professionals who understand and work with type.

The typographic designer

A typographic designer is a graphic designer who specialises in the type side of design communication.

The typographer

A typographer is someone who works almost exclusively with type. Typographers tend to work with long texts, such as books. A typographer will design, lay out and typeset an entire job.

The type designer

As the name suggests, type designers design type. Graphic, interactive media and typographic designers may create typefaces themselves, but most of the time they use typefaces designed by other people. Type designers are those people who create the typefaces. While they primarily design type, they may also be graphic, interactive media or typographic designers as well.

The typesetter

The final type specialist is the typesetter. The typesetter knows how to set type well but is generally not a designer and may not have had much design training. Typesetters are usually not type designers. The skill of the typesetter is in being able to complete a layout and set type quickly and effectively to a template or set of instructions prepared by a graphic designer.

WHAT MAKES A GOOD TYPOGRAPHIC DESIGNER, TYPOGRAPHER OR TYPE DESIGNER?

It goes without saying that to be a good typographic designer, typographer or type designer you need to have a good knowledge of type; but beyond this, you need to know how to use type within a space—for example, on a page, or screen, or sign—and understand how it interacts with non-type elements, like images, empty ('white') space and the larger environment. This chapter will help you develop these skills. It helps to be passionate about type too, but that is not unusual. To be a good designer you should be passionate about all aspects of design, including type.

Having a good knowledge of type involves more than knowing about its technical aspects: it means understanding the value of type in the process of communication. From this you can develop an understanding of how type can add another dimension to communication.

HAND-DRAWN TYPE

While you may spend most of your time setting type using a computer, being able to draw type is a vital skill. Hand-drawing existing typefaces is the only way to truly understand their unique character. If you decide to create your typefaces, the only way to do this successfully is to draw the letters by hand.

EXERCISE   Look around the space you are in right now. Count the examples of type that you can see. What is the function of each example of type? Is it a sign, text on a screen (a website for example), advertising, a book title? How many different typefaces can you see?

117

While it is true that you may never use anything other than computer-based digital typefaces in your career as a graphic designer, the history of type prior to its digital forms continues to have a deep and important effect on type and how we use it today. The effect is in the actual typefaces, how we structure their use, and the terminology.

THE ALPHABET

The story of type begins a long time before Gutenberg created moveable type. It begins with writing.

The oldest known 'written' recording of human ideas and thoughts is believed to exist in northern Australia and is about 50 000 years old. These are marks ground into rock faces. One of the first recorded writing systems was developed by the Sumerians in about 3000 BC. It was called Cuneiform and consisted of groups of wedge-shaped forms. In about 1600 BC the Phoenicians developed a writing system based on sounds rather than ideas or objects (like 'man hunting bison'). This system was adopted by the Greeks, who made their own modifications and formalised the shapes and forms into what we recognise as letters. The Romans also adopted the system and made their own modifications. The result was a system of 23 letters that make up the bulk of the capital letters we know today. (They are known as capital letters because the Romans used to carve them on, among other places, the Capitals, or the top of their buildings.) Today we also refer to these letters as upper case.

In the Middle Ages an alternative system of simpler letters was developed in Europe by scribes who needed to transcribe texts quickly by hand. By Gutenberg's time there were, in fact, two letter systems in use. One was the Rotunda system developed in southern Europe, particularly in Italy. This is the system that we recognise now as our lower case letters. The second system was the Gothic Textura, and it was this that Gutenberg used as the model for his first typeface.

↑ The type that started it all: a page from *Gutenberg's Bible*. Note, all the coloured elements were added by hand after printing.

Designer **JOHANNES GUTENBERG**

Upper case (capital letters, for example 'A', 'B', 'C'), also known as majuscules, are the letter shapes based originally on stone carving.

Lower case (little letters, for example 'a', 'b', 'c'), also known as minuscules, are the letter shapes based originally on handwriting.

The name comes from the positioning of the trays of metal type when hand-setting type.

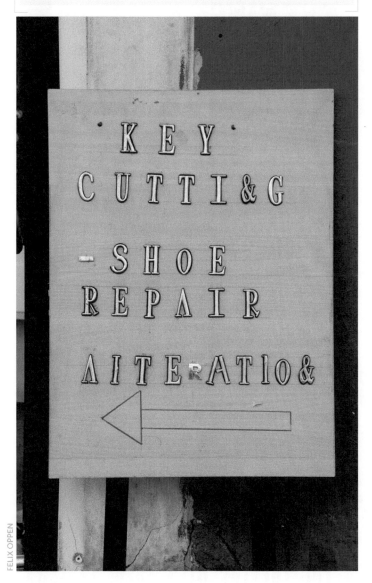

↑ The balance between simplicity and uniqueness of each member of the alphabet (and the supporting symbols) and the fact that each letter/symbol represents only a sound means that the message can still be conveyed even when the letters are not accurately rendered.

Designer **UNKNOWN**

FELIX OPPEN

THE AGE OF TYPE

Gutenberg's great innovation was to use his training as a goldsmith to solve the problem of printing words. Letters could be carved out of a hard metal, like steel, and the resulting 'letter punch' could then be hammered into a softer metal to make an impression (the 'matrix'). A single letter punch could be used to make many matrices. From each letter matrix could be cast the final printing types in their thousands. The individual printing letters—'slugs'—were made from an alloy of lead. They could be used to make tens of thousands of final impressions of ink onto paper, for one printing job after another. The whole combined process of type, press and paper reduced the time to reproduce a book from years to months and dramatically cut the cost of opening up the knowledge contained in books to a much wider audience.

The development of type from the mid-fifteenth century to the present is a dual story. It covers the design of typefaces themselves in response to the needs of the time, and also encompasses typeface design in response to the possibilities of the developing surrounding technologies.

Type in Australia

Unfortunately type does not have a distinguished history in Australia. It began with the arrival of an old press and second-hand metal type on the First Fleet—unaccompanied by anyone with any knowledge of printing. Until the 1970s, the industry was largely dominated by British and American companies. However, with the technologies that have swept the world of type over the last few decades, this limited local history presents you with the opportunity to be part of the creation of an Australian type industry that is slowly but surely emerging. (Apart from the example of the Gutenberg Bible all the examples in this chapter are of Australian and New Zealand typographic design.)

EXERCISE   Choose a letter of the alphabet and research its origins. How did it develop? When did it reach its final, modern form? Design an A3 poster to show your findings. Include several different typeface versions of the letter and the structural components that make up its design (see 'The anatomy of type' on page 125).

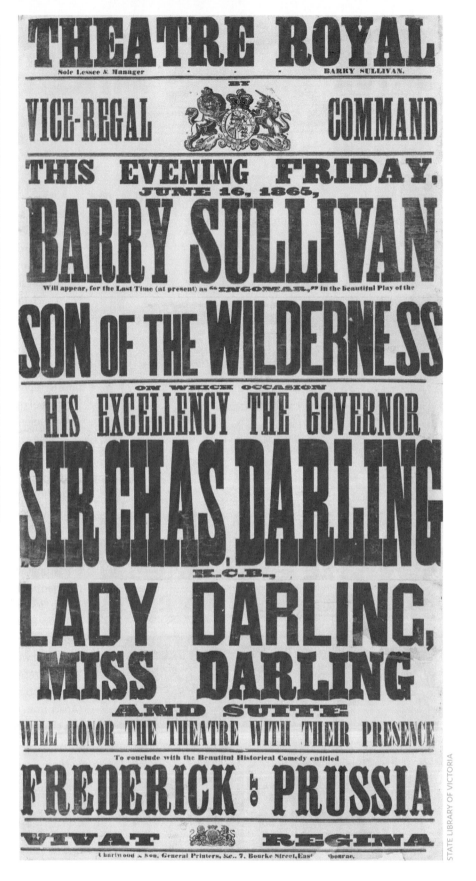

↑ A theatre advertising flyer from 1795. This would have been printed on the old wooden letterpress and with the second-hand type that arrived on the first fleet. Paper was very scarce during the early years so this must have been quite a special event. It was probably printed by George Hughes, who taught himself to use the press.

→ A theatrical poster from 1865. Produced in Victoria, it shows a typical use of mixed wood types that was common both in Australia and the world at the time.

120

EXERCISE

At the end of this chapter is a list of some key figures in the age of type. Choose one and find out why they were important. Research who some of their contemporaries were. Place them in the historical context of typography. Is their influence still being felt today? Create an A3 poster of your findings.

↑ A corner shop in the 1950s. Unlike today, all this work was hand painted. Type was used heavily because it is much more space efficient as a communication tool and also easier and cheaper than images to realise accurately.

→ The first thing printed in the new colony were the rules, known as the General Standing Orders. This is a page from the 1803 edition and is the first book published in the colony of New South Wales. The quality of printing is much better than the theatre flyer of 1795 because it was printed by the first trained printer to arrive in the colony, George Howe, who arrived in 1800. From 1805 he published the *Sydney Gazette*, which eventually became the *Sydney Morning Herald*.

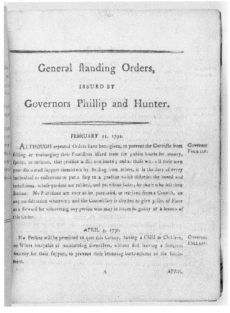

EXERCISE

Before computers, other methods were used for typesetting. These were cold metal (or hand) typesetting, hot metal (or machine) typesetting and photo-typesetting. Research one of these methods. When did it appear and for how long was it used? Were there specific technologies associated with it? What were the advantages and disadvantages of the method? Create a 10 minute presentation of your findings.

Wayne Thompson

www.atf.com.au

Typographer Wayne Thompson's childhood was spent chasing snakes and riding his BMX until his father brought home an old Letraset catalogue and rub-down lettering. From that day he was hooked. He worked his way through design school and up the ranks in advertising agencies to the position of art director in the 1990s. 'During this time in agency-land I became increasingly aware that, despite the wide variety of typefaces available, I was unable to find suitable type for many jobs. So I began to draw my own. With the advent of the internet and digital type foundries, I decided to start marketing my typefaces and began Australian Type Foundry in 2001,' says Wayne.

Since then, Wayne has designed over 100 typefaces for both local and international clients, including NRMA, Panasonic, Kmart, Big W, Sensis, Gloria Jeans, Telstra and Triple J. 'My type work is a combination of corporate commissions, modifications to existing typefaces and new designs of my own,' Wayne says.

Wayne approaches a brief by asking his client a lot of questions. 'As well as the obvious issues of style and appearance, we need to agree on the character set, licensing, naming, distribution and technical considerations. For a personal type design I have much more freedom in the process and often start designing with no particular goal in mind.' Wayne assesses each brief and varies his technique for creating concepts and type accordingly.

When creating a new typeface from scratch, he will over-draw the entire alphabet by hand before digitising. Wayne explains, 'For a client, I sketch concepts on paper. It helps to refine direction before anyone spends too much time and clients love the "artiness" of seeing real hand-made drawings. I generally show my client a few sample characters first, then the whole alphabet, then the first digitised beta version. Most type designers begin with the letters n o H O because these contain most of the straight and curved shapes which will inform the remainder.'

Comprehensive and well thought-out briefs from his clients allow Wayne to quickly understand what is required. This is necessary when working with advertising agencies with tight deadlines. 'I'm usually under a fair bit of deadline pressure. Often I only get a few days, but one job continued on and off for 18 months. A few weeks is the average.'

In this digital age not even the humble typeface is unaffected. Realising a majority of their audience will ultimately view their work only in digital media, typographers like Wayne have become savvy when designing typefaces for print and digital media. 'My primary concern these days is hinting—the process by which digital type displays within the pixel grid of a screen. Even at standard reading sizes, maintaining legibility on screen in complicated letter shapes such as 'a' is quite a challenge.'

When it comes to Australian audiences' reaction to typography, Wayne believes 'Australians are more sophisticated than our mass media would have us believe, and they notice and appreciate when anything creative is done well.'

TOP LEFT | Wayne speaking at the 2010 agideas conference in Melbourne.
TOP RIGHT | A sample of AeroSans Cyrillic
LEFT | Hand-drawn ArumSans alphabet in progress

TOP RIGHT | Custom type for NRMA's 'Unworry' campaign
MIDDLE RIGHT | A sample of ArumSans
RIGHT | A sample of Iperion

WHAT MAKES GOOD TYPOGRAPHIC DESIGN?

Type is a tool. Different typefaces can be used to create different moods and add to the meaning of the words they are being used to display. Type is a bit like drawing with a pencil: when drawing, you can use different pressures and kinds of strokes to create a beautiful image; with type, you can enrich text and create beautiful mental images. When the type truly enhances the text, it tends to work subliminally to produce an appealing effect.

Working with type allows you the possibility of considerable personal expression. Today many thousands of typefaces are available. When you choose typefaces for a job, your personal knowledge and preferences will influence your design.

Good typographic design enhances the communication of the text. The choice of typeface and its structure and arrangement on the page (the layout) all work seamlessly to aid comprehension. Done correctly the typographic design works so well that the reader comprehends the text without noticing the design. Good typographic design is essentially invisible to the reader.

What this means is that as the designer you must understand the needs of the client and their text. You will have to read it, or at least enough of it to understand what it is about. Then, within the budget and design constraints of the brief from the client, you choose typefaces and design a layout. So far this is no different from any other part of graphic design.

It is tempting to think that you can just apply whatever typeface you happen to like at the moment, or choose from whatever happens to be in your font list at the time. After all, all typefaces have the alphabet in them, they all look basically similar, so what does it matter which you use? Anything will do, right? Well, not really. This is likely to result in a poor design decision, as there are many factors involved in choosing the right typeface for the job.

Like snowflakes, no two typefaces are the same. There are subtle differences that a designer can use to convey different tones and voices. These can work for or against the text. Placement of the text

↑ Typographers create sample sheets for their typefaces to display the font flexibility and various uses. This is a sample sheet for the typeface Halvorsen by the Australian Type Foundry.

Designer **WAYNE THOMPSON, AUSTRALIAN TYPE FOUNDRY**

on the page, the number of columns, the length of the lines and the spaces between the lines, the size of the text and the headings are all elements that impact on the text and how it is perceived. There are few limits to what you can do with all of these. Get it wrong and the text could be unreadable, but get it right and you will have created a great piece of effective design.

Good typographic design requires carefully thought-out and skilfully applied creativity. It is a personally satisfying process, and in a sense, the resulting piece of communication is just the icing on the cake.

WHAT IS A TYPEFACE?

In order to be able to use type effectively it helps to know how to describe it, the names of the parts of letterforms or shapes, how it is organised and how typefaces of different styles are grouped. Knowing this information helps you to:

❯ describe the key characteristics of a typeface to your colleagues and clients

❯ quickly find similar or contrasting typefaces

❯ identify unknown typefaces

❯ understand the structure and purpose of various aspects of different typefaces.

THE ANATOMY OF TYPE

This diagram shows the names for the parts of letterforms.

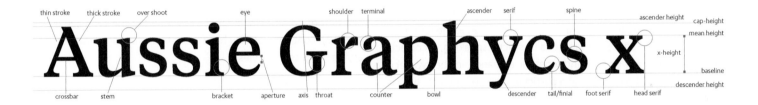

thin stroke · thick stroke · over shoot · eye · shoulder · terminal · ascender · serif · spine · ascender height · cap-height · mean height · x-height · baseline · descender height

crossbar · stem · bracket · aperture · axis · throat · counter · bowl · descender · tail/finial · foot serif · head serif

arm · arch · link/neck · ear · ligature · apex · small cap-height

upper and lower case · loop/lobe · leg · small caps · lining figures · non-lining/old style figures · italic · sans serif · slope 5–15°

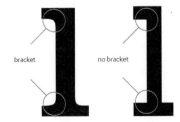

bracket · no bracket

 ↖ Here are the various terms that describe the parts of the letterforms. Knowing these allows the designer to analyse, understand, describe and compare different typefaces.

EXERCISE

The best way to understand the unique nature of typefaces is to hand-draw them. From the list at the back of the chapter, choose two typefaces. View them using the websites provided. Reproduce, using pencil and paper, at least six of the characters that you think best represent the unique elements of the typeface design. Pay attention to not only the shape of the letters but the space between them, ensuring that they look accurately formed *and* evenly spaced.

125

TYPE VOCABULARY

It is important for graphic designers to understand the language of typography. The following terms are used commonly by professionals working with type.

Type/typeface

The word 'type' comes from the Greek *typos*, which means impression. Thus in printing, 'type' refers to the letter shapes that make the impression, and 'typeface' refers to the particular overall design of a collection of type characters.

Font/fount

The word 'font' (fount is the UK English spelling) comes from an old French word for molten. It refers to the casting of a typeface at a particular size. Today font refers to the complete character set of a typeface at a particular size (for example, the font size of this typeface is 10 point). Today font is also often used interchangeably with the term 'typeface' (for example, 'Can you change the font from Times to Comic Sans?'). Though this is, strictly speaking, incorrect, most designers will understand whether a change in the typeface or just the font (the typeface at a particular size, weight and style) is being requested.

Type style

Typefaces that are designed for setting text usually come in two styles, roman and italic. Roman is the upright version of the typeface and italic is the slanted, originally mimicking handwriting.

Type weight

The weight of a typeface refers to how light or dark (how heavy) each member of the family is. The weights can range from ultra light to ultra black. The most common, and really the minimum requirement for a family, are normal and bold. (Note, the term roman is often used to refer to the weight most suitable for setting text.)

Type width

Typefaces may be available in a range of character widths. They range from ultra narrow (or condensed) through to ultra extended.

Font family

This term refers to all the styles, weights and widths of a particular typeface. It is in common use, but is not strictly speaking correct. The correct term is 'typeface family'. Note, the advent of non-letterpress typeface design and manufacture, especially computer typeface design, has seen a significant blurring of the meanings of the terms typeface, font and font/type family. However, it is still important to know the distinctions.

Super family

A super family is just a type family with a large number of weights and styles. With modern computer-designed type it is relatively easy to create a range of widths and weights (though large families did exist before computers, such as Univers—see the typeface list on page 158). Font families may have more than a hundred members (of varying weights and styles).

Character set

The character set is all the individual members of a typeface. It includes upper and lower case letters, numerals (numbers), punctuation and a whole host of other characters, including ligatures (two characters joined together for better spacing—fi fl are the most common), mathematical symbols, dashes, foreign language accents/modifiers, and so on.

A **typeface family** (also known as a font family) is made up of a number of variants of the typeface. Variants include different type styles (roman, italic, thin to heavy), type weights (light to dark) and type width (condensed to extended).

A **character set** is all the elements of a typeface, including letters, numerals, punctuation and all the other accents required for setting type.

Point size

The measurement system we use for font size is the point system. This is a system that was developed hundreds of years ago, and it is not related to the metric measurement system (in Europe different systems were developed but now metric millimetres are the preferred measurement). There are approximately 72 points in an Anglo-American inch. In layout programs, this measurement has been rounded down to exactly 72 points to the inch (2.5 cm). The point size of a font is the height from the bottom of the descender (the portion of a letter such as g or j that extends below the baseline) to the top of the ascender (the portion of a letter such as b or d that extends above the x-height of a typeface). The abbreviation of point is pt, which is how most designers and software programs refer to points (e.g. 12 pt).

Pica

'Pica' is short for pica em. In the mid-nineteenth century, a standard was developed for measuring type. One pica em is equal to 12 pt. The em refers to uppercase 'M', which was the letter with the largest slug size in a character set. Picas are still used, mainly for determining the widths of columns of text.

Leading

'Leading' is the term used to indicate the amount of space between lines of text. It has its origin in the use of actual strips of lead used to separate lines of metal type and it is measured in points. Leading is always described in the form of font size *plus* the actual amount of leading. Thus text set with leading included is described this way: 12/14 pt—this means the font size is 12 pt and the leading is 2 pt (12 pt + 2 pt = 14 pt); in other words, the measurement of leaded text is a measure from baseline to baseline.

Kerning

The letters of the alphabet are all different shapes and sizes. To be easy to read, the letters of a line of text need to look evenly spaced. Kerning is the process by which the spacing between pairs of letters is adjusted by the eye to achieve this. Typeface designers will encode the most important kerning pairs into a digital typeface, so that the set text looks pretty good without extra work required of the graphic designer. Normally, as a designer you would only manually kern part of a text, such as headlines or advertising slogans. Manually kerning text is also referred to as 'letter spacing' text.

Tracking

The space between letters and words is not fixed. The process of increasing or decreasing the amount of space between letters and words is called tracking. Tracking is measured in thousandths of an em (see 'pica', above). 'Tracked out' text (large spacing) is referred to as 'loose set' text and 'tracked in' text (smaller than normal spacing) is referred to as 'tightly set' text.

LAYOUT MEASURES

In Australia and New Zealand we use the point system and the metric system in the typesetting and design of layouts. Points are used for measuring font size and leading. We use either points or millimetres to measure gaps between paragraphs. Columns, rows, **margins** and **gutters** can be measured in either millimetres or picas. Page sizes are measured in millimetres.

A **margin** is the space with no text around an image, a column of text or the edge of the page.

A **gutter** is the space between columns of text or images.

Point size refers to the measure of the size of type. There are approximately 72 points to the inch (2.5 cm).

A **baseline** is an invisible line on which all the letters in a line of type sit.

Leading is the space between lines of text.

Kerning is a method used to add space between letters to give a visually equal space between them.

Serif face

As you can see in the 'Anatomy of type' diagram on page 125, serifs are the little bits that extend from the sharp corners of some typefaces. Typefaces that have these extra bits are called serif faces.

Sans serif face

The word 'sans' means without; sans serif faces are typefaces that do not have serifs.

Display face

In theory all typefaces are designed to be read. Some typefaces are very ornate. Other typefaces have had a designer play around so much with the basic letter shape that they become quite hard to read for longer that very short texts. This does not mean they are bad—visually, they can be quite stunning. These typefaces are called display faces because they are so good at getting attention. They should generally only be used for headings.

Text font/face

Text fonts (or text faces) are designed specifically for long texts and are intended to be easy to read. Good text faces have clear, well-defined letter shapes that do not stray too far from the basic letterforms. While text faces are much plainer than display faces, this does not mean that they lack character and individual style.

TYPEFACE CATEGORIES

Today there are literally thousands of typefaces available for you to use. Virtually all of them belong to one of a small number of categories. There are numerous systems for categorising type, but foremost among these is the Vox System. Table 4.1 outlines this system and shows the key type characteristics of each section.

Developed in 1954, the Vox System is the official system of the Association Typographique Internationale, the premier world typographic body. The Vox System groups type into categories based on historical factors and appearance. This system is not perfect, particularly as it predates computer type design; this means there are many typefaces that do not fall into any, or have characteristics of several, of the categories. The first few categories are based on the historical developments of type design during the first 300 years of the age of type. Virtually all serif typefaces fall into these groups. It is important to remember, however, that these categories describe the structural characteristics of typefaces that just happen to be consistent with changes that occurred during the early centuries of type. Typefaces in these categories were not necessarily designed during that time, but they do have certain features that first appeared during that time.

→ Not all typefaces are serif or sans serif; many, like this one, are display style. 'Django' was created to give the impression of handwriting.

Designer **WAYNE THOMPSON, AUSTRALIAN TYPE FOUNDRY**

A **serif face** is a typeface with serifs, which are small extensions to the sides of the letterforms.

A **sans serif face** is a typeface without serifs. These typefaces tend to have low contrast between horizontal and vertical strokes.

A **display face** is a typeface designed for headings. They tend to be eye-catching and not necessarily suited for use at small point sizes.

TABLE 4.1   THE VOX SYSTEM

Class	Notes	Characteristics	Examples
Humanist (serif)	Originally appearing before 1500, most of the typefaces in this category are in fact revivals and reconstructions from the late nineteenth and early twentieth century. They are good for long texts and book work.	Humanist serif typefaces are characterised by small x-heights (large ascenders and descenders), small counters, angled crossbar on 'e', low vertical/horizontal stroke contrast, strongly angled stress on round letters, calligraphic inflections, heavy angled serifs and caps the same height as ascenders.	Centaur
Garalde	These typeface characteristics first appeared in the 1490s and. They are good for long texts and book work. In other category systems Humanists and Garaldes are grouped together as Old Style Serifs.	Garaldes are characterised by medium x-heights, larger counters, medium stroke contrast, horizontal crossbar on 'e', still pronounced stress on round letters, less calligraphic inflections, squared off serifs and angular forms.	Garamond
Transitional	This group form the bridge between the Garaldes and the following Didones and appeared in the late seventeenth and early eighteenth centuries. Again they are excellent for long texts and book work.	Transitional typefaces are characterised by medium x-heights, larger counters, strong stroke contrast, pointed apex on 'A', minimal stress on round letters, limited calligraphic inflections, flattened and squared off serifs and even more angular forms.	Baskerville
Didone	These typefaces are also known as 'Modern' and appeared in the late eighteenth and early nineteenth century. The high stroke contrast means that they are not particularly suited for long texts or book work and bolder weights should certainly only be used for short text.	Didones are characterised by medium x-heights, larger counters, extreme stroke contrast, pointed apex on 'A', vertical stress on round letters, no calligraphic inflections at all, bracketed and unbracketed serifs* in the same font and more angular forms.	Bodoni

* see page 125

A **text font/face** is a typeface designed specifically for typesetting body text. Letterforms are usually clear, distinct and optimised for reading at small point sizes.

129

Mechanistic (slab serif)	This includes two groups: 'Egyptians' with unbracketed serifs and 'Clarendons' with bracketed serifs. They are characteristic of the industrial age, reflecting the emergence of advertising, the ability of presses to handle larger areas of ink and a demand for heavier types. Ideal for shorter texts.	Slab serifs look black (even the normal/roman weights) and have much larger x-heights, low stroke contrast and pronounced drop forms. They have heavy serifs (bracketed or unbracketed).	**Rockwell Clarendon**
Sans serif or grotesques	These appeared at the same time as the Slab Serifs and were used for much the same purpose initially. In the twentieth century they were adopted by the 'modernist' movement as the type of the future. They are very versatile and can be used for all forms of text; however, for long texts generous leading is recommended.	Sans serif can be highly geometric, constructed from mechanical curves and lines or Humanistic based on more parabolic forms. They have large x-heights, open counters and of course no serifs.	Univers Meta
Glyphic	A small group of typefaces that are also known as 'flare-serifed'. Relatively uncommon, they are often not suitable for long text setting.	Glyphic typefaces are characterised by waisted stems and chiselled forms with only a hint of serif. They give the sense of having been carved.	**Albertus**
Blackletter	These are based on Northern European (Germanic) manuscript handwriting. This is what Gutenberg used for his work. They have continued to this day, being the preferred book types in Germany into the early twentieth century. They are hard to read to our unfamiliar eyes and are not at all suited to long text work. They have also become synonymous with heavy metal music graphics.	Blackletter typefaces still carry many characteristcs of hand-made calligraphy. They tend to have a very vertical visual appearance (narrow letterforms, thick vertical strokes and thin horizontal strokes).	Cloister Black

Italics and scripts	Italics began as freestanding faces but there was a move away from calligraphic forms and they became an adjunct to the roman forms. Today they are not used for long texts but rather as a highlight option within roman text. Scripts and italics were an attempt to bring the free flow of individual human handwriting to printing. Until digital type design, the result was often stilted and lacking in vitality. They are not really suited for anything other than highlights and should never be set in all capitals.	Italics are characterised by sloping letterforms (the degree of slope varies between about 5° and 15°). Scripts generally mimic cursive handwriting and therefore the intention is usually that the letters be linked.	*Snell Roundhand*
Decorated and ornamental	This group encompasses a huge variety of individual display typefaces. They are useful for giving character to headings and for advertising	These are often designed for effect rather than readability. Thus they can be highly ornate and may also not have complete character sets (for example, there may only be upper case letters).	ZEBRAWOOD
Beyond classification	A group also associated with display typefaces. Again, they are useful for giving character to headings and for advertising.	This category is the child of the digital type age in which anything is possible in the design on typefaces including such things as combining the parts of serif and sans serif faces, faces of partial letterforms and many other effects.	Dead History

To set type well, it helps as much to know about design and type history as it does to be familiar with the technology at hand. It is also important to understand the language and visual aesthetics of typography. Successfully using type relies on your ability to solve problems through creativity.

← In certain applications, identities need to be reinvented regularly. Type-based identities are particularly suited to this kind of development.

Designer **MATHEMATICS**
Client **THE AUSTRALIAN RECORDING INDUSTRY ASSOCIATION**

The way type is used can say a lot about the material and information it is displaying. It can help or hinder communication. The conventional view is that the typeface chosen should be 'invisible' and should not in any way interrupt the reader's ability to read or understand the text. The contemporary view, on the other hand, is that the choice of typeface can add to the text in many subtle ways and that even disrupting the reader's ability to read, to some extent, may be an important addition to the communication process.

CHOOSING TYPE

Choosing the right typeface may seem difficult. There are no real rules to apply, as each decision should be based on the job at hand. You need to experiment.

Remember: sometimes even the most experienced designers must make many attempts before they get their type choices just right.

APPROACHES TO TYPE
To find out more about these two approaches to typesetting track down an essay by Beatrice Warde entitled 'The Crystal Goblet' and the writings from the 1980s on postmodern typography from The Cranbrook Academy of Art in the United States. (See *Looking closer* series in reference list.)

{ LITTLE **SPEKTRUM** LARGE }

{ COMMUNITY **SPEKTRUM** CORPORATE }

{ PRIVATE **SPEKTRUM** PUBLIC }

{ COUNTRY **SPEKTRUM** CITY }

CONSERVATION RESOURCES
PRESERVATION — INNOVATION — REALISATION

CHOOSING THE RIGHT TYPEFACE

When you are choosing a typeface there are a number of practical requirements it needs to satisfy, usually driven by the text. Is it a long or a short text? A long text needs a text face. A short text is anything from a few words to a few hundred words. Where and how is the text to be displayed and read—in a book, on a billboard, on screen, or somewhere else? Each of these will have a different impact on your choice. What does the typeface need to be able to display? Is it simple, like a novel? Or complex, like a textbook? Do you need numerals? Will there be a range of weights needed for emphasis, headings, captions, footnotes and so on?

There may also be other practical factors influencing your choice, like the text having to fit into a certain space.

In short, the typeface you choose must be able to do the job required of it and still leave room for your own creativity. This may seem an impossible task but as you look around the world in which we live you can see this task being achieved successfully in many different contexts.

FELIX OPPEN

← Identity for an art gallery. Here the use of ultra-commonplace Verdana (designed for use at text sizes on screen) is used out of context and some of the strengths of the typeface for its screen use have become hindrances when displayed as 50 cm high letters.

READABILITY AND LEGIBILITY

Text is intended to be read. This is the primary goal when you are setting type. There are other issues of course, such as enhancing the tone of the text; but if the text is not readable, at least to the intended extent, the design won't work.

Our eyes jump along a line of text when we read, not identifying every word or letter but rather groups of them. This happens in jumps of a fraction of a second. Then the eyes flick back to the next line and the path begins again. If the spacing between the letters and words is uneven, or the typeface too complicated or not complicated enough, the brain has to work harder to interpret what it is reading. If this result is not intended, then the text has been poorly set.

When you are assessing a typeface for use you need to consider its *legibility*. This refers to how identifiable the letterforms are at the point size you want to use them, how simple or complex the design of each letterform is and how different they are from the standard form of the letter.

Body text is the main text of a document. This means the point size shouldn't be too big so the eye doesn't have to move around the page too much. The lines of text shouldn't be too long or too short. Set your text in a typeface designed for text use and use sentence case (i.e, mostly lowercase letters with capitals used only at the beginning of sentences and for proper nouns) so the letterforms are clear and have enough variation to be easily distinguished. Don't use a weight that creates too much or not enough contrast with the background because both too-high and too-low contrast hinders reading.

Short texts (including headings, advertising and other texts of only a few lines) allow much more flexibility. The same issues with difficulty of reading remain, but because the text is short and read quickly before the brain tires, these issues are less significant. However, poor choices may still be sufficient to make even the shortest text unreadable; for example, by using the wrong size, a badly designed typeface, or having the wrong visual contrast with the surrounding material.

There has been much debate and research into the differences between serif and sans serif typefaces. Unfortunately, it is very difficult to prove which style allows better readability, because the more familiar you are with a typeface the easier it becomes to read. Currently, the general view is that you should be governed by what your intended audience is most likely to be familiar with, balanced by the factors outlined below.

SEEN RATHER THAN READ

Some typefaces are meant to be seen rather than read. For example, the body copy of this book is set in a typeface called Karbon. It is a highly legible and readable typeface especially in the Regular weight.

At 6 pt it is still very readable.

There is also a bold weight

but at 6 pt Karbon bold is not nearly so readable.

And what about Karbon italic at 6 pt?

This is because the latter examples were designed to be used for emphasis and/or at larger sizes, that is in situations where they draw attention to themselves as a way of highlighting text via subtle disruption of readability.

Body copy (or **body text**) is the main portion of text in a document or design. It contains the information being communicated.

FASHION AND TYPE

Like virtually all designed things, typefaces and the way type is used goes in and out of fashion. This is inevitable because we are influenced by, and respond to, what is going on around us and as time progresses these influences change. You can use fashion to your advantage: it allows you to design something that appears up to the minute, or something that appears to be of another era, just by careful choice of typefaces.

July 94

A friend and collector of our books suggests we print a new edition of *Ulysses*. We laugh like drains and explain the logistics of hand setting a 900-page novel. F&C insists. We compromise and say that it would *just* be possible to do the final chapter and even that would take months during which we wouldn't be able to support ourselves, let alone finance such a huge production.

[...] who better equipped for the post of Foreign Correspondent? Though perhaps a Marxist Feminist critique of Ecclesiastes is not what they have in mind.
Susan Furse to JJ, April 1994

F&C says he will pay our bills for the duration and will also ensure a steady supply of bread and water.
We weaken and agree to take on Molly Bloom's soliloquy.
The project is ON.

The creative challenge was to produce a design which would reflect the rich character of an illuminated manuscript, with pages possessed of all the vigour of a mediaeval book without being a pastiche of one. The heavy Italian paper on which for once the deckles were left intact, numerous initial letters cut by Mike in the versal style, and the twenty hand-coloured illustrations gave a luminosity to the clean lines of 20th century typography.

Aug. 94
Not knowing where to start looking re. copyright, I write to Penguin in London as the publisher of the latest edition.

Sept. 94 (early)
Heard nothing from Penguin so make a phone call and get told that *Ulysses* is OUT of copyright.
Start working on layouts (expressionist typography being the name of the game) and order vast amounts of sans serif.

We used red ink for the Latin set in 24 point Old English, blue for the Middle English set in 18 point Bembo, and black for the modern translation. The last, set in 14 point Plantin, used the red Versal initials, pulling the reins on the progressive 'modernisation' and making a bridge to the forthcoming lines of Latin text. The endpapers featured a portion of the original Bodleian manuscript, redrawn and enlarged, and then cut in lino and printed twice in ochre and brown respectively, each run overlapping the other slightly to produce a calligraphic pattern. 20 copies x 10 illustrations each, plus title page and decorated first page added up to an awesome amount of hand painting. We set the process in motion following Alice's tea party example, laying out the pages around our large work table and moving from one to the next, each brandishing a brush laden with a different hue of watercolour paint. Despite the book's large size, multicolour printing and numerous opportunities for knocking over jam jars filled with dirty water, the production was remarkably trouble free, all malevolent inanimate objects apparently on holidays. But the animate ones were as active as ever. [...] the unexpected wonderful weather made the printing of 'Brothels' a breeze. Except — there is always a BUT or an EXCEPT — we still have to print the colophon, which can't be done until we know such minor details like; How will the edition be bound? The book's subject — and hence it's design — being mediaeval, we decided to bind it in a tapestry which we spotted in the window of a local interior decorating shop. Closer investigation revealed it was a real tapestry, imported from Belgium — at $200 a metre. Ouch. So back home to work out exactly how much is needed — at this price we wouldn't want to over-order .... few days later, back at the shop — which has been there throughout the eight years we've lived in Katoomba — and ..... THE SHOP IS CLOSED. THE SHOP IS EMPTY. There is a note in the window saying THE SHOP HAS MOVED. WILL REOPEN AT A NEW, UNSPECIFIED LOCATION.

Sept. 94 (later)
Get a letter from the Joyce Estate's solicitor (to whom Penguin apparently passed my letter) saying *'your request has been passed on to the Estate's Trustee in Ireland'*.

Sept. 94 (later still)
Get a letter from Ireland telling me to write to the Estate in Paris and give details of the proposed edition. (Stephen J. Joyce)

Oct. 94 (early)
Oblige with letter to Paris.

Oct. 94 (later)
Get a letter from Paris consisting mostly of incoherent ravings and accusing us, among other things, of publishing the book without permission and *then* having second thoughts. The general gist of the letter is PERMISSION TO PUBLISH REFUSED.
The project is OFF.

Oct. 94 (same day)
Write to SJJ to set the record straight, i.e: book NOT published.
Nothing to lose so tell the Boring Old Tit that he's a B.O.T.

Oct. 94 (same day)
Write to Would-Be-Benefactor with the bad news.

Nov. 94 (early)
Get second, totally unexpected letter from SJJ in which he makes no reference to previous correspondence and says YES, permission to print granted.
The project is ON.

Nov. 94 (later)
Write back to SJJ, 'Thank you, thank you...'

Nov. 94 (a bit later)
Write to Would-Be-Benefactor with the good news.

Nov. 94 (later still)
Get letter from W-B-B saying that after SJJ's initial refusal, believing himself to be free of his obligation to the project, he had done some Big Spending by telephone at a New York auction and can no longer finance Molly!
The project is OFF.

Dec. 94
Write to SJJ, eating volumes of humble pie.

Dec. 94 - 30 March 95
Suffer much indigestion.

31 March 95
Get a letter from W-B-B saying that Big Spending came to nought (another failure in modern telecommunications?) and do we still want to do the book?
The project is ON.

31 March 95 onwards...
chewing fingernails, smoking and drinking excessively, trying to decide on the approach most likely to be successful when writing to SJJ again.
If we miss the project OFF will be again.
(We are sitting here, after months of inactivity and no income, on a pile of layouts and in possession of a couple of thousand dollars' worth of type specially purchased for the occasion ...)
JJ to John Crombie, 4 April 1995

This sample setting comes from a work in progress at Wayzgoose Press. Compiled in large measure from correspondence, job sheets and well-remembered adventures, the narrative documents life at the press from its inception in 1985 up to the present. As in any creative environment, events here frequently overlap as this extract demonstrates. Our typographic solution was to present them in parallel rather than sequentially, to better suggest the complex interweaving of day-to-day press activities, and to show that a creative life is not at all the picnic it is reputed to be.

EXERCISE   Select five fonts from the list at the end of the chapter. What do you see when you look at them? Do you think they are masculine? Old-fashioned? What market do you think they would suit, and to which typeface category do you think each belongs?

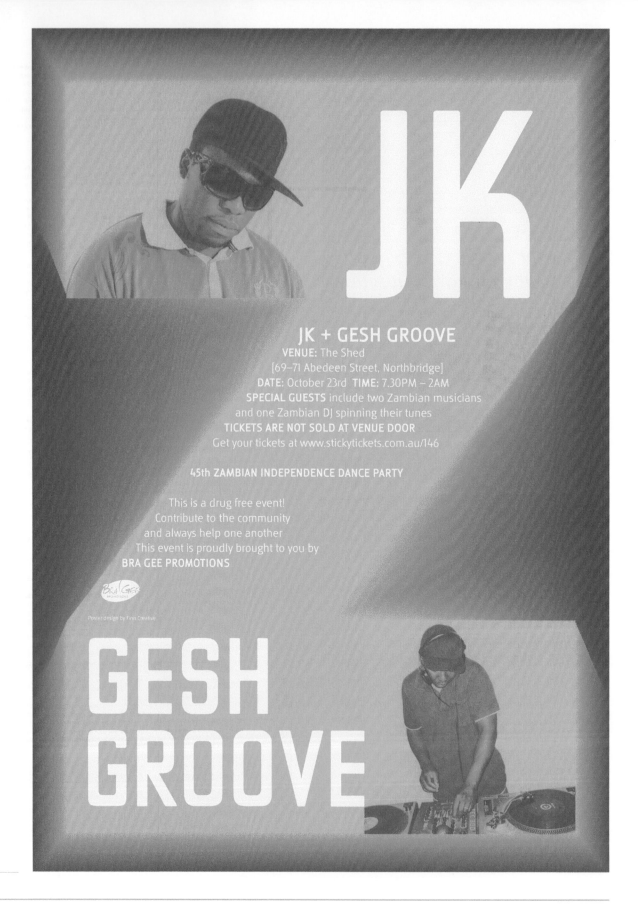

→ *Designer*
FINN CREATIVE
Client **BRA GEE**
PROMOTIONS

↑ In this example the type has be carefully placed to appear on the page edge. This is time consuming to achieve but elegant and effective. The simplicity and familiarity of letter forms makes this far more striking than using images for the same purpose. There is no reason why type cannot be used for its intrinsic decorative value as well as its communicative value. With skill, both can be achieved, even if there is quite a lot of text involved.

Designer **CAMPBELLBARNETT**
Client **FAIRFIELD CITY COUNCIL**

TONE OF TYPE AND TEXT

Every text that you set, be it one or two words or ten or twenty thousand, has a tone. The tone should reflect the meaning of the text, who it is intended for and how it is to be understood. When choosing type, you can work with the tone and even enhance it.

Every typeface that you come across also has a tone. It can convey a certain sense of time and place. The tone of a typeface varies from viewer to viewer and is coloured by the viewer's own experience of it (or of similar typefaces), the time in which the viewer lives and the history that the viewer, and the typeface, have lived through. The tone of a typeface can change over time.

The way you set up a design or layout also conveys a tone. Again, this tone can change over time and be interpreted differently by others when filtered through their own knowledge and experience.

This changeable nature can make choosing typefaces seem like an impossible task. It is not necessarily easy, but if you take time, do research and generally keep yourself immersed in design and life, building experience all the time, then the very flexibility that this brings will provide great possibilities for design communication problem solving, perhaps more than offered by photography and illustration.

In the meantime there are no rules and only a few guidelines to offer. For example, some sans serifs look quite geometric, with curved elements being very round and circular. These faces can be seen as rather cold and impersonal and may be appropriate for corporate business documents needing to convey accuracy and impartiality. On the other hand, other sans serifs with less geometric shapes are perhaps friendlier, more personal, but still convey a sense of responsibility, corporate or otherwise. Or, in another example, some serif faces have lots of soft shapes and almost no hard corners. These perhaps convey a sense of comfortable warmth that is somewhat feminine in nature, whereas the faces with big, chunky serifs convey a sense of brashness that is boisterous and somewhat masculine. Of course, these interpretations are highly subjective: we wouldn't be surprised if you disagree.

TEXT ORGANISATION AND STRUCTURE

When you receive a text to typeset it is unlikely ever to just be a mass of words. It will have a structure that you will need to address in a way that makes sense. Some of the main components are outlined below.

Chapter

Long texts are often divided into chapters based on themes or ideas contained in the text.

Body copy/text

This is usually the main component of any text and forms the bulk of the words to be typeset. Body text is generally set in a font size of 8–10 pt.

Heading

The **heading** is a few words that signal the opening of the body text or a section of it. It will give a general indication of the themes to follow. Headings are generally set in point sizes much larger that the body copy, and they may also be set in a different weight.

Subheading

A body text may be organised into subsections each with a sub-heading. The subheading is set in a size between headling and body text, clearly indicating its position in the organisational hierarchy.

Footnotes

Footnotes are notes that support the body text with additional information. They are generally at the foot of the page or end of the chapter (when they are called 'endnotes'). They are typeset in a way that differentiates them from the body text, usually a point size or two smaller.

Quotes

Quotes are key pieces of text that are reprinted from other texts or reproduce someone's actual words. They are often set in italics to show that they are not written by the author.

Pull quotes

Pull quotes are a small piece of the body text that has been highlighted by a change in font size and style or weight to draw attention to those particular words. They may also be distributed through the text for visual effect, but they should never be created just for visual effect.

Captions

Captions are explanations accompanying images, illustrations, tables, diagrams and figures. They are typeset in a way that differentiates them from the body text.

→ Hand-lettering: does it count as type? Some might say no. Nevertheless hand-drawn type is a valid and useful tool that designers can use to great effect either on its own or combined with carefully chosen conventional drawn type.

Designer **MATHEMATICS**
Client **ON THE BRIGHT SIDE**

A **heading** is a line of type in a larger font that introduces a body of text, for example a headline in a newspaper, or a chapter title in a book.

SECRET SOUNDS & SUPERSONIC PRESENTS

ON THE BRIGHT SIDE

THE STROKES
MUMFORD & SONS
THE TING TINGS
ANGUS & JULIA STONE
BAND OF HORSES
HOT CHIP
BLUEJUICE
THE MIDDLE EAST

SAT 24 JUL 2010
ESPLANADE PARK

UNDER THE SUPERTOP - RIVERSIDE DRIVE PERTH 12-10PM - SUBJECT TO COUNCIL APPROVAL
ALL AGES W/18+ AREAS. NO BYO. NO PASSOUTS. WE PLAY RAIN, HAIL OR SHINE

TICKETS ON SALE FRIDAY 28 MAY

WWW.HEATSEEKER.COM.AU · MILLS · PLANET · STAR SURF · LIVE STORES

WWW.ONTHEBRIGHTSIDE.COM.AU

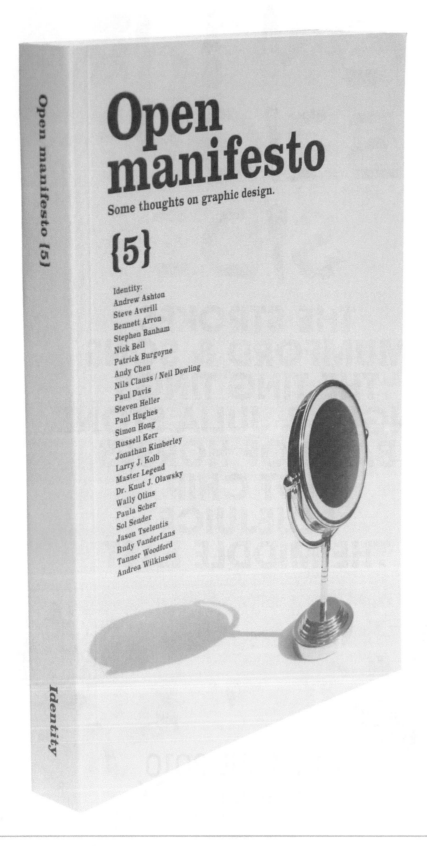

Open manifesto

Some thoughts on graphic design.

{5}

Identity:
Andrew Ashton
Steve Averill
Bennett Arron
Stephen Banham
Nick Bell
Patrick Burgoyne
Andy Chen
Nils Clauss / Neil Dowling
Paul Davis
Steven Heller
Paul Hughes
Simon Hong
Russell Kerr
Jonathan Kimberley
Larry J. Kolb
Master Legend
Dr. Knut J. Olawsky
Wally Olins
Paula Scher
Sol Sender
Jason Tselentis
Rudy VanderLans
Tanner Woodford
Andrea Wilkinson

Open manifesto {5}

Identity

WORD SPACING

If you have properly spaced the words in your line you should be able to insert a lower case 'i' between the words and not have them move closer or further apart.

LINE LENGTH

It may not always be possible to have twelve words or so to a line. You will sometimes have to make adjustments to the leading to help the reader's eye find the next line. This is more important for long lines than short lines. For long lines, increase the amount of leading to separate the lines better.

The setting of type for publications and books often requires a more measured, calmer design approach. If you need people to read a lot of text then you can't make them work hard to understand it. Simplicity is the key, and skill and care are needed to keep the overall design visually interesting.

← *Open Manifesto* This is a journal in which the ideas are by far the most important element, so the design is kept ultra simple

Designer **FINN CREATIVE**

STRUCTURING TEXT ON THE PAGE

In the same way that a text has a structure, its placement on a page needs to have a structure. Everything you will learn about page layout structures in Chapter 5 is equally, if not more important when typesetting text.

As you build the page structure (or 'grid') in which to place your text, the first length of continuous text you need to consider is the line.

The line

A line of text is the smallest unit of continuous text that you need to work with (it may be a headline or a caption or a short section of body copy). To be readable the line should not be too long or too short and the spacing between letters should mean that the words are easily identifiable. The spacing between the words should not be so close that they appear to run together or so far apart that the line breaks into single words. Aim to have your line of text about twelve words long, plus or minus two or three words. This appears to be a comfortable length for the human eye to scan easily.

ALIGNMENT

Long or continuous text is arranged into pages and columns. There may be only one column per page or there may be many. There are four forms of alignment for text in columns.

Flush (or ranged) left, ragged right

In a **flush** (or **ranged left**), **ragged right** alignment, the left end of the lines are arranged neatly to the left column edge and the right end finishes with the nearest whole word to the right column edge. As we read from right to left this is the easiest alignment to read because each new line starts at a predictable place on the page.

Be careful with texts containing lots of long words because they can make the right ends very ragged. This can be a real problem in narrow columns. Also, you may need to add a little extra width to the gutters between the columns so that the columns are clearly separated.

The raggedness of the column gives the text an informal feel.

Justified text

In **justified text** the words in a line are stretched to the full width of the column. This is done by increasing the word spacing, and to a lesser extent the letter spacing, until the lines are of equal length. This means that the word spacing on every line may be different.

When justified text is used in narrow columns, 'rivers' may appear. These are roughly vertical channels running down through the middle of a column of text. They occur because the word spacing has become wider than the leading. Rivers can make text impossible to read. You can remove them by changing column width, justification, point size or even typeface.

Some people think that justified text is easier to set than flush or ranged text, but to work well, justified text needs to have word spaces that are almost all the same. This can be very tricky to achieve.

Justified text can create a more formal or business-like tone.

Centred text

Centred text has all the lines aligned on an imaginary axis down the centre of the column. As a result there is no consistency in where lines begin and end on the page, making it harder to read. This kind of alignment should only be used for short sections.

SHAPING TEXT

You can make centred text easier to read by shaping your text. Start the paragraph with shorter lines, then increase the length until the middle of the paragraph, then shorten them again towards the end.

Flush (or **ranged left**), **ragged right** text is arranged in a column that has a neat left-hand edge and an uneven right-hand edge.

Justified text is arranged in a column that has all lines of equal length.

Centred text is a column of text that has all lines arranged around an imaginary line down the centre. Both left- and right-hand edges of the lines are uneven.

6:55am	A short history of product placement

When Pope Julius II engaged Michelangelo to paint a ceiling at the Vatican, it's fair to say he was expecting product placement in the result. If the artist had painted a bowl of fruit or a bunch of dogs playing poker, there would have been hell to pay. But he didn't. The

Italian stayed on message and worked the God brand into the Sistine Chapel pretty well. Product placement, the paid (or bartered) inclusion of a brand in a work of art or entertainment, has been with us for centuries, but it truly came into its own in the 20th century.

	6:58am

1800s
SOL BLOOM, a teenage promoter, convinced local merchants to pay to have their names inserted into the scripts of theatre shows at the Alcazar in San Francisco.

1896
ONE YEAR after the Lumiere Brothers first exhibited their films in the basement of a Paris café, the first product placement hit the screens. The Lumieres' distributor also represented UK soap manufacturer Lever Brothers. In June 1896, a film of two women hand-washing clothes, with two cases of Lever Brothers soap prominent in shot, was shown in New York.

1905
STREETCAR CHIVALRY. Thomas Edison's movies contained similar early product placement (mostly for the local railways), but this movie took place in a commuter car placarded with posters for Edison products, such as the phonograph. He may have also invented cross-promotion.

1919
THE FIRST known complaint about product placement appeared in movie trade journal, Harrison's Reports. It concerned a scene in The Garage, a Fatty Arbuckle comedy, involving Red Crown gasoline.

1929
AMERICAN RADIO depended on advertising for revenue. By 1929, 55 per cent of the programs were not only paid for by advertisers, they were created by advertisers and agencies. In the 1930s, The J. Walter Thompson Company produced more than 33 programs, more than 60 hours per week. It was responsible for half of the decade's top ten shows.

1931
MGM MOVIE Easiest Way carried publicity for seven national advertisers. One sequence was set in an advertising agency, with artwork lying around for Old Gold cigarettes, Coca-Cola, Phoenix Hosiery, Mallinson Silks, Cadillac, Parker Pens and the Santa Fe Railroads. MGM bragged: "While from time to time pictures have given a free ad to nationally known companies or products, never before has any single feature combined so much as Easiest Way." Variety reported that the idea of paid product placement was "not altogether remote".

1933
MA PERKINS, the first radio soap opera, was created for Oxydol, a Procter & Gamble brand. In the 1950s, many of the successful soaps would switch to television. Brands paid for plugs at the beginning and end of episodes, as well as ads during the shows.

1934
IT HAPPENED ONE NIGHT. Many advertising books and experts will tell you that after Clark Gable took off his shirt to reveal a bare chest in this picture, singlet sales dropped by 75 per cent. He supposedly crippled the undershirt industry. James Dean is widely credited for selling shiploads of Ace combs after using one in Rebel Without A Cause in 1955.

1939
METRO-GOLDWYN-MAYER became the first studio to open a placement office.

1940
ADVENTURES IN DIAMONDS. After pressure from DeBeers, which was investing heavily in product placement, the name of the movie was changed from Diamonds Are Dangerous. In 1941, DeBeers had a scene about diamonds written into Skylark and prominent placement for jewellery in That Uncertain Feeling.

1945
JOAN CRAWFORD drank Jack Daniels liquor in Mildred Pierce, in what is believed to be the first instance of a star plugging a brand-name product in a film.

1949
PRODUCT PLACEMENT was an instant hit on US television. Shows were sponsored. Comedians were known to work plugs into routines. And writers offered to include specific locations in dramas at a price. Camel cigarettes, sponsor of Man Against Crime, set rules for writers, directors, and actors: "Do not have the heavy or any disreputable person smoking a cigarette. Do not associate the smoking of cigarettes with undesirable scenes or situations plot-wise." No one on screen was allowed to cough.

1951
LOBBYIST BILL TREADWELL, who worked for Britain's Tea Bureau, claimed he had scenes involving tea inserted into 83 movies in two years. He said he persuaded Warner Bros to change the name of the musical No! No! Nanette! to Tea For Two. Tea consumption in America increased by 17 million pounds a year.

1957
ONLY A DECADE after television caught on, more than a third of US programs were created by advertisers and their agencies.

↑ Spread from *The Gruen Transfer*, the book accompanying the TV series (ABC TV). This book has to be a physical representation of the (mostly verbal) style of the show.

Designer **DE LUXE & ASSOCIATES**
Publisher **ABC BOOKS**

↗ A spread from *Harvard Business Review*.

Designer **DE LUXE & ASSOCIATES**
Client **HARVARD BUSINESS REVIEW**

142 EXERCISE Analyse this book. What is its page structure? Using the terminology you have just learned in the 'Using type' section, describe the tone and the organisational structure of the text, including how the different components of the text, headings and body text have been used. How has the alignment affected the layout? What about the white space? Present your findings as an 8-page A5 booklet.

ecutives cried out, "Reports! Our kingdom for more reports!" The problem was that what they really wanted—useful, insightful analysis—couldn't easily be produced with the software provided by corporate IT.

Poor Richard. What to do? Work 29 hours a day, 10 days a week, to manually create those reports and the much-needed analysis? No way. He hacked the system. He softened up a vendor, got a password, tapped into the database, and began creating never-before-possible reports for the C-suite.

Would the bank's auditors and IT security guys freak out if they knew that Richard had hacked their system? Uh, yes. But since then, Richard has become incredibly productive and is now a go-to guy companywide. He's a hero to all those senior execs who wanted more than data dumps. If only they knew the full story. Says Richard, "As a result of this hack, I keep senior management off our backs, so we're able to continue doing more for our clients with less."

He's not alone in believing that he has to take matters into his own hands in order to get the job done and achieve better results for the organization. Many in the workforce are coming to the same conclusion. The illusion of corporate control is being shattered in the name of increased personal productivity.

The Promise This kind of work-around isn't new—your company has been hacked from the inside for ages. What is new is that the cheat codes are becoming public, and there's nothing you can do about that. Bloggers are telling your employees how to bypass procedures. Forums give tutorials on how to hack your software security. Entrepreneurs are building apps to help your employees run their own tools and processes instead of yours.

There's only one successful strategy for a hacked world: If you can't beat 'em, join 'em. Change the debate within your company to leverage what your hacker employees know. We're seeing managers in enormous corporations such as Google, Nokia, and Best Buy embrace things that benevolent hackers would pursue with or without them: greater worker control over tools and procedures, increased transparency, and meritocracy. As even senior management begins to feel the pain of outdated tools and structures that refuse to budge, what was once shunned as bad is now the new good.

Bill Jensen is the president and CEO of the Jensen Group, a change-consulting firm in Morristown, New Jersey. **Josh Klein** is a New York-based hacker and a consultant on security and workplace effectiveness. The two are collaborating on a forthcoming book, *Hacking Work* (Portfolio).

---

8 RISK MANAGEMENT
SENDHIL MULLAINATHAN

Spotting Bubbles on the Rise

We have the tools to sound the alarm early

The Problem

Will Rogers had sage advice on investing: "Buy some good stock and hold it till it goes up, then sell it. If it don't go up, don't buy it." The guidance we get today regarding economic bubbles is just about as helpful: If it bursts, it was a bubble. That kind of postmortem analysis is useful to historians, but it does nothing to limit the collateral damage caused by, for example, a sudden collapse in housing prices.

An early warning system would be more valuable. For one thing, it would change the way that regulators go about securing the safety and soundness of financial institutions. To ensure that a financial institution is sound, regulators must discount the value of its assets for their riskiness. Under the current Basel regulatory framework, the discount is determined by looking at market pricing of risk. This has disastrous consequences during a bubble, when almost by definition, the market is underpricing significant downside risk. A financial institution holding $50 million worth of mortgage-backed securities in its trading book in January 2007 was facing far more

risk—and was less sound—than the market price suggested. If we had a reliable metric for pronouncing an asset class to be in a bubble, regulators could dampen the risk. They could more aggressively discount asset values and analyze an entire balance sheet's exposure to the threatening burst.

The Breakthrough Idea At ideas42—a behavioral economics R&D lab that I co-direct—we have taken on the challenge of creating an early warning system. We are asking, "Could a bubbles committee—like the committee that does recession dating for the National Bureau of Economic Research—use the research in behavioral finance to identify bubbles as they form?" The answer appears to be a guarded yes.

Understand that our goal is not to be able to predict when a bubble will burst. That might never be possible. Luckily, in terms of the public interest it isn't necessary. To regulate risks it would be helpful merely to recognize when we are in one—a far simpler task. That is why a public effort must create such a committee. (The market itself is far more interested in the timing of bubbles. Any smart arbitrageur would rather ride a bubble for some time than lean against it; a fortune can be made by riding the bubble up and selling right before the burst.)

How would the committee make the call on a rising bubble? Behavioral finance gives us the perspective to spot telltale signs. We know that when markets work well, it's because they are incorporating disparate views of asset value and distilling them into a single price. When markets fail, as they do during bubbles, that is no longer true. After prices have risen for a prolonged period, the bears have sold all their shares, so their downward influence on price is lessened. If they believe that shares are overpriced and due for a fall, they must bet against them in more expensive (and hence less potent) ways, such as short selling.

This suggests an approach to finding warning signs. Looking at short interest, demand for put options, and trading on a variety of derivatives, a bubbles committee could construct technical measures of those opinions that are underrepresented.

In taking these factors into consideration, the committee wouldn't strictly be going against consensus opinion; it would be discovering times when narrow asset prices alone did not measure the consensus.

A bubbles committee need not be passive. If it suspected a bubble in an asset market, it could selectively recommend introducing derivatives that explicitly target bubble risk. Consider a long-horizon put option designed to pay out only in the case of a significant drop in prices. The market price of that security would help regulators decide how to view that asset class. Of course, the committee's activities might serve to burst a bubble early, but that need not be its primary goal; we should be satisfied if the committee simply minimized the social costs of the bubble's eventual burst.

The Promise Translating these raw insights into a concrete methodology will take some work. Careful research is required. Diverse technical measures must be gathered to quantify contrarian inves-

tors' bets. These must be integrated with traditional indicators of fundamental value, such as P/E ratios. New consumer-sentiment measures, based on insights from consumer psychology, will also need to be explored. All of this must be tested against historical data. In this we are lucky: There is no shortage of data. Numerous asset classes around the world have gone through what in hindsight were obviously bubbles. The steps outlined above are technically challenging but very manageable if we make a concerted effort.

We can't prevent earthquakes or hurricanes, but construction engineers have learned ways to minimize their damage. Similarly, financial bubbles will surely continue to rise and burst around the world, but with one big R&D push we can put tools that contain their effects in the hands of a public-minded committee.

Sendhil Mullainathan is a professor of economics at Harvard University and a cofounder of ideas42.

9 GLOBAL ECONOMY
PAUL ROMER

Creating More Hong Kongs

How charter cities can change the rules for struggling economies

The Problem

Knowing how hard it is to transform a change-averse organization, managers sometimes create a skunkwork, an autonomous corporate division where pioneers can build something new. A leader who starts a successful skunkworks changes the firm by showing rather than telling. Target is a good example: It began as a discount-retailing skunkworks at Dayton-Hudson and eventually remade the entire firm.

Flush (or ranged) right, ragged left

A **flush** (or **ranged**) **right, ragged left** alignment is the opposite of flush left text, with the left end of the line being ragged and the right end being neatly aligned. It is not easy to read, and is definitely not recommended for long texts.

Hyphenation

One of the most useful tools you have for improving word spacing and balancing lines is the ability to break a word at the end of a line and carry it on to the next. This is called hyphenation. Current page layout programs have sophisticated controls that allow you to determine how many hyphens are allowed per paragraph. You can use hyphenation in all four forms of alignment, but it is most useful for justified text. However, try to keep hyphenation to a minimum as broken words are harder to read.

White space

One of the strangest aspects of good typographic design, in fact of graphic design in general, is that a very important component is 'nothing'; that is, empty space. 'White space' (as empty space is known, even though it may not actually be white) is as important to a design as all the elements you actually place on the page. Used correctly, white space can help provide a flow to how the information on the page is revealed and understood by the reader. Using white space effectively takes skill but it is a very useful tool for creating dynamic layouts.

MIXING JUSTIFIED AND UNJUSTIFIED

There is no reason why, in complex text, you can't use both justified and ranged text. In fact newspapers often do just that. They use justified alignments for news reporting and ranged alignments for commentary and opinion pieces.

Flush (or **ranged**) **right, ragged left** text is arranged in a column that has a neat right-hand edge and an uneven left-hand edge.

White space is the space on a page containing no images or text. It provides a counterpoint to the information-rich portions of a page.

Kris Sowersby

www.klim.co.nz

Klim Type Foundry

Tiempos Headline Light Italic 80 Point

Riflincka

Tiempos Headline Regular Italic 80 Point

Dynamo

Tiempos Headline Medium Italic 80 Point

Swarthy

Tiempos Headline Semibold Italic 80 Point

Janacek

Tiempos Headline Bold Italic 80 Point

English

Tiempos Headline Black Italic 80 Point

Akimbo

WWW.KLIM.CO.NZ

New Zealand typographer Kris Sowersby has a big international reputation. Known for his highly successful commercial typefaces as well as his thoughtful logotype, Kris still remains down-to-earth and driven by his love of typography and letterforms.

Graduating from the Wanganui School of Design in 2003, Kris spent time as a graphic designer before starting his own company Klim Type Foundry in 2005. For Kris, type work has come as custom typeface commissions for many diverse sectors, like banks, wineries, newspapers and small pacific islands. He has also created several retail fonts that are commercially available to purchase. His first retail typeface, Feijoa, was released onto the international market in 2007.

The journey from graduate to typographer didn't happen overnight, says Kris: 'It was four years between graduation and my first retail release, Feijoa. During this time I struggled along, trying to teach myself typeface design. As well as a few regular graphic design jobs, my good friend and I started our own graphic design business, The Letterheads Ltd. About the time that started to wind down, Feijoa was released and my typeface design career started proper.'

Almost immediately after the release of Feijoa, Kris started to garner interest from global clients. In 2007 he released his second retail typeface National, which won a Certificate of Excellence from the Type Designers Club, New York. Adding to his award collection he later received Certificates of Excellence for two more typefaces: Serrano and Hardys.

Developing his concept process Kris says, 'These days I rarely draw anything of substance with a pencil or pen. I most certainly don't create final logos or letterforms with ink on paper. I work almost exclusively on the computer. However, I don't consider working on the computer any less "manual" or inferior to pencil and ink.'

Logotype is another area of interest for Kris: creating custom lettering for companies and their branding is a large portion of his business.

Klim Type Foundry

Tiempos Headline Light 80 Point

Chromica

Tiempos Headline Regular 80 Point

Phenoles

Tiempos Headline Medium 80 Point

Zeragiko

Tiempos Headline Semibold 80 Point

Rheumy

Tiempos Headline Bold 80 Point

Scallopé

Tiempos Headline Black 80 Point

Zeitung

WWW.KLIM.CO.NZ

THIS PAGE AND OPPOSITE |
Samples and weights of
typefaces from the Klim
Type Foundry

Klim Type Foundry

Karbon Hairline 70 Point

Thérmogrein

Karbon Thin 70 Point

Microskopial

Karbon Light 70 Point

Nucleosynth

Karbon Regular 70 Point

Hygroscope

Karbon Medium 70 Point

Elektrónica

Karbon Semibold 70 Point

Chémistriia

Karbon Bold 70 Point

Protoplasm

WWW.KLIM.CO.NZ

Klim Type Foundry

Founders Grotesk Condensed Light 104 Point

ELEGANCE

Founders Grotesk Condensed Regular 104 Point

PHYSIKAS

Founders Grotesk Condensed Medium 104 Point

FRESCOE

Founders Grotesk Condensed Semibold 104 Point

CHIMERA

Founders Grotesk Condensed Bold 104 Point

EMPIRES

WWW.KLIM.CO.NZ

Kris's practical approach to typography and design is evident in his awareness of Australian and New Zealand audiences. 'I think they have a lower tolerance for rubbish. They know instinctively if something is "right" or not. They're hungry and the trick is to find what their appetite and taste is for. If a concept isn't taken up, it's not the audience's fault. It's probably simply a bad concept. Designers can lose sight of this, they get embroiled with their own cleverness. Audiences have little tolerance for designer self-indulgence.'

Throughout his type career Kris has worked with many well-known typographers and agencies and recognises the need for collaboration. 'All of my typeface commissions have been collaborative and under instruction from clients. Collaboration is essential for a commission; there is always a fair amount of back-and-forth between the development. This is not unusual for any type of design. If there's no collaboration, it's not really design; it's probably closer to art. This isn't a bad thing, it's just different.'

TYPE ON SCREEN

Good typography is just as important for a web page as it is for any other format. The fact that it appears on a screen rather than on paper is irrelevant. It should still be pleasing to look at and easy to read. Ultimately, typography has the same job to do in this environment as it has in print; namely, to communicate.

NINA DRAKALOVIC

Designing for a computer screen has its own set of problems. Screens are usually viewed at something approaching arm's length, but the very nature of computer screens introduces a whole range of constraints. When you add to these the elastic nature of a web page (which has to work across different computer platforms, different screen sizes and different generations of both) the problems get even worse.

It is your job as a designer to understand these issues and to address them; to maintain some kind of control when everything else is changeable.

The screen environment

The typefaces you normally read have been designed to be printed on paper. Many of the characteristics of type that work on paper do not work on screen. As more people read more type from computer screens, this becomes a problem. That's why type on screen can and often does look terrible (especially italics) and is often painful to read.

Because of the platform and screen generational issues mentioned earlier, web design operates in a 72 **dpi** environment. This is not a good environment for readable type. The core of the problem is that, at even not very small type sizes, the size of the pixels at 72 dpi competes directly with the details and structure of the letterforms of the type. Small type especially can look terrible on the web.

Type size

Avoid setting your type size too small. It is possible (though not easy) to read 4 pt printed on paper, and 8 pt is quite comfortable to read. On screen, 10 pt should be your minimum and something like 12 pt recommended if space allows.

Anti-aliasing

Pixels are a fixed size and, like tiles or bricks, can't be divided. They create jagged steps, which can only be smoothed by using tone and colour. This process is called anti-aliasing. By introducing pixels of a colour somewhere between the foreground and background colours, you can effectively smooth the edges of the lines. Anti-aliasing is a subtle and controlled blurring of the letterforms. It is not a perfect solution.

Hinting

This is a function built into modern web-optimised typefaces. It allows the individual characters to automatically shift slightly so that they align better with the pixels on the display screen. Hinting reduces the negative characteristics of anti-aliasing at smaller point sizes.

IN PRINT VS ON SCREEN

Remember that while the purpose of text in print and text on screen is the same—to communicate— this does not mean that you can treat it the same way in both environments. In many cases the text should even be written differently.

← These frames from a title sequence show how type can be used in screen media other than web pages. By choosing the typeface carefully and integrating it into the images, the designer has created a visually stunning event.

Designer **NINA DRAKALOVIC**

COMPUTER SCREEN RESOLUTION IN CONTEXT

Offset printing on average quality paper operates at 2540 dots per inch (dpi).

Newspaper printing operates down to 1270 dpi.

Your eyes can discern pixelation up to 400 dpi.

Poor quality digital print devices operate at 300 dpi.

Best quality computer screens operate at 96 dpi; but we design for a lowest common denominator of 72 dpi to cater for older screens.

---

dpi stands for dots per inch. It is a measure of image resolution.

'Pixel' fonts

This is a certain group of fonts that are optimised for the 72 dpi environment. They are exclusively fixed size (like the old cold metal type). Most commonly they are described as being 8 px, 9 px, 10 px, 11 px and 12 px. You use them at their optimum size, and anti-aliasing and hinting then become irrelevant. Remember there are 72 points in an inch so at 72 dpi a 12 px font is the equivalent of 12 pt type. Pixel fonts, although extremely dull and characterless, are very functional and they can allow you to get away with using smaller type sizes on screen; but be careful how small you go.

One big problem remains: the number of web-optimised fonts available. If websites could consist completely of JPEG or GIF images, there would be no problem. But we rightly, and of necessity, work with dynamic text. When doing so, we are limited as to the fonts available on the viewer's computer, and we can't be certain what those actually are. This is why we code our fonts as follows:

```
body {
font-family: verdana, 'trebuchet MS', helvetica, sans-serif;
}
```

This sets a preferred choice, then a series of back-up options that are progressively more basic, so that the text will continue to display on the oldest computers using the oldest operating systems and browsers.

Fortunately this is changing, albeit slowly. Sites are being developed that aim to provide a centralised licensed font warehouse so that fonts can be used in websites without them having to be on the viewer's computer.

OTHER KINDS OF SCREEN

Most of what we have just discussed relates directly to how to display websites on computer screens, but there are other kinds of screens to consider: television and film screens. When you choose type for these screens the same basic rules apply (see the 'Characteristics of a good screen font' tip box). The big difference is that you do not need to worry about what typefaces are available on the viewer's screen. You design your film title sequence, for example, choose your typefaces and these are embedded into the film. This means you have a much greater selection of typefaces to choose from.

CHARACTERISTICS
OF A GOOD
SCREEN FONT

Wide letter spacing

Good counter width

Fairly low horizontal/
vertical contrast

A tall x-height

Many people still find reading on screen more difficult than reading printed text. It is advisable to break text up into smaller portions. This process is called 'chunking'. On the other hand, screens allow for animation, which can be applied to type as well as images. This allows for a kind of communication that is impossible in print.

→ *Designer* **MATHEMATICS**
Client **RED RIDERS**

↓ *Designer* **STUDIO PIP AND CO**
Client **PEOPLETHINGS.COM**

Some of the issues we have seen with type on screen also need to be considered when type is used in the environment. 'Environmental type' is type used outdoors or in public places, on walls, signs and so on. Most environmental type applies to urban areas, though it is also sometimes used in the bush.

The most important issues are to do with the fact that these environments are what is considered 'low resolution': the type is viewed for very short periods, at oblique angles and in low light and poor weather. Sometimes it is critically important that the type be legible under the worst conditions; in fact, lives may depend on it.

Environmental type can be grouped into three areas: advertising, wayfinding and general environmental. Let's look at each.

ADVERTISING

This area includes billboards and posters among other things. These may be viewed relatively slowly if you are walking past, or just glimpsed if you are travelling in a vehicle. They are often viewed at oblique angles. They also may be viewed in poor light and weather (both making it much harder to read). Obviously your client still wants their advertising to be effective regardless of the conditions, so:

❯ try and keep the number of words down

❯ choose stronger, unfussy typefaces

❯ use more generous letter spacing, but not too wide

❯ aim for good contrast between type and background.

Posters, particularly for music gigs, which often have a lot of information, require a strong and clear hierarchy so that the essential information can be communicated very quickly.

↖ *Designer* LANGUE/ ALICE WILSON
Client SYDNEY IMPROVISED MUSIC ASSOCIATION

← *Designer* MATHEMATICS
Client VILLAGE SOUNDS AND SECRET SERVICE

WAYFINDING

This is the proper name for directional signage. Type in this role has only a few functions: to give directions and indicate hazards. It is critical that type in this environment be clear and easy to read because lives and safety in general can depend on it. Even in apparently non-critical situations like pedestrian precincts, such as malls, type should be clear, and easy to identify and read. So:

- minimise fuss, use simple strong typefaces, especially those designed for wayfinding
- put your type on a plain background in a strongly contrasting colour
- work on placing your signs consistently within the environment, for example, at a consistent height, to make them easier to find
- set your type in from the edge of the sign—use generous margins
- avoid using only upper case letters; you want to maximise individuality of words to make them as legible as possible
- keep your information as succinct as possible, with short lines and short lists
- use clear but limited hierarchies in organising your information.

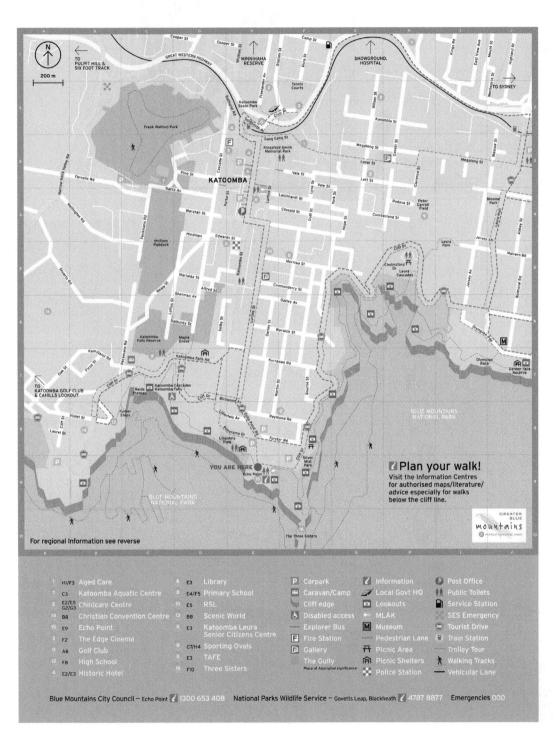

1	H1/F3	Aged Care	6	E3	Library			
7	C3	Katoomba Aquatic Centre	8	E4/F5	Primary School			
2	E2/E5 G2/G3	Childcare Centre	10	E5	RSL			
14	B8	Christian Convention Centre	13	B8	Scenic World			
15	E9	Echo Point	6	E3	Katoomba Leura Senior Citizens Centre			
3	F2	The Edge Cinema						
11	A6	Golf Club	9	C7/H4	Sporting Ovals			
12	F8	High School	5	E3	TAFE			
4	E2/E3	Historic Hotel	16	F10	Three Sisters			

Symbols legend:

- P — Carpark
- Caravan/Camp
- Cliff edge
- Disabled access
- Explorer Bus
- F — Fire Station
- Gallery
- The Gully — Place of Aboriginal significance
- Information
- Local Govt HQ
- Lookouts
- MLAK
- M — Museum
- Pedestrian Lane
- Picnic Area
- Picnic Shelters
- Police Station
- Post Office
- Public Toilets
- Service Station
- SES Emergency
- Tourist Drive
- Train Station
- Trolley Tour
- Walking Tracks
- Vehicular Lane

Blue Mountains City Council – Echo Point ☎ 1300 653 408   **National Parks Wildlife Service** – Govetts Leap, Blackheath ☎ 4787 8877   **Emergencies** 000

← Of the kinds of environmental type that exist, most care needs to be taken in the design of wayfinding systems. These can also be the most complex and require a wide array of cohesively designed elements, including pedestrian signage, vehicle signage and printed maps.

Designer **CAMPBELLBARNETT**
Client **BLUE MOUNTAINS COUNCIL**

Environmental type not associated with wayfinding or advertising allows for the designer to play. They can create monumental type forms if the budget allows. This is also an opportunity to investigate how letterforms originally created to be flat, two-dimensional marks can be translated into a solid three-dimensional shape.

Environmental type can last a long time and make a tangible contribution to the history of the place in which it appears.

↑ *Designer* **LETTERBOX**
Client **HUGO MITCHELL GALLERY**
← *Photographer* **LOUISE HAWSON, 52 SUBURBS**

OTHER ENVIRONMENTAL TYPE

This might include company names placed on doors and buildings, and type simply used as a decorative effect within an environment. In all these situations the text should have some informational value, so it is probably a good idea for it to be informational. Beyond this, you have a lot of scope to play. When working with these kinds of environmental type:

- ❯ be aware that the choice of typeface is much less critical, except where corporate branding rules apply
- ❯ try to use the space you have effectively
- ❯ be interesting—a wall is a big space, so use it well, because if the result is not good it will be hard to ignore.

↑ Constructed from solid concrete, the signage for the North Melbourne Town Hall Artshouse is not only functional, but also sculptural. 'The joy of carefully spacing was not shared by the signage installers, probably because each letter weighs over a ton', reports Letterbox.

Designer **LETTERBOX**
Client **CITY OF MELBOURNE**

DESIGN BRIEF: CREATE YOUR OWN PERSONAL TYPOGRAPHY REFERENCE BOOK

 Summarise the key aspects of this chapter and the margin exercises you have done and combine them into a 24 page, A5 sized book. Particular emphasis should be given to the description and structure of type and typefaces and the application and use of type for setting text. Include any defintitions, diagrams, illustrations and example images that you think are necessary.

This is a design exercise that should allow you to apply what you have learned about type and typography in the actual design of a document, so choose your typeface carefully to set an appropriate tone for your work.

Draw upon information in other chapters of this book to help you decide how you structure your design (with a grid, chapter 5), how you use colour (chapter 3) and how you go about printing and binding the final piece (chapter 6).

SUMMARY

Given its function in the written expression of language, type is arguably the most important tool of the designer for the communication of ideas. However, to be used effectively, considerable skill is required. The basis for that skill comes from an understanding of type's origins and structure, and the terminology of typography. This flows into an understanding of how to place type onto a structured page, screen and three-dimensional space.

As a graphic designer these are vital skills to have and by applying these tools you will become part of a long tradition of the effective communication of our most precious commodity: knowledge.

The power of type as a communication tool is in its flexibility, and to work successfully with this flexibility requires understanding, practice and skill.

TYPE PEOPLE

A few of the many influential people of type and typography:

Johannes Gutenberg	Jan Tschichold
Nicolas Jenson	Emil Ruder
Aldus Manutius	Herb Lubalin
William Caslon	Charles Peignot
Francois Didot	Otl Aicher
Giambattista Bodoni	Scott Makela
Vincent Figgins	Ed Fella
Peter Behrens	Erik Spiekermann
Eric Gill	Jeff Keedy
Frederic Goudy	Neville Brody
Hermann Zapf	Carol Twombly
Wim Crouwel	Zuzana Licko
Karl Gerstner	Martin Majoor
Matthew Carter	Luc(as) de Groot
Morris Fuller Benton	Stephen Banham
William Dwiggins	Kris Sowersby
Margaret Calvert	

TYPEFACES

This list is just a small sample of the typefaces available. These are all relatively common and as a designer you should learn how to use each of them effectively.

Akzidenz Grotesque	Gotham
Avenir	Helvetica
Baskerville	Hoefler Text
Bembo	Joanna
Bodoni	Meta/Meta Serif
Caslon	Mrs Eaves
Century	National
Clarendon	Officina Serif/Officina Sans
DIN	Rockwell
Eurostile	Sabon
Frutiger	Scala/Scala Sans
Futura	Times
Galliard	Trade Gothic
Garamond	Trebuchet
Georgia	Univers
Gill Sans	Verdana

KEY TERMS

For the terminology of letter shapes, please refer to the diagram on page 125.

For a description of the main typeface categories, please refer to the table on pages 128–130.

REFERENCES / MAGAZINES / WEBSITES

Baines, P & Haslam, A 2002, *Type & typography*, Laurence King, London.

Bierut, M (ed) 1994–1999, *Looking closer: critical writings on graphic design*, vol. 1–3, Allworth Press, New York.

Bosshard HR 2000, *The typographic grid*, Verlag Niggli, Zurich.

Bringhurst, R 2004, *The elements of typographic style*, H&M Publishers, Vancouver.

Craig, J, et al 2006, *Designing with type: the essential guide to typography*, Watson Guptill, New York (see also www.designingwithtype.com).

Dair, C 1967, *Design with type*, University of Toronto Press, Toronto.

Lupton, E 2010, *Thinking with type*, Princeton Architectural Press, New York (see also www.thinkingwithtype.com).

Garfield, S 2010, *Just my type*, Profile Books, London.

Hill, W 2010, *The complete typographer: a foundation course for graphic designers working with type*, Thames & Hudson, 2010, London.

Hochuli , J 2008, *Detail in typography*, Hyphen Press, London.

Jury, D 2002, *About face: reviving the rules of typography*, Rotovision, Mies.

Kinross, R 2004, *Modern typography*, Hyphen Press, London.

Spiekerman, E & Ginger, EM 2002, *Stop stealing sheep & find out how type works*, Adobe Press, Berkley.

Willi, K 2003, *Typography: formation + transformation*, Verlag Niggli, Zurich.

Baseline magazine

Idea magazine

Font Magazine

Adobe Fonts (www.adobe.com/type)

Australian Type Foundry (www.atf.com.au)

DaFont (www.dafont.com)

Font Shop (www.fontastic.com.au)

Identifont (www.identifont.com)

I Love Typography (www.ilovetypography.com)

Letterbox (www.letterbox.net.au)

My Fonts (www.myfonts.com)

Typohile (http://typophile.com)

Village Typographers (www.vllg.com)

chapter 5

PRINT DESIGN

INTRODUCTION

After reading the first few chapters, you now know how to design using colour, shape, type and the elements of design. You also understand the importance of the big idea, or concept, in your designs and you're now desperate to create a fabulous finished product. Whether your design is on-screen (web and digital design) or in a book, brochure or magazine, you need to think about layout and pulling all the visual (and sometimes sound) elements together. This chapter looks at the print side of layout. We will look at the principles of design, including grids, and at page characteristics, the proportions of layout and the importance of active space. We will consider the design requirements of different kinds of printed publications, presenting to clients and refining final designs.

CHAPTER OVERVIEW

Layouts and grids

Active areas of design

Publications

Presenting to clients

Final design refinement

PROCESS:
Reuben Crossman

PROFILE:
Monster Children

LAYOUTS AND GRIDS

The organisation of pages might seem like it should be a simple thing. You might assume you just need to throw a few shapes, text and images together using software such as Adobe InDesign® or Illustrator®. But given the way these programs are structured, you will still need to give careful consideration to aspects of your design before you create 'the page'. You may not think that sketching the design first is necessary, but most good designers still sketch a general **layout** first. Additionally, if the end product has multiple pages, a mock-up or dummy showing the pagination of the finished publication should be produced to plan the pages. If you're working on a magazine, the editor will have clear guidelines on the breakdown of pages and formats for each issue, and you will need to keep to these guidelines.

PRELIMINARY THOUGHTS

What size is my page? What margins will I need? Is there going to be more than one column? And if there are multiple columns, how big is the gutter between each column? For most forms of printed material, there are guidelines and protocols to answer these questions.

For instance, business cards, possibly the smallest thing you will ever design, can be any size your client requests. However, they are generally trimmed to 90 mm × 55 mm. If you change these standard measurements, the cards may not fit into a card holder. The **bleed** needs to be 5 mm larger on every side than the page; in other words, it must be 5 mm larger than the **trim size**. The **print area** needs to be 5 mm within each edge of the page in case the paper moves or slips slightly in the printing press. These measurements are consistent no matter how big the business card is. So decide on a document size and then think about all the different elements that make up the page. The figure at left shows the components that make up a page.

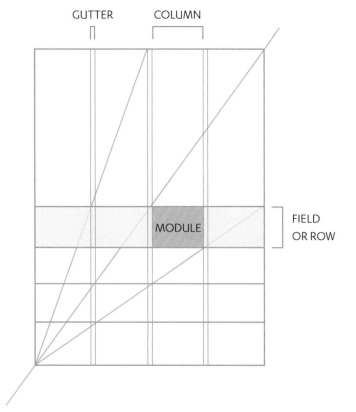

← Layout elements of a page design. The diagonal lines help to identify the width of the printed area and the size of the exterior margins.

Layout refers to the general appearance of the design of a printed or digital page. It covers the management of

form and space that creates the relationship between images and text.

Bleed is the area of an image that extends past the trim lines, so that there is no white space between an image and the edge of the page.

→ EyeSaw book spreads

Designer **NAUGHTYFISH**

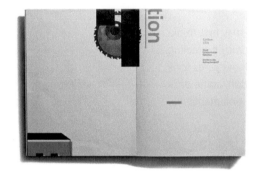

MARGINS

Margins create a lineless frame around the layout. The bottom margin of a page should be the largest, while the inside margin of a double-page spread should be the smallest. Appropriate margins contribute to a document's readability.

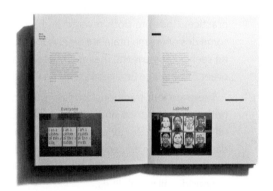

GUTTERS

Although gutters (the spaces between columns) are often set to 4 mm or 5 mm wide, this will depend on the type size. If the gutter isn't wide enough, body copy will be read across columns; if it is too wide, it will look unsightly.

Trim size indicates the final size of a publication. It should be communicated to the designer as part of initial specifications.

Print area is the area of a page that is within the margins. Print area is usually defined in books and magazines so that pages retain consistency throughout the publication.

163

The person's name and company are the two most important pieces of information on a business card and can be typeset in up to 10 pt type. Often the company name is included as part of the logo and will not need to be typeset again. The rest of the type can be typeset as small as 6 pt. As the designer, you may prefer to set it all in the same size.

Business cards are harder to design well than you may first think. Depending on the results of your first attempt, you may be feeling elated or wondering how designers ever make business cards look any good. Even if you are happy with your first creation, come back to it in six months, or a year, and you may find lots of elements you would like to change.

GRIDS

The use of grids, which are frameworks that divide a page into columns and rows, is ingrained in current Australian graphic design practice. Grids are both revered and reviled for the absolutes that some designers maintain are essential to their integrity. The grid can be seen to possess the means to obtain clarity of thought (design), order of language (images vs text) and precision.

There are four traditional kinds of grids: manuscript grids, column grids, modular grids and hierarchical grids. Each one is used in different ways, for different types of publications, and can be designed to have endless flexibility. If you think that the use of a grid will make your design boring, then you're not using your imagination to consider all possibilities.

Do magazines, newspapers, websites or the iPhone interface have a grid? Yes. Grids are used in all of these designs, and more. Good grids are designed to be flexible: elements of the grid can be combined as needed, hidden within the overall structure, or even omitted where necessary. It all depends on the informational requirements of the elements in your design brief.

↓ Grid development process.

ANATOMY OF A GRID

BUILD APPROPRIATE STRUCTURE

ANTICIPATE IDIOSYNCRACIES OF CONTENT (IMAGE, AMOUNT OF TEXT)

TEST THE LIMITATIONS OF THE GRID STRUCTURE

EXERCISE

CREATE A BUSINESS CARD
Using the standard specifications discussed in the text (trim size, bleed, print area and type size), create your own business card. Use your name, title (Graphic Designer), address, phone number, email address and web address (if you have one). Use two colours (black, plus a colour of your choice), with an illustration, logo or photographic image. The card can be one- or two-sided.

↑ All printed material should be designed with print area, **trim lines** (or crop marks), bleed lines, columns, gutters, margins and **slugs**.

Designer **LANDOR ASSOCIATES**

← Business cards

Designer **NAUGHTYFISH**

Trim lines (or crop marks) are lines or marks that indicate to the printer where the edge of a page should be trimmed.

A **slug** is an area that is printed but does not appear on the final document as it is outside the trim area. It is used to send instructions to the printer and contains file names, printer's colour bars, and trim and register marks.

A brief history of the modern grid

The Bauhaus School operated in Germany from 1919 until 1933. It combined craft and fine arts but is most famous for its approach to design. Many journal articles were published by the Bauhaus practitioners. In its relatively short life, the Bauhaus made such an impact on the creative arts that it is now credited as being the innovative leader of modern graphic design thinking. Designers including László Maholy-Nagy, Herbert Bayer, Jan Tschichold, and particularly Ludwig Mies van der Rohe and Walter Gropius are credited with bringing different influential fields of design into the twentieth century.

In the years between World Wars I and II, Bauhaus staff and students experimented with design, typographic placement, photomontage and the highly characteristic use of bars, rules and asymmetrically composed type. Although columnar layouts were used in newspapers, magazines and advertisements in parts of North America and Europe, most of the world had not been exposed to these radical design concepts. The Bauhaus officially closed in 1933 after the Nazis arrested these 'degenerate' designers or forced them to leave the country—some going to North America, and Tschichold leaving for Switzerland where the advocacy of asymmetry and grid-based layout flourished.

↑ Designers still utilise the grid in contemporary design.

Designer **LANDOR ASSOCIATES**
Client **AUSTRALIAN GRAPHIC DESIGN ASSOCIATION**

Design collateral refers to all the components that make up the promotions for a company, product or service. This could include brochures, business cards, letterheads, fliers and advertisements.

A **text block** is a shape created in a software program to hold text, which can carry over multiple pages or sections of a publication.

Experimentation continued in Switzerland, at Neue Grafik in Zurich, and also at the Basel School of Design, with an emphasis on taking the Bauhaus ideas further. Although the two groups took different paths, the end result was driven by the desire to produce balance (between type and open space, and between form and function) and the need to produce proportional guidelines. The pervasive ideas of these radical designers still permeate graphic design today.

Paul Rand, born in 1914, is attributed with introducing the Swiss style of design. He was initially educated at the Pratt Institute, New York, but considered himself mostly self-taught. He felt he gained most of the relevant design information he needed from European magazines such as *Gebrauchsgraphik*. Rand made a great impact on American audiences where, as early as the 1940s, he was utilising design constructs in business communications. The need for visual uniformity led to the creation of design style manuals where all components of a business's corporate communications were described in detail. Corporate identity and the idea of branding across different design collateral, including print advertising, packaging and television, utilising complex grids became standard in the 1960s.

The overarching principle of utilising grids in graphic design is as quoted above, to create a balance between freedom and conformity.

Manuscript grids

The most simple grid structures, manuscript grids are used for many reports and often in books (i.e. manuscripts). The primary structure is a text block with margins. The size of the margins defines the placement of the text block on the page. The location and size of the header and footer, chapter title and page numbers define the look of the publication. Variation and interest can be achieved through shifts in typographic leading, alignment, size and colour, use of extra wide and asymmetrical margins and use of imagery.

↑ Front cover of Gelganyem promotional book.

Designer **FINN CREATIVE**
Client **GELGANYEM TRUST**

A **header** is the publication title, chapter head or other information that 'runs' at the top of every page of a book.

A **footer** is the publication title, chapter head or other information that 'runs' at the bottom of every page of a book.

167

→ Some designers specialise in
newspaper and magazine design.

Designer **DE LUXE & ASSOCIATES**

↓ Modular grids are used in
all phone software as well as
catalogues and advertisements.

Designer **LANDOR ASSOCIATES**
Client **CITY OF MELBOURNE**

EXERCISE

Look carefully at a few different newspapers and assess what their base column grid is—you may have to look
at two or three different pages to work it out. Also make an estimate of how many typefaces they use in the
design. Are there any other special elements in the layout?

→ The masthead is the title of a newspaper or magazine or, in this instance, the top section of a website design.

Designer **NAUGHTYFISH**
Client **SIRCA**

Column grid

This grid type is very flexible with some columns joining for wider text blocks and images. This means columns can be independent of each other for small blocks of text or joined to create variety. The width of the column relates directly to the size of the text. Larger type requires a larger column, with 10 words per line being the optimal, for ease of reading. The challenge is to avoid large amounts of hyphenation by creating the right proportions between the column width and size of type. In a traditional column grid the margins are assigned a width that is twice the width of the gutter.

Page structures can be created of 2, 3, 4, 5, 6 and up to 9 columns—just look at most newspapers.

Modular grid

This grid type is often seen in catalogues and complex publications including charts and schedules. Modular grids often have a mathematical or technological feel, and hence seem very 'modern'. A modular grid is essentially a column grid with horizontal lines that create a matrix, or modules. Although this grid feels very structured, a more postmodern approach is created by combining modules together to hold large images, or pull out text or headlines. Module size should relate to the width and depth of one average paragraph of text at a given size. Gutters and margins must be considered, along with the size of the modules, for the overall page layout to work as a coherent design. Although small modules provide a designer with greater flexibility and precision, too many divisions can be confusing to the reader and are inevitably redundant.

Hierarchical grids

Magazine covers and web pages are two examples of the most common use of hierarchical grids. Magazines need to have their **mastheads** or titles at the top of the publication for easy identification in racks by consumers. Brochures also often need to have their subject heading at the top of the cover panel for easy identification. Scrolling web pages can be designed so that the masthead stays at the top of the screen while the content can be scrolled through. Generally, hierarchical grids conform to the information that needs to be organised but the organisation of information is intuitive and less rigid than other grid structures.

Magazine mastheads are carefully designed and constructed to attract their target market's attention. Colour, size, type and position are extremely important to compete with other periodicals.

A **masthead** is the title of a newspaper, magazine or website, generally located at the top of the front page or in the top section of a website.

169

Studying graphic design in Wellington, New Zealand, at Victoria University and Wellington Polytechnic School of Design, Reuben Crossman found himself drawn to typography, illustration, photography and printmaking. 'I was also very interested in fine art and painting, so was always exploring ideas that enabled me to combine these in a commercial sense,' says Reuben.

After starting his career in corporate design and advertising, Reuben was offered a project through Murdoch Books. From there he made the switch effortlessly to become one of the most inspired book designers in Australia today. 'I am fortunate that the clients I work with are also all passionate about what they do and are successful in their own fields. I've created books for many of Australia's top authors, chefs and restaurants, interior stylists, photographers and many other creative professionals.'

Within a publishing team, Reuben works with the publisher to create the concept direction. 'The publisher will set the design budget and initial footprint for a title so it will be up to me to create a solution based on these parameters. Once I have developed several concepts or directions I will finalise the design with the publisher and then work with the author and creative teams to produce the final product. The one area a publisher will generally be more involved with would be the cover design. It will usually be a broader discussion with a sales and marketing team for their feedback on how they anticipate a particular solution working in the current market.'

Relishing the challenge to translate the passion of an author to print, each project is treated as, Reuben says, 'a unique graphic extension of the authors' story'. To approach each graphic extension, Reuben researches his subject thoroughly. 'I try to find out as much about the subject and the author as possible before I start to put anything down on paper. I will usually spend time with them and try to understand as best I can, what exactly they are hoping to communicate to a consumer audience. This will obviously influence my design direction but I will also look at what is out on the shelves and figure out how we can produce something that stands out from the current range,' explains Reuben.

THIS PAGE | Three different creative solutions for cookbook covers. *Quay* won the Australian Publishers Association Best Designed Book of the Year in 2011

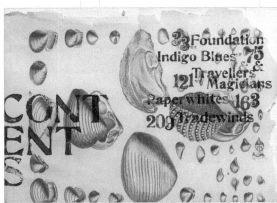

With the research completed and a spark of an idea, Reuben commissions photographers, stylists and other creative talents to help create the visual content. 'I normally work quite closely with these teams art directing the larger projects, but it can also be a great chance to bounce ideas around and sometimes develop the concept further. Some projects are short and tightly concepted, others can run for over a year, so it gives you time to really consider an idea and push the boundaries for that subject matter.'

Developing a grid structure for each book's layout can become quite complex, but is essential to allow the information to be easily understood. Finding inspiration from his research and exposure to fields outside of design, Reuben is constantly refining the techniques he uses to create a visual interface. 'I am always looking for new and exciting ways to present graphic information and have been fortunate to have worked with some very creative chefs who were also keen to push conventional cookbook styles aside and develop something that was not just a recipe book but more of a sensory experience.'

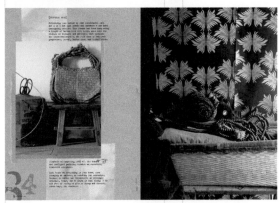

A style Reuben has developed for certain books is the scrapbook look. 'The titles I have designed that required a scrapbook style were developed by identifying the author's own style and extending this onto a page,' explains Reuben. 'I worked with the author to collect a body of material I can then design with. This involved collaging backgrounds and textures, creating type from old stamp sets, building all sorts of graphic elements that can then be layered into the final design.'

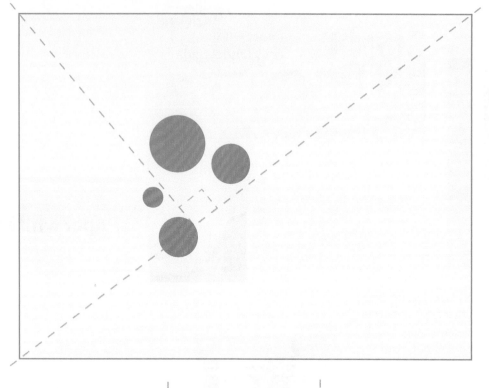

← This diagram of dynamic symmetry utilises the diagonal to illustrate the 'hot spots' that are the focus for the reader. The red dots illustrate where focal images and text should be placed to maximise a reader's interest.

← This diagram illustrates the 'hot spots', which are the focus for the reader's interest. The size of the red dot illustrates the areas that are identified in the rule of thirds. However, each area does not have the same focal strength.

→ A designer can create a harmonious spatial relationship by using the Fibonacci pattern to space objects, text and even white space.

172

EXERCISE

Have a look at any software program and note how the most important information for the program is situated in the top left-hand side of the layout on the screen.

ACTIVE AREAS OF DESIGN

The amount of text, number of illustrations or images, number of available pages and the width and depth of the columns as decided in the grid structure, will all have an effect on the type size of the text and the management of white space within the layout.

Management of the space on pages is a fundamental aspect of being a good designer. Recognising that some areas of a page attract the viewer's eye more strongly enables a designer to use this information to focus attention on a page element. In general, people from Western countries are trained, when they start reading at an early age, to view and process information from the top left-hand corner before moving right and descending down the page to the bottom right-hand corner. Using this active/passive theory of page layout design along with grid formats enables a designer to create pages that have increased readability; however, there are other components that also need to be considered—visual relationships and proportions of elements as well as information hierarchy.

THE RULE OF THIRDS

A significant amount of study has been done on the best layout of pages. Most of the studies have been related to the composition of paintings and photography; however, it is still useful to apply this knowledge to the composition and layout of page design. The 'rule of thirds' recommends dividing the page into thirds, horizontally and vertically. The points where the lines meet are known as the 'hot spots' of the page. It is believed that the eye lingers on these as it scans the page. Many designers have used this principle to create strong design layouts and it is particularly evident in corporate identity designs where logos appear in the top left-hand corner. This 'sets the scene' for the viewer to read further information on the page. Other applications of this compositional device are websites that have navigation bars at the top and left, many newspapers that have the least important information on the right-hand side of the page and the layout of menus on most software programs

THE FIBONACCI PATTERN

The Fibonacci pattern is a sequence of numbers that is closely related to the 'Golden Ratio'—a ratio often observed in naturally occurring patterns, such as in the structure of the nautilus shell, flower petals and bee hives. Designs that use a Fibonacci pattern in their layout are proportionately true and pleasing to the eye. The pattern series always starts out with 0 + 1. By adding the two numbers together you obtain the next number. Therefore, the sequence is:

0, 1, 1, 2, 3, 5, 8, 13, 21, 34, etc.

The 8:13 ratio is believed to be the most important and many designers use it to decide on the shape of their book or page sizes. As most paper sizes within Australia are based on the A series paper size, it is more expensive and often wasteful to use other page sizes, but designers can still utilise the Fibonacci pattern, or the Golden Ratio, in their designs by dividing up the page based on its own proportions.

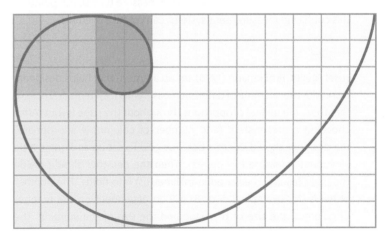

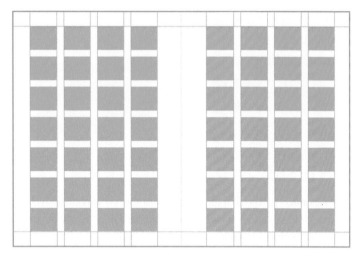

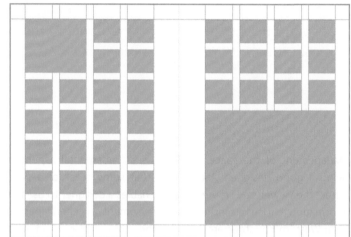

BASELINE GRIDS AND FIELDS

Most typographic characters, including capitals, sit on the baseline. Baselines are horizontal guide lines and the distance between baselines is the type size plus the leading. Therefore, 8 pt type with 2 pt leading will require a 10 pt **baseline grid**. Creating a design with a baseline grid enables the designer to line up all elements (type and images) within the page design. However, we measure page and image sizes in millimetres, whereas we measure type size in points—this conflict in measurement systems can create a dilemma.

Page fields

Josef Müller-Brockmann (1996) set up a system that helps designers work with the dilemma of different measurement systems and ensure that there are unified proportions throughout the page layout. After choosing a grid system (and number of columns if appropriate) the designer should select a baseline grid to set up and guide type alignment (measured in points). Then the designer should divide the page (usually measured in millimetres) into fields. The number of fields (for example 3, 5 or 8) will be dependent on the number of columns, the size of the page and the size of the margins. The

↖ EQUAL FIELD GRID
This illustration features an asymmetrical grid of equally spaced modules of uniform size arranged in four columns This is a simple variation of the asymmetrical four-column grid.

↑ ALTERNATIVES
This grid is also based on the asymmetrical four-column grid, but it features modules of different sizes that create larger and more dynamic picture spaces.

ideal result is having the tops of capitals align with the top **keyline** of images, and descenders of type (whether body text or captions) that align with the bottom keyline of images. These considerations will create a more harmonious and rhythmic result in the graphic design layout.

It is important to note that few even very experienced designers can create a well-constructed page without trying out a number of options with reference to the specific criteria of the project. As every project is different, each best result will need different solutions.

A **baseline grid** is an invisible grid that allows the baseline of type (lines of text) to line up from column to column and page to page.

Keylines are lines used to indicate placement of images as well as special printing requirements, e.g. die lines and fold marks. They generally do not print.

> 'Every difficulty standing in the reader's way means loss of quality in communication and memorability.'
>
> JOSEF MÜLLER-BROCKMANN, *GRID SYSTEMS IN GRAPHIC DESIGN*, 1996

↑ Fields can be diagonal as well as horizontal.

Designer **LANDOR ASSOCIATES**
Client **DESIGN INSTITUTE OF AUSTRALIA**

SNAP TO GRID
Use 'snap to grid' in your software options if you have set up a grid and baseline alignment. It is more difficult to accurately achieve the best result by eye alone.

→ An asymmetrical design of
a double-page spread.

Designer **FROST* DESIGN**
Client **RIZZOLI INTERNATIONAL
PUBLICATIONS**

LEGIBILITY VERSUS READABILITY

Legibility is concerned with the characteristics of a font and describes whether each character of a font is easily discerned from the rest. Readability is concerned with the complete process of communicating meaning and involves navigating a page of information easily. Space on a page needs to be assessed for the shape that it forms and that shape's ability to not only attract the viewer's attention but also enable maximum readability.

STYLE SHEETS

Setting up style sheets not only encourages consistency but creates reoccurring signals to the reader that they can interpret almost unconsciously. Well-constructed style sheets signal that sections belong or don't belong to each other, that one heading is more important than another heading, or that a certain chunk of text is an interlude.

THE SYMMETRICAL VERSUS THE ASYMMETRICAL GRID

The verso and recto (left and right) pages of a symmetrical grid are mirror images of each other with equal inner and outer margins. On the other hand, an asymmetrical grid uses the same layout on the recto as the verso pages. Most books tend to favour a symmetrical grid to aid planning for the space lost in the inside margins due to binding issues as well as the placement of asymmetrical page numbers and other page elements.

STYLE SHEETS

Because every client brief is different, every brief requires a new design and layout, with a new grid and **style sheet**. The look and feel of a document relies heavily on the use of positive and negative space, and the activity within the positive space. When information is well laid out, it is better retained in the memory, and it can also be read more easily and quickly. Clarity of design adds to the credibility of the information.

A **style sheet** defines a consistent approach to the size, font, spacing and colour of different type within a document. Style sheets can be set up in most publishing software programs and are a great timesaver when changes need to be made across a large document.

A style sheet is a system that identifies the different hierarchy of headings and the space around them in a document. The hierarchy of type is dependent on size, weight, colour, boldness, italics and underlining. A style sheet enables a designer to set up a code for the reader of that particular document. If there is no consistency in the look and feel of certain headings, then there appears to be no logic in the sequence of text and the reader can become confused. The chosen typeface needs to clearly indicate at each weight and size of a heading whether it is important, very important or crucial. This code gets the reader ready for the next series of information.

The space between paragraphs is also important, as well as the shapes that columns and images create. The negative space (or white space) created by these elements is the component that allows the page to breathe and directs the reader's eye through the material from beginning to end. A heading placed too high above its body text no longer acts as a heading, but as a statement unattached to its explanation. Space in paragraphs allows the reader to pause before continuing. Lack of space can be exhausting and uncomfortable for the reader as they are carried through reams of text. Badly designed newspapers, for example, can give the reader the feeling that they are being dragged along with the text.

Style sheets can also create texture on a page that might otherwise be conservative and boring. By introducing more space and differently weighted or coloured type, you can create emphasis and importance. But the best thing about style sheets is that they can be set up in a multipage software program relatively easily and changed even more easily.

Style guidelines

When a brief is given by a client for an existing publication or corporate identity, the designer may have to work with existing style guidelines. These guidelines can include everything from the typefaces to be used, type of grid, editorial content and approach, to the ratio of images to text. In organisations, there will be different preferences for the use of a number of design elements including the colour palette and the designer's approach to imagery. It is best to be aware of these guidelines before you start the design process so that any conflict with your design is avoided.

DECIDE ON A TYPE HIERARCHY OR STRUCTURE
Are there three, four or more levels of headings? You may need to collaborate with the writer or editor to identify the hierarchy.

WHAT SORT OF GRID WILL BE USED?
If it's a column grid, how many columns? And, therefore, how wide are the columns? This will indicate how large the type needs to be to allow eight to ten words per line.

CREATE FIELDS
Correspond the number of fields to the components of the text and images and the look and feel of the document.

DECIDE ON A FONT FAMILY
Select the typeface that is most appropriate for the look and feel of the document and legibility.

CREATE A TRIAL LAYOUT OF THE TEXT
See if the components of font, size, colour, space, alignment and leading work in the grid and field structure to maximise legibility.

CHANGE WHERE NECESSARY

TRY COMPONENTS AGAIN

↓ A book may have pages with
no text and bleeding images, and
therefore no need for a grid.

Designer **NAUGHTYFISH**

PUBLICATIONS

All **publications** need a code of composition and legibility in order for readers to understand where to go on a page and to make sense of the information. Sometimes there doesn't seem to be any sense in a design structure or layout. Cheap weekly magazines often avoid the use of structure in their layouts to convey the feel of a massed amount of information, which gives the audience the sense of getting their money's worth. To generalise, the higher the design ideals, the simpler the structure appears to be. Not only will the structure be simpler, but also the use of colour, number of fonts, and the general design theme.

The best work portrays only the elements that are essential. Every element is purposeful and nothing distracts. Good design doesn't jump out or call attention to itself; it does not divert the reader from the content.

ELEMENTS OF A PUBLICATION

There are many elements of a publication that you will need to take into consideration in your design.

Design collateral

Design collateral refers to all the components that make up the promotions for a company, product or service. This could include brochures, business cards, letterheads, fliers and advertisements.

Text block

A text block is a shape created in a software program to hold text, which can carry over multiple pages; or the block of printed signatures or sections of a publication.

Headers and footers

A header is a publication title, chapter head or other information that runs at the top of every page of a publication. If this information runs at the bottom of the page, it is called the footer.

Structure/layout

The terms structure and layout refer to the arrangement and treatment of type and images on a page.

Double-page spread

Books and other multi-page documents have spreads where two pages are visible together. It is important to design your layout with consideration of the verso (left-hand) and the recto (right-hand) pages and how they relate when viewed together.

Headlines

The largest title on a page is the headline. It will communicate to the reader the tone of the information to follow.

Page numbers

Page numbers, also called folios, make it easier for readers to navigate a text. Sometimes page numbers are left off full-page illustrations or photography pages. They should still be considered an aesthetic as well as functional aspect of the page design. Thought should be given to how they are aligned to the grid or field structure.

Keylines

Keylines are lines used to indicate placement of images as well as special printing requirements like die lines and fold marks. They generally do not print.

A **publication** is a magazine, newspaper, catalogue, brochure or book. Typically, a publication is a multi-page document that is offset printed and bound.

179

…The white man history has been told and it's today in the book. But our history is not there properly. That's one way to tell 'em. We've got to tell 'em through our paintings. They might see it through there.

Clifford Brooks, Martu, Tjukurba Gallery.

↑ *Designer* **FINN CREATIVE**

Picture boxes

Usually square or rectangular, picture boxes can be any shape. They are indicated in a hand-drawn layout by a box with a cross through it. In a computer layout they are indicated by a keyline, which is usually black but is not always visible. When used in a column with ragged type, the picture box needs to be set approximately 5 mm smaller than the column width, otherwise it will look too big.

Captions

Most images need an explanation or reference so that readers understand what they are and why they are included in the text. Captions are often set in different type to body text and traditionally were set in italics. They usually appear underneath or to the side of the image they are describing.

Diagrams

A diagram is an illustration that describes an object.

Headings and subheadings

In a style sheet a heading will be the largest text in a hierarchy of different type. There are also different levels of subheadings within publications, depending on the hierarchy of information. This book has three levels of subheadings.

Rough/visual

A rough or visual is a thumbnail or the draft of a layout for a page with all the information in place. The level of finish of the rough will depend on the visual literacy of the client.

Mock-up/dummy

A same-size or miniature version of a final design that can be shown to a client, printer or manufacturer to communicate the look of the end product. For example, a multiple-page document could be constructed of the selected paper stock, bound and hand-rendered or digitally printed to indicate the final design; or a package design could be created in an alternative material but with the correct dimensions to indicate the look proposed by the designer.

EXERCISE

Research a theatre production to promote. Brochure specifications—size (trim area): 210 mm × 297 mm; bleed: 5 mm; print area: 200 mm × 287 mm. Decide whether to use a concertina or single-gate fold as part of the document grid. Choose information and imagery to create a balance that intrigues the audience. Choose a hierarchy of headings and substitute 'Lorem ipsum' (dummy) text for the body text.

4 page

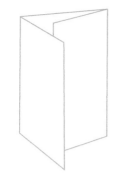

6 page letter

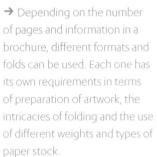

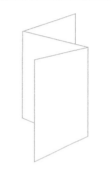

6 page accordian

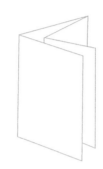

8 page parallel

← ↑ The layout of most magazines is more structured than you may realise. Even youth magazines use grids to maximise use of space. For a regular publication it is much easier to design quickly and well if you are working to a structure.

↑ *Designer* **TIMBA SMITS**
Client **WOODEN TOY MAGAZINE**

→ Depending on the number of pages and information in a brochure, different formats and folds can be used. Each one has its own requirements in terms of preparation of artwork, the intricacies of folding and the use of different weights and types of paper stock.

8 page gale

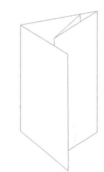

8 page roll

BROCHURES

Brochures have been one of the most successful ways that companies advertise their products and services. Although web pages have become increasingly more useful in terms of currency (which is vital in communicating up-to-date information such as interest rates, accommodation rates or flight timetables), there are still a lot of brochures and small booklets published by companies for their clients. Brochures can take many forms but the traditional brochure in many industries is DL sized—it fits into a DL envelope and is a proportion of an A4 sheet, usually 210 mm × 297 mm folded to 99 mm × 210 mm. Many industries, such as tourism, use standard-sized display cabinets, which is why standard brochure sizes have been so widely retained.

No matter which format you end up using—and there are many—brochures can be an interesting challenge to design well because they are constructed of panels that must work individually and jointly. Designers still need to manage the **dynamic symmetry** of a relatively small design while clients require them to be economical with space.

16 page broadsheet

Dynamic symmetry is the relationship between positive and negative space, and form and counter form.

181

→ As well as being useful within publications, the grid, combined with clever layout, can assist in organising information and images for cover designs. This cover features multiple illustrations, which could easily look messy; however the designer has used the grid and pieced the elements together to create a harmonious, attractive book cover.

Designer **ZOË SADOKIERSKI**
Client **PIER 9, MURDOCH BOOKS**

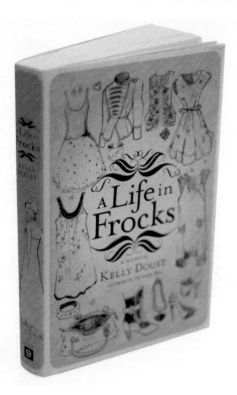

ASTRED HICKS

SO YOU WANT TO BE A MAGAZINE DESIGNER?

Key staff in magazine editorial design include:

editor—ultimately responsible for the content

art director—responsible for organisation and commissioning content including journalism and pictorial

production manager—sets the production schedule and oversees all special print requirements

sub-editors—edit the copy to ensure stylistic coherence, correct spelling, grammar and punctuation; cut copy and rewrite all badly written copy

picture editor—responsible for sourcing images, commissioning photographers and ensuring there is copyright clearance on images

designers—responsible for laying out the publication according to the art director's instructions; can be senior and junior designers, or design assistants; seniority, the working practice of the art director, the lead time to publication, and the ratio of staff to number of pages all affect the responsibility given to each designer on the team.

MAGAZINES

There is thought to be a magazine produced and printed in Australia for everyone. Magazine design is a multi-billion dollar industry and there is so much competition that one badly conceived cover design could make or break a magazine's and a designer's future. Walk into a newsagent and you are often confronted with hundreds of titles competing for your attention through the use of cover image, cover lines, masthead or branding. Consumer titles include women's, men's, children's, leisure, special interest, news and fashion. Each successful publication has been designed for a specific **market segments** and contains advertising by companies that are targeting that segment.

A magazine's masthead is very important, as it is the initial driver in setting the scene for the unique image of that publication. Popular magazines have lost significant subscriptions just due to the change in the font of a masthead. The masthead is usually the one stable element from one issue to the next and is the essence of the publication's identity. Content, images and themes can change from issue to issue and these changes are reflected on the cover to signal to readers that it is a new issue and encourage them to buy. This means that for magazine staff there is a constantly changing body of work to interpret and organise.

BOOKS

There are many different types of book: fiction, biographies, children's books, cookbooks, 'How to' books and textbooks, to name a few. Each type of book has a format that helps people feel comfortable when they start to read the book. Fiction books often have strongly coloured and well-designed covers that are intended to stimulate interest in potential readers. However, the inside pages are usually only filled with text. The typesetting of these pages is vitally important, as the reader will react negatively (fatigued by bad readability) if it is not done well.

The content of children's books depends very much on the targeted age group. A book targeted at a young audience will have more images than one targeted at an older audience. The number of pages in the book will also directly relate to the targeted audience, as will the type size, the number of words per line and coloured or dramatised text and headings. Textbooks, on the other hand, are about information, and include images and diagrams to help decipher information for the reader.

The binding, paper stock, use of coloured images and number of pages will directly relate to the budget for the book as the costs will increase depending on the use of these elements.

→ A fiction book that contains no imagery, only text, relies on its cover to spark interest in a potential reader. Book designers will often work on many concepts before the right cover is developed, as illustrated here by a first concept (left) and the final cover design.

Designer **DESIGN CHERRY**
Client **RANDOM HOUSE AUSTRALIA**

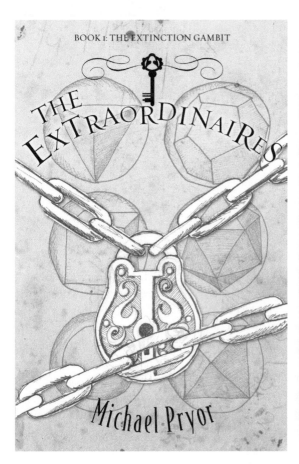

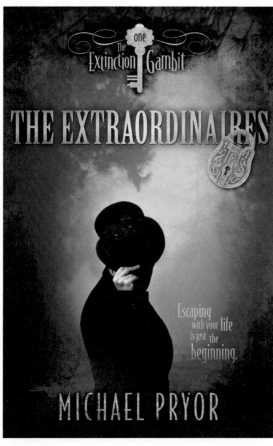

A **market segment** is a group within the broader market that has similar wants and needs, or similar behaviour towards products and services.

Monster Children
www.monsterchildren.com

Taking a long route to arrive at a career in design didn't deter Campbell Milligan. Together with co-publisher Chris Searl, Campbell has created one of Australia's most forward-thinking and engaging magazines, Monster Children. 'I actually failed art in high school, more for my lack of interest in theory than talent,' Campbell says of his design background. 'Did a brief stint as a carpenter's apprentice after leaving school, but soon realised that the early mornings weren't my scene. I luckily could draw and got my first job illustrating airports for a cartoon book company at a local printers; from there I landed a job in a small design studio. This was to be my first lesson in design, and type.'

The idea for the magazine came from personal experience and lifestyle as well as the idea to experience more. 'Having worked in surf and skate magazines for a while, I think we just got to a point where we were thinking that if you skate, you don't just want to know about skating, you have an interest in music, art, photography—whatever. So the basis was, we make a magazine that has no real set limit to what we put in it, if we like something or someone—it's in. So simply, the vision was to open our eyes to everything and anything,' explains Campbell.

So how did the magazine get off the ground? With no other publication in Australia connecting to Campbell and Chris on an individual level, they felt compelled to put something together.

Examples of the ever-changing masthead for the magazine. Breaking away from magazine-style branding, the landscape format of the publication replaces a masthead as the recognisable identity on shelves.

'We got a couple of $5000 credit cards, borrowed the same amount off our parents and printed the first issue,' Campbell tells us. 'Luckily we had done some work with a few of the advertisers in the first issue so they knew we weren't too suss. Once that first issue was done it made things so much easier, if anything, just to show people the general idea of what we were doing. Nowadays we can't stand the sight of the first issue.'

The combination used for the magazine content has been a successful one and has drawn much interest from the intended audience as well as the graphic design community. The idea that there is no set formula for the content has created a publication with a unique perspective, one that is very much driven by its publisher's own individuality and lifestyle. 'Everything you see within the issue is something we have a passion for, it's why the [*Monster Children*] gallery started also, all these people we were showing in the magazine and at the gallery were people we grew up watching and admiring. We fan out all the damn time.'

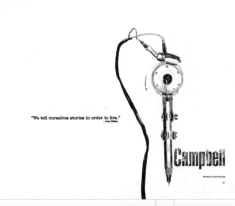

"We tell ourselves stories in order to live."
— Joan Didion

Campbell

Written by Kate Wilson

Scott

The buzz emanating from Saved Tattoo on a rainy afternoon is enough to set a tattoo junkie's teeth on edge. It's a quiet sound, likely to go unnoticed or ignored by anyone who can't identify it.

But this is Williamsburg, and here—in what is perhaps both New York's hippest and most modest enclave—you'd be hard pressed to find someone who would mistake the rattle of a tattoo gun for a dentist's drill. You'd also have a hard time finding someone who hasn't heard of Scott Campbell. The founder of Saved Tattoo, Campbell has illustrated Canni ole and been the subject of a New York Times 'Consumed' column. His tattoo work is like a badge of identification for New York's downtown cognoscenti. Having his filigreed lettering etched into your skin signifies that you either know somebody who knows somebody or—as is the case with Marc Jacobs, Sting, Heath Ledger, Lily Cole and the like—that you actually are somebody. Lately, Campbell is also a greeting art world star, having held solo shows at O.H.W.O.W. in Miami and Lazarides Gallery in London in the past year.

However, most of this—the press, the celebrity, the status—and if I told Scott Campbell doesn't 'really care about. What's important to him, what he'll remember's probably their relationship.

subverting
expectations
deanne cheuk
written by

In a way, we should thank Deanne Cheuk a lot... of Children, because she's one of the reasons that Campbell started fooling arou... 'arkXpress. Deanne is a genius graphic designer, illustrator and artist. Largely kn... for art directing TOKION she's been relentlessly creating since she started work as art di... of Perth's REvelation magazine when she was, ahem, 19 years old. Since then, Deanne's been working across so many different projects that it's easier to get this mag out than pin her down for an interview. Clearly working with Vogue Japan, the New York Times Magazine, Conan O'Brien, and getting ready for an upcoming exhibition are more important than answering our blockhead questions. Yet somehow she managed to find time to both humour us and start from the very beginning, and that beginning is Perth.

— works records —

With such strong vision the design of the magazine needed to be able to present the editorial in the same unique manner. 'Well, we don't have a set masthead, the magazine is landscape and we change the department headers each issue, so we have managed to give ourselves a bunch of extra work each issue. Each magazine is usually based around say 3–4 fonts max; Helvetica is the body copy font for now. With the features, we endeavour to let the story do the talking. I really try to let the photography and words breathe without over-designing any of the pages. The main design idea is to complement the work we are showcasing, and then also to fit 1000 words, a picture, heading, subhead and by-line on a single page. Ha!'

Like the cover, the editorial pages within *Monster Children* have no set template, allowing Campbell and Chris to experiment with the design to best illustrate the subject of each article.

185

PRESENTING TO CLIENTS

The process of producing a printed project initially requires a designer to analyse the brief or client's requirements, research the competitors and environment of the product or service. The designer then uses their imagination to brainstorm as many ideas as possible that relate to their research and analysis. These ideas need to be refined and developed until there are three possibilities that can be presented to a client. The design process includes creating a structure, often a grid, deciding on the format of the publication and selecting the paper and print techniques to be specified for a quote from the printer.

Well thought through presentation backed up by research and analysis

+

Three good ideas presented professionally on boards and in PDF format

+

Assist the client to choose the best solution by reasoned argument

+

Accept feedback and criticism graciously - present again another day if needed

=

SATISFIED CLIENT
(and a great finished product)

Although client presentations can be quite stressful to designers, they are essential in providing the client with the visual, verbal and written results of the designer's work so far. Once the designer has client approval to proceed, final images and copy needs to be formatted using a style sheet for large documents. The designer sends the final client-approved designs to the printer who will produce a proof which should be checked and signed off by the client. Final printing and finishing can then proceed.

↑ Guidelines for the best outcome in the print layout process.

→ *Designer* **PAUL GARBETT, NAUGHTYFISH**
Client **EYESAW 2009 EXHIBITION**

FINAL DESIGN REFINEMENT

Once you have refined your final ideas for the design layout of a publication, it is time to consider all the components of the production process. You will need to select paper stock, decide on the general format of the design, get quotes from printers (with consideration to embellishments like die-cutting, embossing, ink usage and publication format), work out how you will source your images, and communicate the required delivery date to printers and finishers to make sure that production within the time frame is possible.

Once your design is finalised and ready for production, there are a number of final requirements involved in preparing your files for printing. We will look more closely at pre-press requirements in Chapter 6.

JOSHUA MORRIS

INFORMATION FOR PRINTERS SHOULD INCLUDE:

Document size—flat and folded

Quantity—total to be printed

Stock—paper or other, weight (gsm), satin, matt or glossy

Print—1 colour, 2 colour, 4 colour (CMYK), 5 colour (CMYK plus a special) etc.

Special print requirements—details of embossing, die-cutting, add in pages, folding etc.

Delivery—where and when (printers will deliver straight to the client if requested)

DESIGN BRIEF: CREATE A BOOK OF FACT

 Prepare a document that illustrates examples of column grids, modular grids and hierarchical grids.

Size (trim area)

90 mm × 50 mm

Bleed

5 mm

Print area

80 mm × 40 mm (or within 5 mm on all sides from trim area)

Production

Multi-page book

1. Source examples of different grid formats from printed publications (and web pages for hierarchical grid) and scan them. Your document should contain traditional and non-traditional examples of each of these page structures.

2. Look for examples of 2, 3, 4, 5, 6 and 7 column pages with modular grids in at least two contexts (for example, newspaper, photographic chronicle or catalogue) and hierarchical grid (website and newsletter).

3. In your document, discuss in detail why and how you think these layouts are successful or unsuccessful. Also, indicate the different components the designer has used to successfully integrate the many parts of the document to create a cohesive design. Describe whether you consider the use of the grid as traditional or non-traditional and why you think the designer has used that structure.

4. Lay out the document itself as a manuscript grid with set margins, page numbers, page headings and text with a consistent style sheet across all pages. The style sheet should include consistent paragraph spacing, body text, subheadings, sub-subheadings and caption text. If your book consists of traditionally folded pages, printed on two sides, it must have multiples of four pages, possibly with some pages left blank.

SUMMARY

Understanding the design process is a very important component of being a graphic designer. During your career as a designer you may come across many different design processes – each designer will find the best way for them to develop designs and work with each client. Some designers spend a lot of time on the research and analysis phase while others hardly spend any time at all. Each job and each client will have different needs, and this is the challenge. The reward is always doing something different.

A spark of an idea can form at any time—perhaps when you first meet the client or when you put pen to paper. When you're faced with a job that is a real challenge, and you're having trouble coming up with ideas, it is the design process that will help you create the vision.

KEY TERMS

REFERENCES

Ambrose, G and Harris, P 2007, *The layout book*, AVA Publishing, Lausanne, Switzerland.

Ambrose, G and Harris, P 2008, *The production manual: a graphic design handbook*, AVA Publishing, Lausanne, Switzerland.

Avella, N 2006, *Paper Engineering: 3D techniques for a 2D material*, Rotovision, Mies, Switzerland.

Dabner, D 2004, *Graphic design school: The principles and practices of graphic design*, Thames and Hudson, London.

Gerstner, K 1968, *Designing programs*, Arthur Niggli, Switzerland.

Heller, S. and Fernandes, T 2006, *Becoming a graphic designer: a guide to careers in design*, 3rd edition, John Wiley and Sons, Hoboken, N.J.

Hembree, R 2006, *The complete graphic designer: a guide to understanding graphics and visual communication*, Rockport Publishers, Minneapolis, MN.

Kenly, E. and Beach, M 2004, *Getting it printed*, 4th edition, F&W Publications, Inc, Cincinnati, Ohio.

Müller-Brockmann, J 1996, *Grid systems in graphic design*, 4th edition, Niggli, Switzerland.

Samara, T 2005, *Making and breaking the grid*, Rockport Publishers, Minneapolis, MN.

Zappaterra, Y 2007, *Editorial design*, Laurence King Publishing Ltd, London.

chapter 6

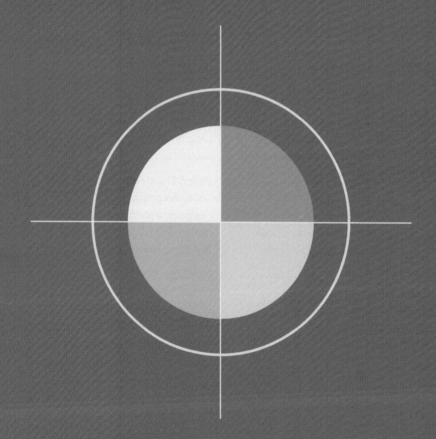

PRE-PRESS AND PRINT

INTRODUCTION

As a designer, every few years you will hear someone say or write that 'print is dead!' This is not true; in fact, we produce more printed material than ever before. In this chapter we will be looking at the process of preparing design work for print. You will learn about who is involved, the different parts of the process, available printing options and, finally, what you need to do to ensure that your vision translates to paper in a way that gives reliable, optimum results.

SETTING THE SCENE

It is almost inevitable that a significant proportion of what a graphic designer produces will be printed. Even interactive media designers should have some knowledge of print production. The process of translating work into a printed object is relatively uncomplicated, if you understand what you are doing. The real risk for the designer is that mistakes can be very expensive to fix.

As an understanding of what is involved will help to avoid mistakes, this chapter will focus on the process of printing from a number of angles.

First, we will look at who is involved; no, it is not just you, the designer—there are clients and suppliers to consider as well. Then we will look at the interaction of the design process and print production, and examine the role of the production manager. Normally the term **'pre-press'** refers to the part of the process between the completion of the final design and the beginning of actual printing. However, there are parts of a larger pre-press process that affect this small part of the design to production process. This is now referred to as print production and we will look at some aspects of it and how it interacts with the design process, with which you should already be familiar.

Next, we will look at the importance of having some understanding of what is involved with printing before we send design work to print. Printing is often about transferring a design from the computer on which it was designed into some sort of hardcopy form. On one level it seems easy—ring a printer, organise a print run, send them the files. To get this process right, though, it is essential for the designer to know about the printing process. They need to know which device to use, how inks work and what is the best medium on which to print. They should also have knowledge about the myriad other processes and effects available to the designer, collectively called 'embellishments'.

Having looked at the process as a whole, we will then focus on the designer's role in the pre-press process from final design to the beginning of printing, and discuss the procedures and checks that are necessary to ensure a design is printed successfully.

Two examples of offset printing: the brochure on the left uses the four-colour process, while the brochure on the right uses one colour (black) on a coloured paper stock

Courtesy **SPICERS PAPER**

PRE-PRESS

Literally speaking the term 'pre-press' refers to everything that happens before printing begins. Normally, however, we use pre-press to refer to the part of the job between the completion of the final design and the beginning of actual printing.

Pre-press refers to the work required to prepare for printing client-approved artwork. It includes final artwork preparation, checking, proofing and printing plates.

THE STAKEHOLDERS

The designer plays a key role in the pre-press process. They have created the design, so they understand how the design works, how it should look and how it is 'put together'. The designer needs to be aware that the client is part of the pre-press process too, not least because they supplied the brief and they will be paying for the printing. The printers are obviously also involved, as are other related service providers who will take the artwork and turn it into the finished product. These, then, are the stakeholders in the pre-press process; let's look at each in a little detail.

THE DESIGNER

The designer is in the business of communication. They are a vital component in the dialogue between the client and their audience. They also need to be able to communicate with the client about the design and print production process. They are hired by clients to use their specialised design skills and knowledge to provide timely and cost-effective results.

THE CLIENT

The important thing that a designer needs to remember about clients is that they pay the bills. Quite rightly, they expect the designer to deliver what they have asked for on the date that they need it. However, it is very important to remember that design and the print production process involves specialist knowledge and terminology. This may mean that the client can have unrealistic expectations about what can be done within a certain timeframe and for a certain cost. They may also not be very good at communicating what they need or understanding what the designer is trying the produce for them.

It is the designer's duty to explain very clearly what they are trying to achieve, how much it will cost and how long it will take to produce. If the client is unsatisfied with any of these factors, the designer will have to change what they are doing. Communicate with your client; usually, things can be worked out to the satisfaction of all. Remember too, if there are problems cropping up during production (delays, for example) then the designer must discuss these with the client as soon as the problem is known. It may be possible for the client to adjust their deadline, but never assume that they can.

DESIGNERS IN A NUTSHELL

You, the designer:

- get paid by the client
- have certain skills
- provide a service based on those skills
- are a vital component in the communication process between client and their audience
- are allowed to have opinions based on your skills and knowledge.

CLIENTS IN A NUTSHELL

Remember, your client:

- pays the bills
- expects their job to be delivered on time
- may not have the same technical knowledge as you
- may have unrealistic expectations about cost and timeframes
- must be communicated with frequently and in detail
- may be able to accommodate delays if notified ahead of time.

THE SUPPLIERS

In the overall production process, once the designer's part is completed with the final artwork checked, approved and ready to print, it is time to hand the project over to one or more suppliers. The main supplier will be the printer, but binders, embellishers and a delivery company could also become involved. These suppliers may be contracted and initially paid by the designer, who will include these payments when billing the client for the work. They are also part of the communication between the client and their audience.

It is important to establish good working relationships with suppliers. They have skills that the designer can use, which can reflect well on the designer in the eyes of the client. Talk to any designer who has been in business for a while and they will say that they have been saved by the quick and clever thinking of a supplier at least once.

The relationship between the designer and their suppliers must be one of mutual respect. Communicate with your suppliers about their needs and take the time to ensure you meet these needs. For example, printers will have specific technical requirements regarding artwork; make sure you prepare the artwork to exactly suit these needs.

The designer can expect to be quoted a good price by their supplier, keeping in mind the client's final budget. However, it is not a good idea to force the supplier so low that they may start cutting corners or bump the job because a higher paying customer has come through the door. Remember, a designer cannot control suppliers other than by being professional, which means showing them respect. If a supplier does a bad job or delivers late, then it will be you, the designer, who will look bad to the client.

KINDS OF SUPPLIERS

Suppliers who may be involved include:

- paper suppliers
- printing plate makers
- printers
- embellishers
- specialist finishers and assemblers
- binders
- couriers
- direct mail houses.

SUPPLIERS IN A NUTSHELL

Suppliers:

- are also paid by the client—often through the designer
- have certain skills and knowledge and are therefore a useful resource for the designer
- can be a vital component in the communication process between the client and their audience
- deserve to be treated with respect.

PRODUCTION MANAGEMENT

You have now been introduced to the various stakeholders in the printing process. You are probably beginning to understand that because there can be quite a few people involved, potentially a lot of money and also a significant amount of time, the process of getting something printed requires good project management: this is referred to as 'production management'. Production management involves parts of both the design process and the production process and begins with the development of the brief. Remember that the design process and the production process (and outcome) influence each other, as the diagram overleaf shows.

HEIDELBERG DRUCKMASCHINEN AG

A look inside a commercial offset printing house. Here, two technicians load large sheets of paper into a Heidelberg printing press, which is capable of printing up to 10 colours at a time.

WHAT DOES PRODUCTION MANAGEMENT INVOLVE?

While the design process may be the fun part of any design job, production management actually gets the job done and means that the designer gets paid. A designer who is production managing a job is first involved in the development of the brief and ensuring that all aspects of it are met.

Following this, they have the role of choosing the most appropriate suppliers, and then ensuring throughout the process that the supplies meet the client's needs in terms of delivering the job on time, at the right price and of the right quality.

A freelance designer or a designer working in a small office may have to be both the 'creative' (the one who actually creates the design) and the production manager. In larger design practices, there may be specialist production managers.

THE DESIGN PROCESS

The design step is the creative/conceptual side of meeting the client brief. The implementation step is turning the design into something real. The process ends with the final sign-off and the pre-press process.

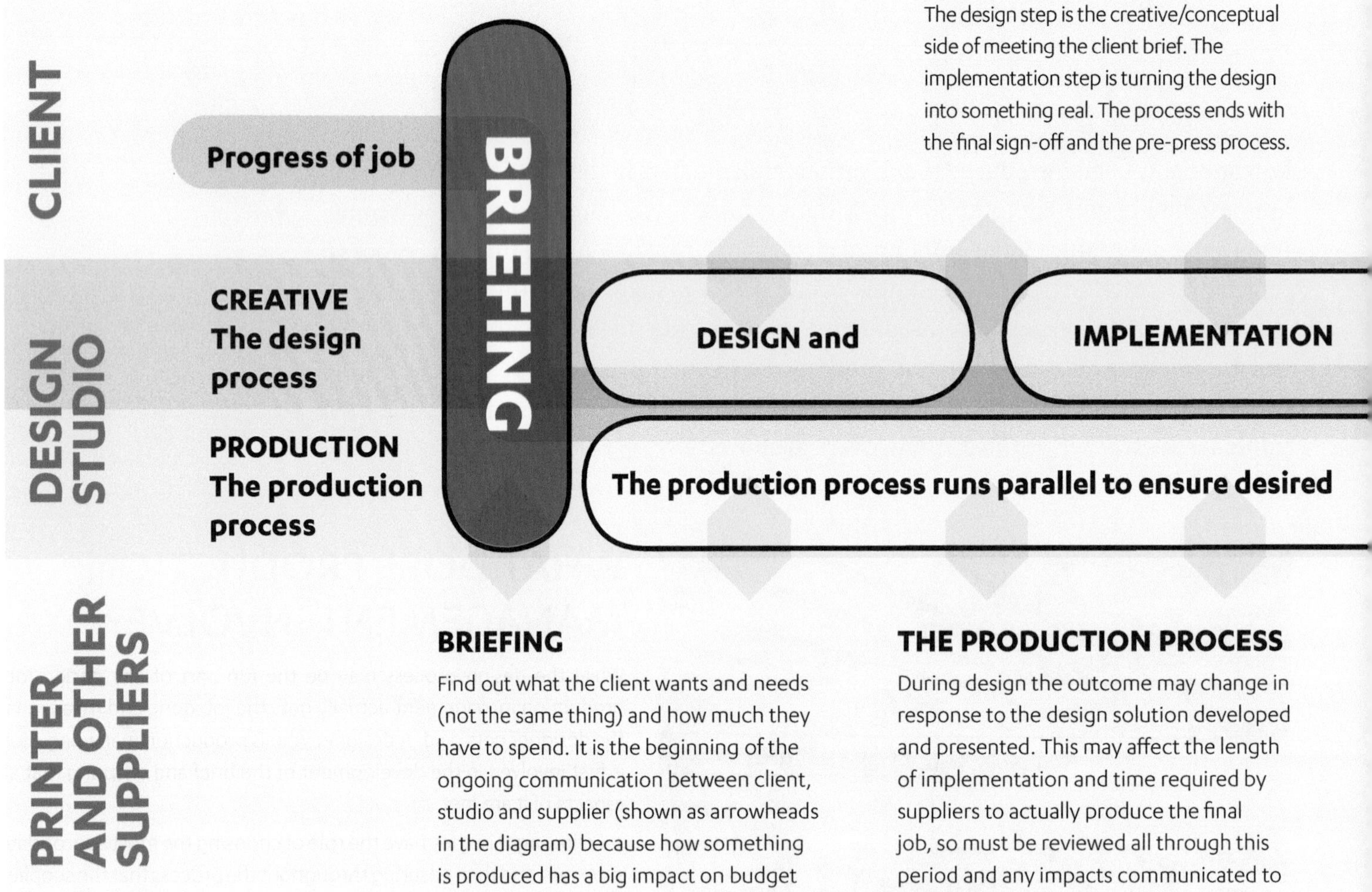

CLIENT

Progress of job

BRIEFING

DESIGN STUDIO

CREATIVE
The design process

PRODUCTION
The production process

DESIGN and

IMPLEMENTATION

The production process runs parallel to ensure desired

PRINTER AND OTHER SUPPLIERS

BRIEFING

Find out what the client wants and needs (not the same thing) and how much they have to spend. It is the beginning of the ongoing communication between client, studio and supplier (shown as arrowheads in the diagram) because how something is produced has a big impact on budget and time.

THE PRODUCTION PROCESS

During design the outcome may change in response to the design solution developed and presented. This may affect the length of implementation and time required by suppliers to actually produce the final job, so must be reviewed all through this period and any impacts communicated to all stakeholders.

This diagram shows the relationship between the design process and production management. The design process runs between the briefing and pre-press; the production process runs from briefing to the completion of the job.

Pre-press and briefing represent the two critical transitions of a job between the stakeholders.

form the bulk of the design process.

result can be and is achieved.

PRE-PRESS

Job delivered to client

REVIEW

Physical production of job by printers and other suppliers

REVIEW

Are there any lessons to be drawn from all processes that affect how the design team works, the client, or the interaction with service providers? This step also includes documenting and archiving the work.

Good organisation is important

The successful production manager is highly organised and has well-established systems in place. This means the job is followed through and structured in the same way every time, from the order in which each stage occurs, to the way files are named. Established systems allow the production manager to track jobs, no matter how complex. Good organisation and a tracking process are also vital for working with teams, so everyone knows how the elements of the project fit together. When a job is handed to a supplier, such as a printer—who may have little or no knowledge of the job to start with—it is important that they are able to understand how the job is organised. We'll look more closely at setting up systems and processes in the section 'Preparing for print'.

How to order printing

Ordering printing is not difficult if the needs of the job are known. The designer must determine the job specifications, such as how many copies, what size, what paper and what colours are needed. When these have been decided—in consultation with the client, other designers and even the printer—the printer can prepare a quote, which the designer will then communicate to their client before confirming to the printer that the job will be coming their way. Then a purchase order is prepared based on the final specifications and sent with the artwork to the printer. The purchase order confirms the price, the delivery deadline and the artwork specifications (quantity, paper and colour).

Finsbury Green
www.finsbury.com.au

Finsbury Green is Australia's leading environmental, printing and solutions group, using clean efficient processes. Established in 1973 Finsbury Green operates in Adelaide, Melbourne and Sydney and employs 190 staff. They specialise in sustainable and green printing. Rod Wade, the National Environmental and Technical Manager, tell us about this philosophy: 'At Finsbury Green we believe that to achieve long-term success we must take responsibility for the economic, social and environmental impacts of our policies, practices and decision making. Our objective is to exceed environmental demands made of us as a company, without impairing the performance of our products and services. We actively pursue a policy of alleviating environmental impacts by adopting green technologies, eco-advantaged products and devising new methods and processes.'

To reinforce their commitment to producing high-quality products, Finsbury Green operates ISO9001:2008 Quality Management and ISO14001:2004 Environment Management Systems certifications. 'Additionally, we comply with ISO12647 Colour Management standard enabling us to maintain high-quality colour standards,' adds Rod.

Along with green technologies Finsbury Green is an independently audited carbon-neutral printing and solutions group. They measure, monitor and actively aim to reduce CO_2 emissions from their operation, then offset the balance

THIS PAGE | Bound books are transported to be trimmed.

RIGHT | Applying ink to rollers.
FAR RIGHT | A close up look at the inked rollers on one of Finsbury Green's offset printing machines.

through Greenhouse Friendly™ certified companies. 'To help clients make informed decisions, CO_2 savings are listed on our quotations,' says Rod.

While focusing on environmental benefits in their printing work, Finsbury Green also works closely with the graphic design community and design students, providing educational presentations and workshops, along with their own publication *The Challenge*. One of their workshops that students may find beneficial is printroduction. A four-hour workshop that teaches a basic understanding of the essential printing processes for designers, managers and marketers of print, printroduction covers colour theory, proofing, file delivery, printing and finishing processes, paper selection and much more.

Happily, as designers become more accustomed to the print process and communication between themselves and their printer improves, so does the final product. 'Collaboration is alive and well, and it is fair to say that the earlier we are involved in a project, the better the outcome, in terms of the cost, quality and time required to deliver the end product,' says Rod.

Rod continues: 'At Finsbury Green we are definitely witnessing the trend, from expert to novice, in terms of the specialised designer print buyer role, but have also learnt that it's not enough to just to go with the cheapest option—clients want more. They want to be more involved and want to remain responsible for their decisions, but they want those decisions to be better informed. So for aspects like paper type and size, print process, lead times, the use of colour and what represents good value, the solutions provider should be discussing and advising their clients; this can and often does mean from the beginning, when some of the creative decisions are made depending on what suits the product best. It also means examining if there is a better way of communicating and working in synergy with other media to drive results. In that way the designer gets a partner rather than just a supplier.'

UNDERSTANDING HOW PRINT WORKS

In order to specify what sort of printing your design jobs will require, you'll need to understand how the print process works. This process has a number of areas that we will consider separately:

- ❯ the press or the printing device
- ❯ the paper onto which the ink is printed
- ❯ the ink or how the colour is put down
- ❯ embellishments.

↑ Where digital printers excel is in the in-device customisation. This mailer is personally addressed to its intended recipient. It was produced on a commercial non-office type digital printer that can actually produce an equivalent to a white foil on this black paper stock.

Courtesy **SPICERS PAPER**

THE PRESS

Printing devices can be divided into two broad categories: digital devices and analogue devices.

Digital printers

With digital printers, artwork is transferred directly from a computer to the print device and exists in the print device's **RIP** only as a digital file for the duration of the print run. Each print is, in effect, an original. Once the print run has ended, the artwork is deleted from the printer memory. Your artwork has no independent existence apart from the files you have created or the printed object. The highly automated nature of digital printers means that on-press manipulation of the artwork is extremely limited.

Table 6.1 compares the two main types of digital printer—inkjet and laser.

Analogue printers

With analogue printers, the artwork file is converted (via a RIP again) to a physical form—the printing plates—prior to printing. The printing plates are loaded into the press, inked paper runs through and the image is created. Therefore, the artwork has an existence independent of the artwork you created and the printed object. These plates can be used multiple times (in theory).

Analogue printers still require a considerable level of human control. Thus on-press manipulation of the artwork is possible and can be done to significant levels—from minor variations of ink density (thickness), to how the colours fit together (registration), to changing one or more of the colours completely.

The two most common analogue print processes you are most likely to come across are **offset** and screen printing.

RIP stands for raster image processor, which is the software that converts electronic artwork into printable files, suitable for output onto printing plates.

Offset printing (or offset lithography) is a printing method in which ink is transferred from a plate to a smooth rubber

'blanket' roller that transfers the image to paperboard.

FELIX OPPEN

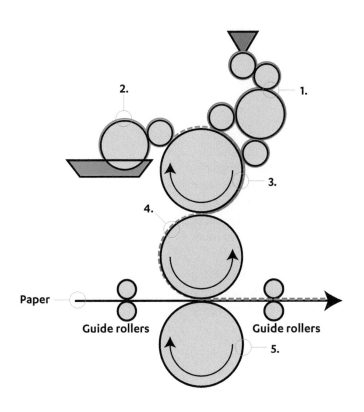

1. Ink tower transfers oil-based ink to areas of printing plate with no water on them. Numerous rollers ensure highly controlable and uniform delivery of ink to plate.
2. Water fountain coats water-sensitive parts of printing plate
3. Plate cylinder has the printing plate wrapped around it. It picks up the water and ink needed in the lithography process and transfers the ink to printing blanket on the offset cylinder.
4. Offset cylinder and blanket wrapped around it ensures much longer life of the printing plate because the plate never contacts the (rough) surface of the paper.
5. Impression cylinder provides the pressure needed to transfer ink to paper.

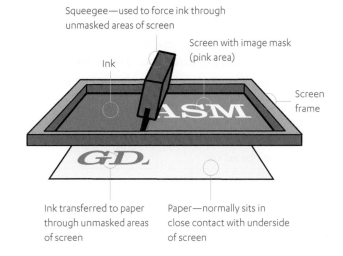

Squeegee—used to force ink through unmasked areas of screen

Screen with image mask (pink area)

Ink

Screen frame

Ink transferred to paper through unmasked areas of screen

Paper—normally sits in close contact with underside of screen

↑ Offset printing is highly mechanised and uses a lithographic process that works through the interplay between water and oil (ink).

→ Screen printing is often still very manual. Ink (water or oil-based) is squeezed through a masked screen onto the paper.

TABLE 6.1   THE TWO MAIN TYPES OF DIGITAL PRINTER: INKJET AND LASER

Inkjet	Laser
Uses liquid water-based ink	Uses a dry toner that is heat set
Slow—produces few pages per minute	Still relatively slow but the heat-setting unit limits size of prints (most common are A4 and A3, but also A2 and A1 can be found)
High cost—machine usually cheap but ink and paper very expensive	Higher cost of machine but toner very cheap so cost of prints lower
Suitable for short runs and large format printing (like advertising billboards)	Limited range of papers for optimal results
Limited range of papers (and other substrates); suitable for optimal results	Suitable for runs of up to about 500 (depending on complexity)
Calibration (maintaining colour accuracy) can be difficult	Calibration (colour accuracy) can be difficult to maintain
Print head sprays dots down so they tend to be more random ('stochastic')—a process favoured by photographers	

All large-volume commercial printing companies use offset presses (short for 'offset lithography press'). On this kind of press the artwork has been transferred to a number of metal plates, one for each colour. It is called offset because the paper does not come into direct contact with the printing plates. These presses are very fast and accurate and can perform tens of thousands of impressions (transfers of ink onto paper) per hour. The presses can also print up to ten colours in a single pass of a sheet of paper through the press.

Screen printing is used for short-run work where custom (or 'spot') colours are involved. In screen printing the artwork is transferred to a number of fabric mesh screens stretched in frames (one for each colour), the ink is squeezed through the screen and the image is transferred to the paper. This process is still often done by hand. Street posters (particularly music) are perhaps the most common example of its use.

Table 6.2 compares offset printing and screen printing.

TABLE 6.2. **THE TWO TYPES OF ANALOGUE PRINTER: OFFSET AND SCREEN**

Offset	Screen
Uses oil or soy-based ink	Uses oil- or water-based ink
A great range of colours possible	Greater opacity of coverage is possible—suitable for printing on non-white substrates
Colour vibrancy/brightness is generally better than digital	Colour vibrancy can be very good
Calibration can be modified during the print run	Calibration and colours can be modified during the print run
Large range of papers available	Suitable for many materials (paper, fabric, plastics, glass, metals, etc.)
Expensive to set up but ink per impression is extremely cheap	Relatively low set-up cost
Sheet-fed (cut sheets of paper through the press) is suitable for up to about 80 000 impressions per hour	Very slow, highly manual process
Web-fed (continuous roll of paper through the press) is suitable for 150—200 000 per hour	Manual process means that registration is rough

Letterpress

Commercial printing began with the letterpress: it is the kind of press that Johannes Gutenberg used (see Chapter 4). Although it is an antiquated method, it is still possible to find letterpress printers in operation. Many of the more recent machines (built in the middle of last century) have been converted to produce embellishments—die-cutting and foil stamping (see below).

There are several other printing methods in use in very specialised areas, such as gravure for very high resolution image reproduction, lino and woodblock printing, intaglio or etching, mezzotint and lithography (the latter few of these are mostly used by artists, require quite specialised skills and are highly manual with very little automation involved). Occasionally, these processes may be useful for a commercial job.

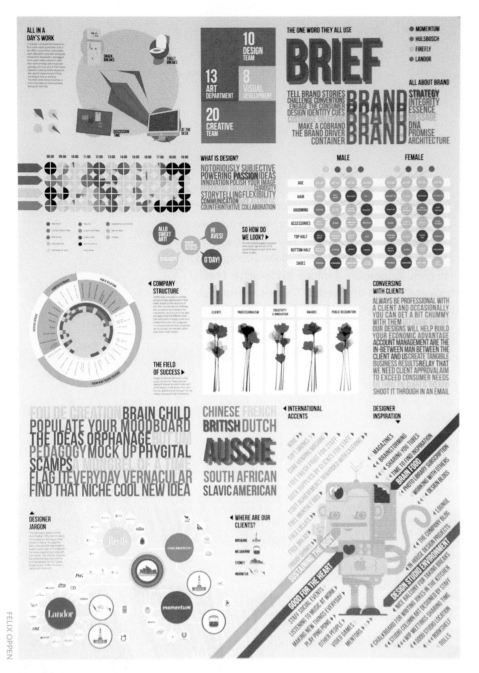

← Numerous colours make up this information graphic, but in fact only four coloured inks were used to render the image on this page. Look closely at the image with a magnifier to see this.

Designers **SABINA OLSZANOWSKA, FIBI RUSLI, AVA THOMSON AND KAT WICKES**

INK

Most of the discussion in this section is related to offset printing, and some of it is relevant to screen printing. Because you have almost no control over the application of ink or toner with digital printers, there is little point in discussing ink in relation to these devices.

It may seem obvious, but ink is what is used to create colour on paper. In all the printing devices mentioned above, with the exception of digital laser printers, ink is a liquid (digital laser printers use a dry powder called toner). There are two ink collections that are used in printing: the four-colour process and spot colours.

Four-colour process

Look closely, perhaps with a magnifier, at the photograph above. It appears to be made of hundreds, if not thousands of colours. In fact this has been achieved with only four coloured inks. The four colours of the **four-colour process** are cyan, magenta, yellow and black.

The **four-colour process** can be abbreviated to '4cp'. It is also commonly called CMYK, which stands for cyan, magenta, yellow, and K = black (originally black ink was just for keylines, which are the boundary lines separating coloured areas of printing on a printed page).

Spot colour

A **spot colour** is a uniquely mixed colour. A system of formulas is used to mix up individual base colours in much the same way an artist mixes their paints. To make life easier for designers and printers, a number of systems have been developed for which a swatch book of formulas and examples exist. In Australia, we use the system developed by Pantone®. In this system, each colour is numbered. This allows a designer to consult their Pantone swatch book, then tell a printer to print, for example, Pantone 485 (which is a red); the printer will then go to their own Pantone swatch book and look up the formula. This ensures that you both know that you are talking about the same colour.

↓ Each of the colours in the spot or solid colour swatch book is a unique colour. They are made by mixing various base colours in proportion. Because designers and printers use the same system it is easy to specify spot colours—by quoting the Pantone number for the chosen colour.

FELIX OPPEN

A **spot colour** is an ink that is used in offset printing to produce a solid non-CMYK colour using one plate.

← Combining CMYK and spot colours can be very effective. Here, black and process yellow are combined with a spot blue and spot red. The result is great colour vibrancy, especially of the blue, which is normally difficult to achieve in the four-colour process.

Designer **YELLOWFORK DESIGN**
Client **PCYC NSW**

↓ In this booklet both CMYK and spot colours, in this case fluorescent inks, have been used to great effect.

Courtesy **SPICERS PAPER**

The final full-colour image.

CMYK separations

CMYK separations: yellow, cyan, magenta and black in print order. Left to right.

Spot colour separations

Two spot colour separations. Pantone 137 on left and Pantone 485 on right. Note, light colour is always printed first.

Combined into a duotone image.

Separations

Look at the picture above. This image existed as a digital picture made of millions of different spots of colour. In order for it to be printed in this book, the image has been broken up into four **colour separations**, one for each of the four process colours. The artwork for each of these colour separations was then etched into the offset printing plate. To print in any combinations of colour, your artwork is separated into one printing plate for each colour. This is the case for both CMYK and spot colour.

↑ The colours required in a print job are separated into layers and a printing plate is created for each layer. The green portion repels water (one component of the lithographic process) allowing the ink to be picked up selectively as required by the artwork.

Colour separations are the result of separating coloured artwork into single colours; this is necessary because printing operates with inks of fixed colour that are laid down one at a time. The colours of artwork are separated into up to six base colours.

Registration

After dividing the colour of an image into separations, making a printing plate for each and loading the plates onto a printing press, the next challenge is to have the ink print in exactly the right place on the paper. This is called **registration**. When the inks are printed in the right place they are said to be in register and when not they are out of register. To check inks are printed in register, registration marks are added around the edges of the artwork.

↑ Because the inks are printed in sequence, in order to get them in the right place registration marks are also printed—shown here as a cross and circle overlaid. You can also see the trim marks to guide the cutting down of the printed work to the final specified size.

Registration is the process by which the inks are printed in the right place in relation to each other. When this occurs, they are said to be in register. When they are not in the right place, they are out of register.

Trapping, spreads and chokes

Even with registration marks, it is possible for the inks to not match up perfectly. This happens because registration is largely done by eye by the printer; also, as a sheet of paper moves through the press, it can move fractionally. Usually this is not a problem, but when two solid areas of ink butt up against each other a white line can appear, and the registration is not absolutely perfect. To deal with this, a process called **trapping** has been developed. Trapping involves creating **spreads** and **chokes**. Spreads and chokes mean that when the inks are in register, areas of colour actually overlap by a tiny amount. The size of spreads and chokes are usually about 0.014 pt.

↓ Trapping is an essential tool to combat the unavoidable movement of paper as it passes through a printing press at speed. You should always ensure that you have set up appropriate trapping.

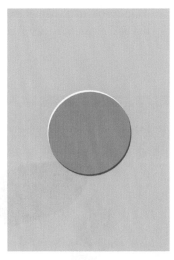

In register. No trapping, however this kind of exact fit is almost impossible to achieve even with the very best printing presses.

Out of register. No trapping and white line of mis-register is very obvious.

In register. Including trapping with both spreads and chokes. (Size of traps has been exaggerated in this example.)

Out of register. Including trapping with both spreads and chokes that effectively hide mis-register.

TRAPPING
We discuss trapping because it is something designers should know about. Modern page layout programs now set up the trapping, creating spreads and chokes automatically. However, do not assume that pixel image manipulation vector graphic programs will also automatically create them.

Trapping is the use of spreads and chokes to aid registration.

Spreads are outer edges of an area of ink that have been enlarged by a tiny amount.

Chokes are constricted inner edges of an area of ink.

How do you get tones in printing?

When ink is printed by a printing press it is laid down as a continuous layer of even thickness. In this respect, using ink is a binary process, which means you have two options: you can either have a solid layer of ink or no ink at all. To create shades of tone, therefore, you need to use a trick: break the **solid ink** up into dots so that the paper shows through. The smaller the dot, the more paper shows and the lighter the apparent shade of colour. The viewer's eye then blends the dots and white paper and tricks the brain into seeing a shade of the colour.

When you looked at the image on page 203 with a magnifier, did you see the dots? Did you see how they varied from very small, separate dots in the lighter areas to larger, connected dots in the darker areas?

The printing of ink is subtractive, which means that if two or more inks are printed on top of each other, the result is darker than the individual colours. Thus, again looking at the image on page 203, if the four process colours were printed exactly on top of each other, the resultant image would look almost black, white and grey. To avoid this problem the **halftone screens** are printed at slightly different angles, referred to as the **screen angle**. Fortunately, modern page layout and pre-press software will set up the screen angles of CMYK printing for you, though for multi-colour, spot-colour printing you may have to set up the angles yourself.

Line screen refers to the measure (in inches or centimetres) of dots required to reproduce the fine detail and tonal shades of a reproduced image (it comes from a time when actual mesh screens were used to produce the dots). A line screen of 150 lpi (lines per inch) is the standard screen for print work. Line screens are not perfect. If an image has fine detail that happens to be in a regular pattern, it can interact, causing a moiré pattern (irregular wavy lines), which can severely interrupt the image. An alternative is to use a stochastic screen, which is made of randomly placed dots.

LPI

In normal quality offset printing the most common line screen is 150 lines per inch (lpi). (We use non-metric measurement for line screens in Australia.)

Newspapers, due to cheap paper and higher speed printing, may have only 120 lpi.

Fine-quality art printing may have 200 lpi.

It is possible to go higher, but above 200 lpi even people with the best eyesight have difficulty seeing the dots.

Solid ink is ink that has been printed in a continuous even layer of 100 per cent strength.

Halftone screens are applied in areas where the ink has been printed as a series of fine dots, creating shades of tone.

Screen angle refers to the method by which the orientation of the dots in halftone screens are varied to ensure colour fidelity of the separations in multicolour printing.

Halftone screens

300 dpi greyscale image at 100 per cent, printed with 150 line screen

150 line screen enlarged 1000 per cent to show how the halftone effects of the greyscale image are achieved

← The enlarged image on the right shows the separate dots of ink that the eye is tricked into seeing as shades of grey in the image on the left. The wider the separation and smaller the dots, the paler the shade appears.

Screen angles

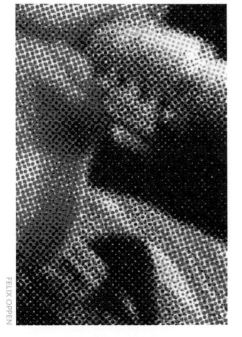

FELIX OPPEN

Screen angles of the CMYK separations at their default angles of 108°, 126°, 90° and 45°

All screen angles set at 45°. Note that the richness of colour is greatly reduced

← It is necessary to vary the angles of the halftone screens of each ink printed to ensure that true colour tone and richness are achieved.

PAPER

What do you think of when you hear the word 'paper'? Not much? Paper is paper, right? Actually, no: paper is much more than white stuff that gets printed on. Different papers have quite different kinds of characteristics, from texture to colour (yes, even white paper has colour—some have warmer tones and some have cooler tones). The careful choice of paper can enhance a design or contradict it.

Choosing the right paper

If the paper used has the potential to become part of a design solution, the designer needs to spend some time selecting the right type. The best way to do this is to get samples of different papers. Look at them and touch them—paper is very tactile. Fortunately, paper suppliers produce sample collections of the papers they sell. They also often supply printed examples on their papers so it is possible to see how they print.

What is paper?

Part of being able to choose the right paper is understanding what paper actually is: a sheet of matted fibres sourced from plants. The plant fibres mostly come from trees, increasingly from sustainably managed forests. They can also come from cotton plants, sugar cane and other plant sources that produce cellulose fibres. The plants are chopped up and the non-cellulose material is removed. To be made into paper the remaining fibres are whitened, and suspended in water; then this pulp is strained through a sieve and then dried into paper.

Paper characteristics

During the manufacturing process of the paper it is given its various characteristics. The more significant of them are outlined below.

Categories of paper

There are two categories of paper, each with two or more sub-categories. These main **paper types** are coated and uncoated papers.

COATED PAPERS have a layer of chalk (calcium carbonate) bonded to the surface of the paper. This gives a very smooth finish that is excellent for printing images on. This surface can be shiny, or gloss, partly shiny, or satin, and not shiny at all, or matt. All coated papers are white in colour.

The quality of the coating comes in three grades—A1 to A3—and relates to the thickness of the coating, with A1 having the thickest (and therefore being the best quality and most expensive) and A3 having the thinnest (and therefore being of the lowest quality). (Note, these 'A' quality categories are completely unrelated to the 'A series' of paper sizes.)

UNCOATED PAPERS are just made of paper fibre and come in two basic quality grades (the grade is determined by the quality of fibre and the care taken during manufacture, and can greatly affect cost). The lower grade papers are called commodity papers. Traditionally, these have not been used for fine print work, but this has changed because designers have come to like the inherent crudeness of the paper. Commodity papers are only white in colour.

The higher grade range of uncoated papers are called specialty papers. They tend to be made in low volumes from the best raw materials, which means they tend to be the most expensive papers. They are often available in a range of colours, and may also have textures (see below) applied to them during manufacturing. Because of their cost, it is often not possible to use them for large print jobs, but they are ideal for stationery.

Lift

Perhaps the biggest difference between coated and uncoated paper is something we call lift. This is how bright the colours look when the ink has been printed. Ink, being a liquid, tends to soak into the surface of the paper, losing its brightness as it does so. The clay used on coated papers is not very absorbent, so coated papers have greater lift than uncoated papers.

If your design includes bright, vibrant photographs that are intended to 'jump off the page', always consider printing on coated paper.

 EXERCISE

DETERMINE THE GRAIN DIRECTION
Method one: Tear a strip off a sheet of paper. Does it tear in a reasonably straight strip? If so, you have torn it along the grain. If the tear is ragged, then you have torn across the grain.
Method two: Take a small piece of paper and dampen one side. The paper will curl, with the 'valley' of the curl indicating the direction of the grain.

Grain

Because of the way the paper pulp is drawn out of the water, the fibres tend to align in one direction. This gives the paper a grain. The grain of the paper is important for things like how it takes to folding. On printing papers the grain direction usually aligns with the long edge of the sheet.

Paper thickness

Some paper is thicker than others. Thicker papers use more fibre than thinner papers. Thinner papers are lighter and more flexible while thicker papers are heavier and more rigid. Both thin and thick papers have their uses. For example, lighter papers are used in digital printers, for writing on, in brochures and for the insides of magazines; thicker papers are used for cards, magazine covers and presentation folders. There are two ways to consider the thickness of paper: weight and bulk.

Weight is a direct measurement of how heavy a sheet of paper is. In uncoated papers, the heavier the paper, the more fibres it contains. With coated papers, the coating adds to the weight without adding to the thickness. In Australia we measure the weight of paper in grams per square metre, or gsm.

Bulk is another way to consider the thickness of paper. It is purely subjective, based on how thick the paper actually 'feels'. You may have three different papers that each weigh in at 150 gsm: one is coated, another is uncoated with a lot of calendering (see below) and the third is also uncoated but with little calendaring. Even though they all have the same weight, the first will feel less bulky than the second and the second will feel less bulky that the third.

There is no definitive measure of bulkiness, but it is something to consider as part of a design. For example, using a bulkier paper for stationery may convey a sense of luxury without necessarily being more expensive for the client.

Showthrough

One of the side effects of thinner paper is **showthrough**. This is when something that is printed on one side can be seen through the paper. This can be a distraction for the reader. Showthrough is mostly likely to occur with thinner uncoated papers than thinner coated papers because the coating is quite opaque.

Texture, tooth and calendering

The final aspect to consider in choosing paper is the quality of the surface itself. During manufacture the paper may be given a deliberate texture. The two most common textures are laid, in which fine ridges are pressed into the surface, and linen, in which the paper is given a surface similar to woven fabric. These two finishes appear exclusively in specialty papers.

All other papers that do not have a manufactured texture are basically smooth to the touch. However, there is quite a lot of variation in the degree of smoothness. All coated papers are smoother than uncoated papers, which can vary greatly in their degree of smoothness or roughness, known as **tooth**. A toothier paper has a rougher surface than a paper with low tooth. Again, this is quite a subjective assessment, but it is a quality that will affect the final outcome of a job.

A less common way of considering the smoothness of the paper relates to how much it has been calendered. Calendering occurs at the end of the papermaking process, when the paper is run through heated rollers under pressure. The higher the pressure, the more a paper is said to have been calendered, so very smooth coated papers and very shiny, or glossy, coated papers have both been highly calendered.

> **PAPER SUPPLIERS**
> At the end of this chapter, websites are listed for a number of paper suppliers in Australia. Look them up, contact the companies and get their sample kits.

The two main **paper types**: coated, which has a chalk coating and can be gloss (shiny), satin (semi-shiny) or matt (dull); and uncoated, which has a dull surface.

Weight refers to the heaviness of a paper due to the amount of fibre and/or coating it has. **Bulk** refers to how thick a paper 'feels'.

Showthrough is when something printed on one side of the paper shows through to the other side. **Tooth** refers to how rough a paper feels.

Spicers Paper

www.spicers.com.au

Spicers Paper is one of several large paper merchants in Australia, purchasing product directly from paper mills and selling it to printers and resellers. Today Spicers Paper is part of PaperlinX, an Australian company listed on the Australian Stock Exchange, but they originally started out in the UK in 1796 and opened here in 1896. Spicers sells approximately 2.9 million tonnes of paper in 26 countries around the world and employs about 6500 people.

As suppliers, Spicers has account managers calling on printers throughout Australia. Spicers also recognises that designers are an important side of the market. It's the printers who buy paper, but it's designers who choose what stock they want their jobs to go on, the look and feel they want to achieve for their client.

Representatives (or 'reps') of Spicers assist designers and printers in paper choice. A rep can provide printed samples,

mock-ups and swatch kits, as well as give invaluable advice on issues such as bulk (the amount of paper you order), showthrough and the ever-increasing environmental aspect of print and paper.

Brownen Black, a Spicers paper consultant, offers this advice: 'A job will work best when paper is considered at the start of the process rather than at the last minute, when there's no time or budget left. The paper is what is carrying your message and can make or break a job. Coated paper prints very differently to uncoated paper, and looks and feels very different too. If you know what you want at the beginning of the process, all sorts of problems can be avoided. Communication early on with both your paper rep and your printer can help enormously. Considerations are the size of document, the weight, look, feel, touch, price and availability.'

Spicers Paper distributes a large range of paper that can be used in a wide variety of applications. There are embossed papers, recycled, metallics, translucents, coloured stocks, toothy or smooth. Most of these are imported, but Spicers also supply unique Australian-made stocks such as Stephen and Tudor. Spicers' global reach means they have access to a variety and breadth of range not otherwise available in Australia. If a job requires something a little unusual, it can be sourced and brought in.

Environmental considerations are increasingly of concern to designers and end users, and leading the way are recycled and carbon-neutral products. Many paper mills use recycled content, sustainable plantation timber and well-managed forest in the production of paper, and the industry is strictly regulated. Certifications such as the Forest Stewardship Council (FSC) and the Programme for the Endorsement of Forest Certification (PEFC) provide chain of custody guarantees of sustainability and good practice.

Digital technology has had a huge impact on print and allows designers much more versatility in providing print solutions for their clients. There are now digital varnishes and foils, embellishments that have traditionally been reserved for offset and letterpress processes. And the boundaries keep being pushed. Digital machines are slightly more limited in the stocks they can use than offset printing, so this is something that has to be considered in terms of the final result required for the end user.

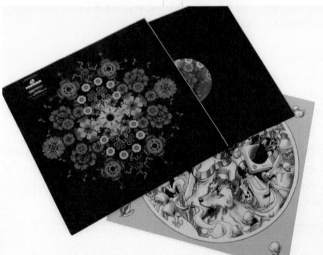

OPPOSITE | Promotional booklet with loose pages commissioned by Spicers to showcase a new paper stock.

ABOVE | This LP record cover uses three different Spicers paper stocks.
TOP RIGHT | A selection of paper stock sample books.

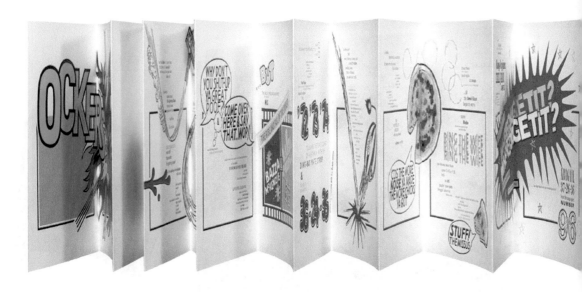

FINISHING, BINDING AND EMBELLISHMENTS

There are other processes that can be applied during the printing process that do not involve ink. These are generally called **finishing binding**, and **embellishments**, and they offer a variety of effects that can't be achieved by printing ink alone.

Before we describe the most common embellishments, let's look at other kinds of finishing and binding.

Finishing

When developing specifications for a printer, be aware that they also need to know about any finishing requirements in order to provide an accurate quote. Finishing requirements can be very difficult to show a printer accurately on a digital artwork file. You may need to make a model or mock-up (or dummy) of your intended end result to show them how you need the additional finishing to look.

Outlined below are the most common finishing processes. Most printers offer these services in-house.

Collating

This is the process of gathering pages of a multi-page document into the correct order. It is usually a process that is assumed to be part of any document binding and may not be referred to specifically in the designer's specification or the print quote, unless there is something particularly unusual about how it is to be done.

Folding

Pages are printed as flat sheets and then folded, after the ink is dry. All sorts of things need to be folded; folders, brochures and so on. Even some things that are supposed to be flat, like a poster, might need to be folded for mailing.

Perforation

Perforation involves placing a partial or broken cut into the printed sheet. A perforation is used whenever you want to include a part of a page that needs to be removed, but without it being completely loose, such as a detachable application form.

Scoring (or creasing)

Scoring is the process of adding a fine indentation into a page to aid folding. This is a vital step for virtually all paper weights above 150 gsm, but especially coated stocks, to minimise cracking during folding.

Folds, perforations and scores are indicated by a dashed keyline. Care must be taken to avoid this line appearing on the printed part of the page. If you are combining, for example, a fold and a perforation, you will need to use different styles of dashed lines.

Trimming

Trimming is the term used for cutting the printed job down to its final size. Trim marks are short lines placed near the corners of the page.

Finishing refers to any final steps of a printing job required to prepare it for delivery.

Binding is what is required to gather pages into a book or booklet.

Embellishments are the effects and processes that are not printed but can be applied to a printing job.

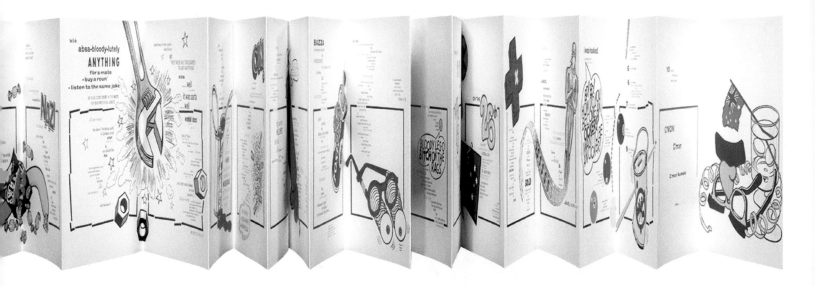

Binding

Any printed document of eight pages or more is usually bound into a brochure or book. The pages of the document are first roughly folded, trimmed and collated into the correct page order, then bound. There are numerous binding methods. The most common are described below.

Saddle-stitching

A saddle-stitched booklet is stapled along the spine. As wire rather than staples are used, the number of stitches is indicated on the print specifications as, for example, 'saddle-stitched with two wires' (meaning it will have two stitches in the spine). This is a very cost-effective binding but should not be used for documents of more than 80 pages.

Glued bindings

There are a number of glued bindings, but the most common are the following:

- **BURST BINDING** The binding edges of the pages are roughened (that is, the edges are burst) then glue is smeared on the edges and the cover is pushed on. This is also a cost-effective binding but should be used for documents of less than 32 pages.
- **SECTION-SEWN BURST BINDING** A book is printed in sections of 16 pages, with each section sewn with cotton thread. These sections are then glued in the binding method. It is a very durable binding but is more expensive because it is a more complicated process.
- **WIRO, COMB OR SPIDER BINDING** Holes are drilled into the binding edge and either a wire spiral or plastic comb are threaded into the holes. Pages are loose and can be laid very flat. Calendars and note books are good examples of this type of binding. Because this binding method is most often used in offices for low-cost internal documents, it presents as being quite cheap (rather than cost-effective).

Trimming is the process of cutting a printed sheet to a smaller size, including the final size required by the client.

→ This cover was
printed in spot
red, with a spot
UV varnish and
then embellished
with red foil. The
section-sewn
binding has been
left exposed.

Courtesy
SPICERS PAPER

ASTRED HICKS

Embellishments

Now let us look at the processes that are considered to be real embellishments. As the name suggests these processes are additional and are definitely non-essential to the completion of the printing process. As all of them add to the cost of production, the designer needs to specify their use carefully, ensuring that they really do add meaningfully to the end result in a way that could not be achieved with normal printing.

Celloglaze

Celloglaze is a thin, clear plastic sheet stretched over then squashed onto the printed page surface. It can only be applied to a whole surface (not small patches of a surface), therefore it need only be mentioned in the print specifications and no special artwork is required. It is available in matt and gloss surfaces. Celloglaze is particularly good for protecting the printed surface of a product.

Die-cutting

Die-cutting is a process for cutting holes in, or creating oddly shaped, printed pages. A metal blade is used to cut away portions of the page. There are limitations on the fineness of detail that it is possible to cut out with die-cutting knives—nothing smaller than 3 mm.

Artwork should be prepared for the knife as a thin, unbroken keyline.

Laser cutting

For fine or detailed cut-outs, use **laser cutting**. As the name suggests, laser is used to cut (by burning) the printed page but the end result is similar to that achieved with die-cutting. However, it is quite an expensive process and the smoke from the burning can stain the paper. Prepare artwork in the same way as for die-cutting knives.

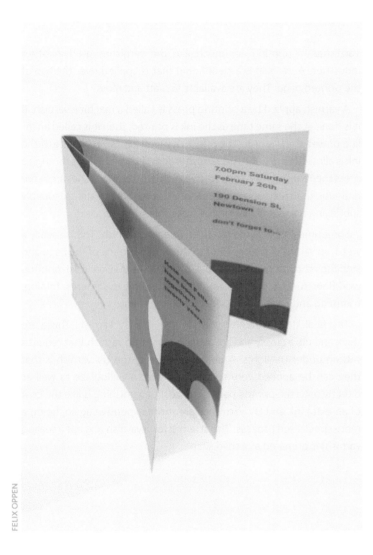

FELIX OPPEN

↑ Never underestimate the value of simplicity: a strong design can survive with minimal embellishment. This is a one spot colour invitation. The embellishment? It has been designed in the form of an eight-page booklet.

Designer **YELLOWFORK DESIGN**
Client **KATE RILEY AND FELIX OPPEN**

Celloglaze is a thin plastic coating bonding to the surface of paper after printing. It is good at protecting the printed surface.

Die-cutting is the use of a sharp-bladed die (cutting tool) to cut shaped holes in paper.

Laser cutting is the use of a laser to cut shaped holes in paper.

Embossing

Embossing is a process of creating a raised surface on a page (called an emboss). Almost any shape can be embossed into the surface of the page. The printed page is pressed between two engraved plates (one 'male' with a raised surface and one 'female' with a recessed surface) to create a raised surface on the page. A blind emboss is when the emboss does not match up with a coloured part of the printed artwork. Embossing works best on heavier weights of paper stock because there is a greater thickness of paper to deform and the results can be quite strong and dramatic. The artwork for an emboss is prepared as a solid shape.

Debossing

This is a bit like a simplified version of an emboss, except the end result is effectively a dent in the front surface of the printed page with the back remaining flat. A single (male) plate is stamped down onto the surface of the page. A blind deboss is when the deboss does not match up with a coloured part of the printed artwork. Debossing works best on heavier and bulkier paper stocks; even so, the results are usually quite subtle, with significant limitations to the amount of detail possible. The artwork for a deboss is prepared as a solid shape.

Foiling

Foiling is when a very thin sheet of metal foil is placed over the printed surface and the pressure of stamping with a deboss plate causes the foil to bind with the surface. Most options are metal foils but there are also non-metal foils, with clear, white and black being the most common. Foils are totally opaque (except the clear foil) and completely cover any underlying printing. Results are usually quite strong but with significant limitations to the amount of detail possible. The artwork for a foil is prepared as a solid shape.

Varnishing

Varnishes in printing are much like the varnishes used in other industries. A **varnish** is a clear liquid that is applied over the top of the printed page. They are available in matt and gloss.

A varnish applied by a printing press is called a machine varnish. If it is done at the same time as the ink is printed, then it is called an in-line or wet-trap varnish. The effect of a wet trap is very subtle. If the ink is allowed to dry and the varnish is added on a later pass through a press then this is called a dry-trap varnish. Dry trap varnishes are more dramatic than wet-trap varnishes but the results are still reasonably subtle and fine detail may be not be visible.

Sometimes printers will lay down a sealing varnish. This is usually a wet-trap varnish that is applied to the whole surface of the page and stabilises the ink more quickly allowing for a quicker post-printing workflow, such as the application of other embellishments, folding, trimming and packaging up to send to the client.

The final kind of varnish you can use is a UV varnish. These are thick and ultra glossy and are a kind of dry-trap varnish that requires setting under UV lights. A unique feature of the UV varnish is that they can be applied very successfully over a Celloglaze as well as directly onto the printed page. The cost of varnishing is like the cost of an extra ink and UV varnishes are more expensive again, being a more specialised process. The artwork for a varnish (except a sealing varnish) is prepared as a solid shape.

Embossing is a process of creating a raised surface in paper that matches parts of the printed artwork. If it intentionally does not match printed elements, it is called a blind emboss.

Foiling is the application of thin, originally metal, foils onto printed artwork. It creates a totally opaque and often high-gloss surface effect.

ASTRED HICKS

↑ A small range of paper stocks is available pre-foiled. This slipcase has been made using this stock, then printed in one colour, matt varnished and finally embossed. Each element contributes to the construction of the visual design, avoiding a sense of over-indulgence.

Courtesy **SPICERS PAPER**

A **varnish** is a clear liquid that can be applied to printing for effect or to stabilise the printed surface. If it is printed at the same time as the ink it is called a wet-trap varnish; if printed in a separate pass on dry ink it is a dry-trap varnish. A thick high-gloss version that dries under UV lights is called a UV varnish.

↓ For very short runs, such as design competition or bid documents, it is possible to explore unusual production methods as a form of embellishment. This case, which did indeed contain a bid document, is made from wood and printed in spot yellow and blue using hand-carved lino-blocks.

Designer **YELLOWFORK DESIGN**
Client **SPACKMAN+MOSSOP**

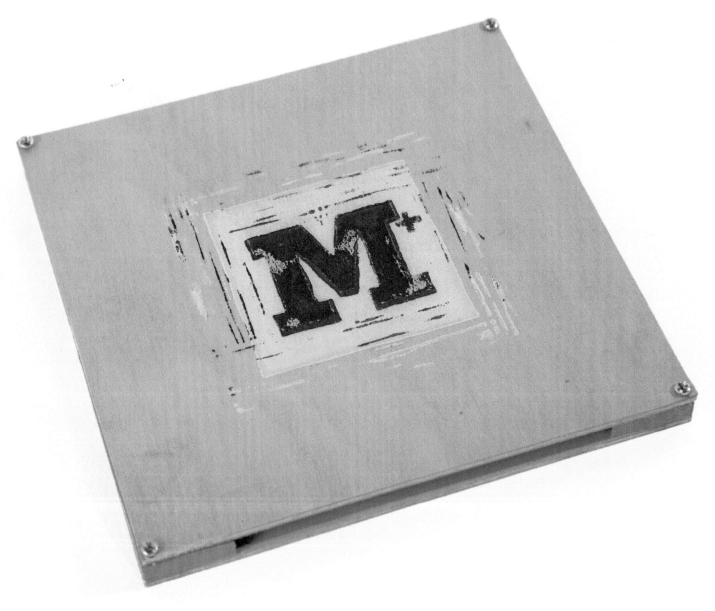

FELIX OPPEN

EXERCISE

LOOKING AT EMBELLISHMENTS IN USE
Go into a newsagent or bookshop and see if you can identify embellishments in use. Make a list of the embellishments you have found. Are there some that are more popular than others? Why do you think that is? *Hint: they are most likely to be used on covers of magazines and books.*

FELIX OPPEN

FELIX OPPEN

← ↑ Binding without binding:
a two-colour poster is folded
down carefully to form a double
pocket folder to hold a series of
A5-sized cards. The end result
is as intriguing and tactile as the
imagery used in the design.

Courtesy **SPICERS PAPER**

223

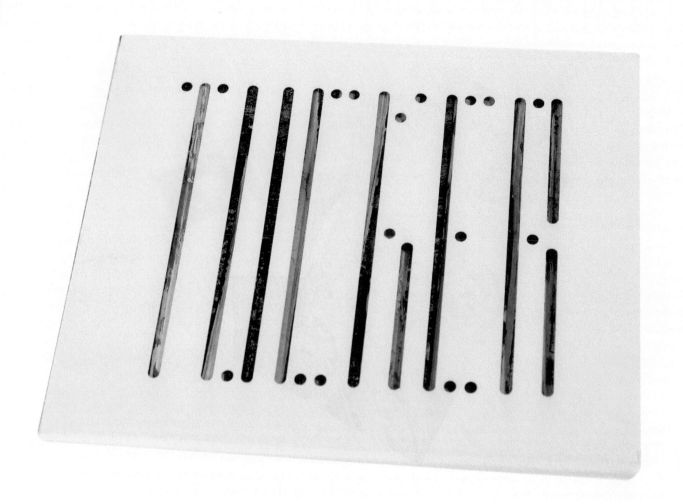

← This strong custom-designed question mark is created by a deboss and holographic silver foil. Such embellishments really only work with this kind of very elegant treatment, otherwise they can look very tacky. The book has a wire binding to accentuate the fact that this is a technical manual about a paper stock called Curious.

Courtesy **SPICERS PAPER**

← This slipcase has been laser-cut. The shapes are large enough that it could have been die-cut. Looking closely, you can see that the laser-cutting process has discoloured the paper. This often unwanted side effect is actually intended and indeed effective here, and is probably why the more expensive laser-cutting was used over die-cutting.

Courtesy **SPICERS PAPER**

← ← Here a gloss celloglaze has been used on the cover of this document. It is very shiny and has the same effect as a gloss varnish in increasing the apparent vibrancy of the ink underneath, but it also protects the printed surface.

Courtesy **SPICERS PAPER**

← A very common embellishment is a gloss varnish over full-colour images. The gloss this provides gives the colour an extra lift.

Courtesy **SPICERS PAPER**

FELIX OPPEN

225

 This is an example of the simplest binding method: saddle-stitching with staples punched through the spine. Also shown are large cover flaps, which make it possible to use a thinner cover stock but still achieve a stiff feel to the cover.

Courtesy **SPICERS PAPER**

← This booklet was printed using just black ink. Colour was introduced with coloured paper stocks. The true embellishment is in the use of different page sizes.

Courtesy **SPICERS PAPER**

↓ One colour and a blind emboss have been used here. Simple, tactile, elegant, striking and quite possibly very cost-effective to produce.

Courtesy **SPICERS PAPER**

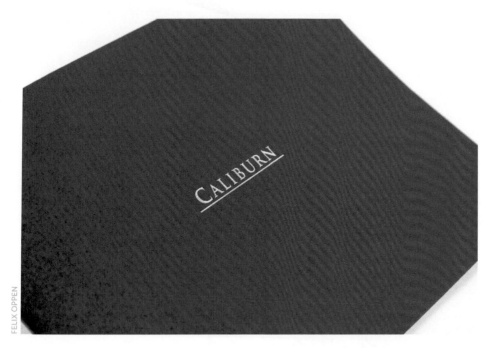

FELIX OPPEN

← This is a very simple design, made effective by the combination of a silver foil on a textured coloured paper. The intention is to be striking but retain a certain solid conservatism that is required of the financial institution that produced the brochure.

Courtesy **SPICERS PAPER**

↓ White inks are usually used for mixing spot colours. However here, white has been printed on to a pearlescent translucent paper several times to get the right opacity (this is called giving the ink a double or triple hit). The page underneath shows through, allowing the mission statement and company name to appear together in a striking way.

Courtesy **SPICERS PAPER**

FELIX OPPEN

↓ Only one embellishment has been used here—die-cutting. Every page has a different shape cut out, so that parts of all pages can be seen once the cover has been opened.

Courtesy **SPICERS PAPER**

FELIX OPPEN

↓ Fabric-covered hardcover books also allow for other effects. Here, the cover illustration, title and author have been embroidered into the cover fabric. This uncommon type of embellishment can be extremely effective when used for the right job, but is unlikely to be cheap.

Designer **DEANNE CHEUK**
Publisher **DEANNE CHEUK**

ASTRED HICKS

↓ This is a slipcase holding a series of smaller booklets inside. The slipcase has text printed in black and a spot UV varnish. Booklets are printed in black, each with a a different spot colour, allowing the same design to be used but without compromising the individuality of each.

Courtesy **SPICERS PAPER**

NEPTUNE ORIENT LINES
EAST LINE

BLUESCOPE STEEL
LINFOX LOGISTICS
HAYMAN RESIDENCES
PRIVATE COLLECTION

PHOTOGRAPHY BY JEAN-MARC LA-ROQUE

FEATURING INTERVIEWS WITH
JEAN-MARC LA-ROQUE AND HIS CLIENTS

PHOTOGRAPHY BY JEAN-MARC LA-ROQUE
PHOTOGRAPHY BY JEAN-MARC LA-ROQUE
PHOTOGRAPHY BY JEAN-MARC LA-ROQUE
PHOTOGRAPHY BY JEAN-MARC LA-ROQUE
PHOTOGRAPHY BY JEAN-MARC LA-ROQUE

FELIX OPPEN

↓ This hardcover book (meaning thick cardboard has been used for the cover and spine) is also covered in fabric—a very sturdy combination. The white illustration has been screen printed on the red fabric, the only way to achieve a really opaque effect. The paper wrapped around with the book title is called a belly band.

Designer **TRISHA GARDNER**
Publisher **HARDIE GRANT BOOKS**

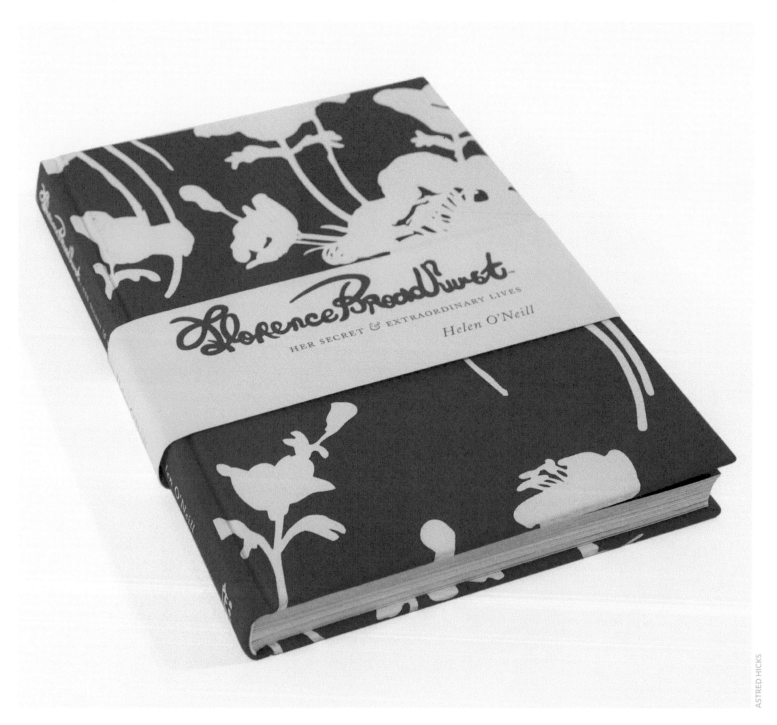

ASTRED HICKS

PREPARING FOR PRINT

In this section we are going to look at the designer's part in the pre-press process. You may be asking yourself 'Why is this important, can't I just send my files to the printer?' But if you neglect your part in this process, it is likely that files will not be correct, or 'print-ready'.

SPELLING

When checking spelling, make sure that the correct dictionary is loaded. In Australia, that means using an Australian English dictionary, not the US English dictionary. If you find any incorrect or ambiguous spellings, check with the editor or copywriter before making any changes, as there may be a valid reason why a seemingly incorrect spelling has been used.

In a sense, the riskiest part of any design job is when the work is handed from one person to another. This is the time when things can go seriously wrong: information may not be passed on, or assumptions may be made. When a design job is handed over to a printer, it is important that it is in a format that the printer understands, because: (1) this ensures the designer will get back what they have asked for; (2) errors, once printing has commenced, can be very expensive to fix; and (3) it demonstrates respect for a fellow professional.

The best way to prepare for print is to set up a methodical process.

THE DOCUMENT

The first thing to do in preparing work for print is to look at the document as a whole. But before even this is done it is necessary to:

❯ check that the work meets final approved specifications and client's brief

❯ prepare a purchase order.

The content

When the work has been checked against the final specifications and the client's brief, and a purchase order has been prepared, consider the document itself and what is in it. First:

❯ check the dimensions are correct—they must match what the client has asked for and what the printer has quoted on

❯ if there are scores or folds, perforations or embellishments, ensure the relevant artwork is set up and correct.

Next look at the colours. Ensure that they will separate into the correct plates. Because the inks are laid down one at a time, include registration marks so that everything can be aligned properly by the printer. So:

❯ check that your CMYK and spot colours are set up correctly

❯ delete any colours that are not required

❯ make sure registration marks and trim marks are showing in the final file.

Images

Now look at the images. There are two kinds: pixel images (photographs) and vector graphics (or digitally created illustrations). To get the best results from pixel images, they need to have image resolution equal to twice the line screen. These days it is likely that most of the photos used will have been taken with a digital camera, but not necessarily all of them. If photos have been scanned, they may have blemishes like dust marks or small scratches. Photos taken at different times and with different cameras will have different colour balances. Check the following:

● for a 150 lpi line screen check all the images are 300 dots per inch (dpi) at 100 per cent (the size they appear in your document)

● check for blemishes and remove them

● check the colour balance of all the images and adjust any variation so that all images appear similar (this adds to the visual unity of the document)

● check that none of the images are in RGB colour: they all need to be in either CMYK or spot colour to separate correctly.

Vector graphics are easy to prepare mostly, because they are not resolution-dependent and they are always created digitally so they cannot get dirty. However, embedded typefaces can be a problem, so:

● convert all embedded typefaces to **outlines**

● check that none of the graphics are in RGB colour: again, they all need to be in either CMYK or spot colour to separate correctly.

Finally, if the images **bleed off the page** you need to include bleeds. Set up bleeds of at least 3 mm wherever an image runs off the edge.

TO THE PRINTER

The safest way to send the artwork files to a printer is as PDF files. If they have been generated correctly, and it is necessary to understand how to do this, the printer will receive the artwork exactly as it was sent. Don't forget, the printer will also need the printed mock-up and a purchase order.

Text

While the text should have been checked and corrected by an editor or a copywriter, it does no harm to run some final checks. Things to do include:

● checking the spelling, with at least the in-built spellchecker on the computer, but especially checking special words, like names

● searching for and deleting any double spaces in body text

● making sure em and en dashes have been used consistently throughout

● checking that apostrophes have been used correctly

● making sure there are no **widows** and **orphans** in the text.

As the designer, it is also your responsibility to check that all necessary fonts are loaded before generating the final file.

PROOFS

It is always a good idea to create a mock-up or proof of the final work. This can help with the checking process. It is also something to show the client so that they have an idea what the completed job will look like and it is a useful part of handing the job over to the printer because it gives them a clear idea of what they will be producing.

The first thing a printer will do with the artwork files will be to check to make sure there are no digital errors and that they can create the printing plates to the specifications on the purchase order (and what they have quoted on). The second thing they will do is generate their own set of proofs and send them back to be checked.

It is important to check the printer's proofs carefully. Run through the whole checking process in the same way as you did for the original artwork. It is also a good idea to have the client check and approve them too. This is the last time changes can be made at relatively low cost.

Convert to **outlines** means turning the typeface from an editable form into an image.

Bleed off the page refers to images, type or blocks of colour that are printed right to the very edge of the page.

A **widow** is a short line at the end of a paragraph.

An **orphan** is the opening line of a paragraph that is separated from the rest of the paragraph at the bottom of the previous page.

THE PRESS CHECK

There is one final thing a designer can do to check the work and this is to do a press check. A press check involves actually going to the printer and looking at the job as it is being printed. The purpose is mostly to check that the printer is matching their own proofs accurately, but a final check for any other problems can be done too. It may seem obvious that the printer should do this but it is not necessarily as easy as it seems. On large presses, pages will be printed several pages at a time (up to eight). If there are images spread over the pages (images are usually areas of high ink coverage) they can affect how the ink goes onto the paper and it may not be possible to match all of the proof accurately. In these cases, the job of the designer is to decide which parts it is more important to match.

There is one other personal reason for doing a press check: there is nothing quite like seeing a printing press, especially a large, multi-million dollar one, being used to print your work. For a print designer it is a most enjoyable thing to see.

NON-PRINT-BASED OUTPUT

So far, the information in this chapter has been about getting artwork printed. However, in the field of environmental design—directional and general signage, for example—many things are not actually printed, but are made from other materials, such as plastic, wood or metal.

Broadly speaking, the process of setting up and preparing artwork for output is no different from what has been discussed so far. Perhaps the biggest difference is that having found out what the client wants, a designer may need to discuss the job with an appropriate supplier sooner, more frequently and in greater detail during the design process. The designer may find that the artwork needs to be supplied differently, but essentially there will be an equivalent of the pre-press process, where the designer or production manager must make sure that everything is correctly prepared so that the desired outcome is achieved within the right timeframe and at the right price.

EXERCISE It is best to be methodical when checking. The best way to achieve this is to create a checklist that you can follow every time. Create your own checklist for pre-press checks. Design it so it is easy to follow. Make sure it is comprehensive and covers everything in this section.

235

DESIGN BRIEF: CREATE A GUIDE TO PRE-PRESS

 Prepare a document that illustrates what is involved in preparing work for print.

Source material

Select what you feel to be the most important material outlined in this chapter, and include it in your guide.

Production

Book of at least 12 pages plus cover

1. Use both CMYK and spot colours.

2. Choose two embellishments to be applied to the document.

4. Choose an appropriate method of binding.

3. Create final artwork (think about how you can create artwork for the embellishments and how you would instruct the printer to deliver what you want).

4. Use the checklist you created earlier (on page 235) to ensure that your work is print ready.

Size

(trim area) 150 mm × 100 mm

Bleed

5mm

Print area

140 mm × 90 mm (or within 5 mm on all sides from trim area)

SUMMARY

While the creative side of the production process may be relatively free and unstructured, the process of actual translation into a physical object is quite different. Throughout this chapter, we have emphasised that pre-press is about ensuring an accurate and reliable end result in the design and production process. The understanding of the need for this comes from an understanding of the technology involved. The ability to reliably give consistent accuracy and attention to detail comes from the establishment of logical, repeatable mechanisms and checking processes for the preparation for print.

Considering it purely from the viewpoint of ensuring accuracy, pre-press may seem like a rather dull process, one that, for a large job, can take days to complete. However, in a broader sense, whereas the brief connects the designer to the client, pre-press connects the designer to the manufacturer (i.e, the printer or other supplier) of the client's needs, thus completing the link between the client and their audience. Further, on a more practical level, pre-press is about understanding how to turn ideas into reality, taking something that began as a few mental images and turning it into something that exists independently of the designer, client and supplier.

One of the joys of being a graphic designer is in seeing ideas realised in a physical printed form. Watching a large printing press produce your work at 100 000 impressions an hour is a magical experience, especially the first time. There is also nothing quite like holding in your hand, or seeing on a bookshelf, samples of your own work, printed and finished just the way you envisioned it, and knowing that you have created something that is very real not just for you, but for others too. The pre-press process is what ensures that this will happen.

KEY TERMS

REFERENCES / WEBSITES

Lawler, B 2005, *Print publishing guide*, Adobe Press.

Pipes, A 2009, *Production for graphic designers*, 5th edn, Laurence King Publishing, London.

PrintWiki (www.printwiki.org/Front_Page)

Pantone (www.pantone.com)

Spicers Paper (www.spicers.com.au)

CPI (www.cpigroup.com.au)

Raleigh Paper (www.raleighpaper.com.au)

Dalton (www.dalton.com.au)

chapter 7

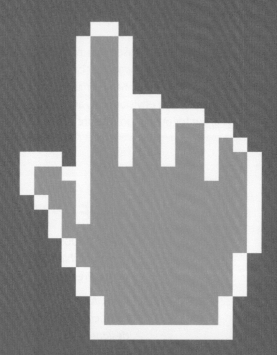

DIGITAL DESIGN

INTRODUCTION

Digital design creates design outcomes that are delivered to the end user—the audience—through an electronic or digital device. Digital design, also referred to as new media or multimedia, covers a broad range of design outcomes, such as websites, applications, games, videos, motion graphics and animation. It draws on the principles established by the traditions of graphic design, film-making and animation, and uses tools and processes developed in the areas of computer science, programming and engineering. It is a combination of design and science.

In this chapter we will focus on some under-represented parts of the website design process, such as information design. We will also explore different design principles and explore the motion graphics design process. Finally, we will discuss the principles of animation in relation to motion graphics.

PROCESS:
Soap Creative

PROFILE:
Alister Coyne

DIGITAL DELIVERY

The potential channels for digital delivery are enormous. People primarily think of digital design as web-based design, experienced through a **web browser**, but there are many other digital delivery mechanisms. These include television, DVD, blueray, streaming media, **kiosks**, touch screen, outdoor projection, installation, LCD screens, digital **adshell**, handheld devices, mobile phones and **PDAs**. The list is ever expanding. Everywhere you can think of to place a screen, people are placing them—the back seat of a taxi, in-flight entertainment—the list goes on.

The design outcomes that can be delivered over these devices are endless. There are websites, videos, motion graphics, games, applications, electronic books, information systems, guides, advertising and much more.

← Websites are no longer static pages of basic information. They can be highly interactive portals like this one, which features video footage, social media widgets, a news feed, an online store and regularly updated game information.

Designer **ALISTER COYNE**
Client **BLUES RUGBY**

EXERCISE

1. List all of the screens you have come across in one day.
2. List all the different design outcome you view digitally today.

A **web browser** or internet browser is an application that can retrieve and present information on the world wide web.

INFORMATION DESIGN

The main point of digital design is to communicate information to an audience for a specific purpose. Understanding the information that needs to be communicated informs the design process. To understand the information, you must interrogate it using a rigorous process. This process is referred to as information design.

← Specialist iPhone app development studio Image Mechanics uses sticky notes to establish the needs and structure of each project.

Information design was developed in areas such as computer science and programming. As digital design applications such as websites became more complex, information design processes were adopted by digital designers and developers as a proven means of understanding information. This led to the development of areas such as usability, information architecture and user experience design. In Australia, companies such as the Hiser Group pioneered these specialist areas in the early 2000s and now they have been adopted widely throughout the web industry.

A **kiosk** is a computer terminal designed to retrieve specific information.

'**Adshell**' is the brand name of the advertising shells around bus and tram stops. A digital adshell is enabled to display digital content or allow user interactions.

PDA stands for 'personal digital assistant'— handheld devices used to view digital content, e.g. iPads, and smartphones such as BlackBerries and iPhones.

Information design begins with recording and ordering information in terms of its importance. Complete the 'Simple portfolio' exercise, which focuses on information listing.

INFORMATION DESIGN: NEWSPAPER WEBSITES

A portfolio is a simple website. A more complex website with a lot more content would be a newspaper website. These sites can be great examples of information design. Information is clearly broken down into levels of importance, such as breaking news or major headlines down to minor stories. Information is grouped together in categories such a local, national and international news.

They can also be good examples of the uses of the principles of graphic design. Newspaper websites use scale to define important information, not only with large fonts, but by devoting large areas of the webpage to headline stories. They use proximity to clearly define associated information.

The documented information design process for a newspaper website would be as follows.

1. Creating content list

All the potential pages of content for the newspaper website must be listed. This is best done with a large pad of sticky notes. After each note is written, it is posted up on a wall or other large surface. At this stage in the process it is important to capture as many ideas for pages of content as possible

2. Categorising content

Once an exhaustive list of the content is compiled, it needs to be sorted. **Card sorting** is used to organise information into categories. The cards in the newspaper scenario are the sticky notes listing each potential piece of site content. They need to be grouped into categories, which, for a newspaper website, might be local, national and international news. There may be areas that cover lifestyle items such as movies, restaurants and entertainment reviews. New sticky notes can be used to create category titles for each page of content that has been listed. The end result is that all the notes are now arranged into a number of categories. Some pages may need to be duplicated in order to go into a number of different categories.

3. Ranking pages by importance

To decide which information is most important, the cards need to be ranked. Using a scale of 1 to 6, 1 being the most important and 6 being the least important, each sticky note is reviewed and ranked. Once each note is ranked, the categories are reorganised so the most important note is at the top of the category and the least important is at the bottom.

How do these tasks relate to design?

There are a number of ways in which the tasks described above are relevant to design. When designing, it is good to have an understanding of the content you need to design, and the best way to understand it is to examine it.

The purpose of the first task is to create an exhaustive list of content. This helps ensure that there is a thorough understanding of the scope of the design project.

The purpose of the second task is to understand the information that has been generated. Putting information into categories helps create chunks of information. This is helpful when it comes to creating the visual design.

The third task creates hierarchy within the information that has been categorised. This allows the designer to use design principles to visually communication the importance of the information to the audience.

After these tasks have been completed, the final organised list becomes the beginning of a website design project: it gives a complete picture of all the content for the newspaper site, and the categories provide a good breakdown of all potential navigation elements. The list of categories could even provide a potential **site map** of the website.

---

242 **EXERCISE**

SIMPLE PORTFOLIO
1. On separate sticky notes, list each piece of information that you would place on a portfolio website. This should resemble a simple **site map**. **2.** Rank the information by writing a number from 1 to 6 on each note (some information may be at the same level). **3.** Rearrange the notes with the most important at the top, and the least important at the bottom.

→ Fairfax newspapers have developed a strong template for their news website. A prominent image box on the left shows the top-rating stories while type size is used to emphasise article importance in the centre column.

FAIRFAX MEDIA

↓ The ranking of information will help in applying the principles of design to the layout of the page. The ranking of the information from 1 to 6 also correlates directly to the ranking of the **header tags** in html, beginning the first steps in the coding of the website.

HOMEPAGE

A brief description of the contents of this page

SERVICES

A brief description of the contents of this page

ABOUT US

A brief description of the contents of this page

FAQ/BLOG

A brief description of the contents of this page

CONTACT US

A brief description of the contents of this page

SERVICES 1.1

A brief description of the contents of this page

SERVICES 1.2

A brief description of the contents of this page

SERVICES 1.3

A brief description of the contents of this page

Card sorting is a simple technique where a group of users are guided to create categories for information listed on cards or notes.

A **site map** is a visual representation of the navigational links within a website.

In html there are six **header tags** that define the importance of the header text, from <h1>, being the most important, down to <h6>.

← The designers of this textile design website have used scale to showcase the character photos on the right, while the information panels appear on the left. This creates a unique experience that echoes the personality of the designer.

Designer **FLOATINGWORLD**
Client **CAT RABBIT**

→ This website illustrates a number of the design principles in action: it follows a strong grid, it also has rich interactivity, makes good use of time and movement and has well thought out social media tools.

Client **INTHEMIX**

As with print and layout design, the core principles of graphic design are important in digital environments. Without them there would be no thought, readability or cohesion in the design. In fact, it would not really be design at all. Understanding the different principles is integral to easily communicating your message in an environment that encourages short attention spans, like the internet. While some principles of print design—like emphasis, balance and rhythm—translate well to a digital environment, new principles are introduced for this area that aren't necessarily relevant to print, such as time and interactivity.

EXERCISE

Have a look at some websites, such as www.apple.com, www.theage.com.au, www.theguardian.co.uk and www.nyt.com. What is the most important piece of information, and what design principles are used to communicate this? How would these inform how you would display the different levels of information and your different categories?

POSITION

If one design element is more important than another, its position should be more dominant. It should be above things of lesser importance, and should also be the first thing that grabs your attention. In left-to-right reading cultures, we would assume that the most important thing, be it an image, type, or illustration, should be near the top of the screen and to the left, as that's where a reader's eye would start reading. Within each chunk of information there may also be different hierarchies. How are these hierarchies communicated using position?

Emphasis

Emphasis helps guide the eye around the screen area using various levels of focal points. These levels form a hierarchy that gives direction and organisation to the design. For example, the element that is most important in the design should be dominant.

Balance

Balance is achieved in a design when the hierarchy between elements is well thought out. The dominant focal point, while emphasised, should not pull too much attention, and the smaller elements should not fade away. For example, websites where everything shouts and competes for attention are not well balanced and can often confuse your audience, leading them to quickly navigate away from your site. Balance can be either symmetrical or asymmetrical.

PROXIMITY

Elements that are in close proximity are likely to be interrelated. Taking the groups of information and positioning them close to each other will allow the user to quickly read and understand these groups of related information.

SCALE

If a design element is big, it is generally more important than other elements on the screen.

There are two approaches to working with size—making the most important element bigger, or making the less important elements smaller. There needs to be a balance between the larger elements and the smaller elements. There should be one or two dominant elements, which become the most important. The other less important elements should be much more subdued in their design. There may be a different emphasis within each chunk of content, depending on the levels of importance within that piece of content.

→ Using typography, stop-
motion animation and JavaScript,
Something Splendid created an
online game where users can
type words and have them
appear on a board spelt out
in cocktail umbrellas.

Designer **SOMETHING SPLENDID**
Client **COCKTAIL TYPES**

CONTRAST

By having contrast within a design, different levels of importance can be communicated. The use of high contrast for headings, reversed-out text, and images on black rather than white background are all techniques employed to achieve a greater level of contrast. Again, the other option is to decrease the contrast in the less important information, for example, by using dark grey rather than black text, or an off-white background. These subtle changes will help create different levels of contrast that match the level of importance of your information.

DIGITAL CONSIDERATIONS

The following are not traditional principles of design but are considerations that should be addressed when undertaking the web design process.

Time

Time is an important aspect of digital design that often gets overlooked. When designing for a digital outcome, the end product is not static. There is the potential for the use of time-based media, such as animations, video, audio and interactive objects. In some of the example sites you looked at, you may have noticed scrolling tools or clickable content boxes. These design outcomes allow the website to communicate a number of different high-ranking pieces of information in the same area of the screen, rather than restricting it to one story or headline.

Tickers were originally electronic machines that printed data onto strips of paper. The most common use was for news or stock market reports. These days, tickers appear on television screens as well as websites.

Movement

Movement is an extension of the design principle of rhythm. Rhythm refers to the use of motion in digital design to draw attention to a particular item. Movement is most visible when it is used for annoying banner ads on websites. Movement can also be used to provide subtle animations for photo stories. A sliding door effect is used to display multiple headlines in the same space on news websites—these are often referred to as **tickers**. Tickers have developed from their text-based origins on newspaper websites to include the use of images and headlines.

Movement can be used to catch the eye, drawing the audience to the most important piece of information.

Interactivity

Interactivity plays a key role in digital design. Interactivity is the ability of the user or audience to control their experience of the **digital design outcome**, which may be, for example, a website, game or application.

The most basic level of interactivity is how the interface functions; in other words, what happens when you click your mouse on a button? There can be many different interactive areas on a website; these can be referred to as **widgets**. There are widgets that play slide shows, audio or video files, or maps. More complex widgets, such as 'accordion' widgets, reveal further information.

Interactivity isn't limited to the web. There are many different digital design outcomes that incorporate high levels of interactivity, from computer games to ATMs.

Users can interact with digital design outcomes using computer mouses, keyboards, keypads, touch screens, voice, and even web cameras with **motion tracking**.

With the increase of touch-screen devices, interactivity is no longer limited to clicking and pressing keys. With multiple touch devices, users are no longer limited to single-finger interactions that replicate the mouse—instead, they are able to perform a range of gestures, such as swiping, pinching, zooming and rotating. There are a growing number of devices that use sensors to measure movement. Devices can respond to users' shaking, rolling or other movement.

↑ With the constant evolution of technology, designers are presented with new and interesting ways to interact with their audience. Augmented Reality uses computer cameras and object recognition to make the surrounding real world of the user interactive and digitally manipulable. This example saw the agency brand promotional cases of product with special Augmented Reality codes. The codes could be viewed through a special iPhone app or online. By viewing the marker the user was able to turn their case into an interactive game device.

Agent **TEQUILA\KWP!**
Creative **COOPERS BREWERY**

A **digital design outcome** is a design outcome delivered digitally, such as a website, video, animation, application, DVD or CD-ROM.

A **widget** is a component of a user interface that operates in a particular way.

Motion tracking is the ability to track a user's motion with a camera.

↓ Interactivity is all about user experience. Online stores like this one need to have a high level of usability. Clear images, strong grids and easy navigation aid the buyer in completing a fuss-free transaction.

Designer **PIXEL FUSION**
Client **MUMMADE.NZ.CO**

login/register

your cart
0

SITE of
the DAY

shop   blog   about us   contact

the boutique

browse our beautiful boutique of the best homemade wares
new zealand mums have to offer.

page 1 of 15   ● ○ ○ ○ ○ ○ ○ ○ ○ ○ ○ ○ ○ ○   Next page

 categories

christmas decorations

modern cloth nappies

clothing

shoes, hats, mittens and sets

amber necklaces

girls accessories

bibs

wraps and newborn essentials

extras

toys

dress up and aprons

nappy and hand bags

balms and creams

laundry and cleaning

current sales

bum bum balm
$14.00

bubbly boo bath
$16.00

daisy and rosie the cow
(in 2 colours)
$26.50

eczema balm for baby
$28.00

verite spa bebe starter kit
$30.00

bye bye mozzie - for babies/children
$13.50

← ↙ Clever integration of social network features on websites like this one, for band Architecture in Helsinki, allows fans to spread the word about tours, news and songs. Listed alongside tour dates are Twitter icons, which allow users to automatically update their twitter feed, telling people which shows they will be attending.

Client **ARCHITECTURE IN HELSINKI**

Social media

A growing area for digital design is the use of social media for promotion.

With a blog or website design, this may involve designing a **share widget**. The share widget allows users to share or promote a story they find interesting with their friends via the many existing social media websites.

It is important that these features are incorporated holistically when designing a site, not bolted on as an afterthought. A well-incorporated share feature makes for a more visually pleasing design, whereas one added as an afterthought can appear jarring and detract from the site design, or draw attention away from the site content.

Motion graphics, video or animation digital design outcomes can be promoted and shared within a social media context by posting copies to YouTube, Vimeo or other video sharing sites.

A **share widget** is a user interface element that allows users to share content on various social media websites.

Soap Creative
www.soapcreative.com

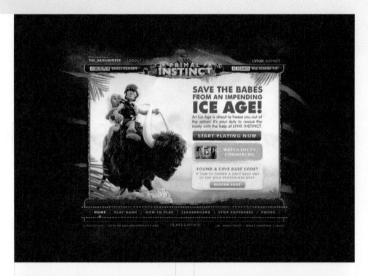

Brad Eldridge studied graphic design at Charles Sturt University, Wagga Wagga, before cutting his teeth on annual reports and typesetting jobs as a junior designer. When the dot com boom went bust he started his own company, which eventually lead him to become creative director and partner at burgeoning interactive agency, Soap Creative. 'Our mission has always been simple: create world-class digital work. That hasn't changed— but a lot has since we opened shop in 2002,' says Brad.

Brad explains the genesis of Soap: 'Soap emerged from humble beginnings as three guys sharing the corner of an office and a 160 GB hard drive. Today we are a full-service digital agency with offices in Sydney and Los Angeles servicing a range of great clients that skew towards **FMCG** and entertainment. We pride ourselves on being strategic, effective, proactive, diligent, thought-provoking, truthful, authentic, analytical, methodical— and we're still cooking up a weekly BBQ every Friday after eight years. We love what we do.'

Understanding the multilayered field that is digital design is key to producing innovative solutions. This can be difficult in an area that is constantly changing and evolving. 'Portable devices have become ubiquitous and have changed the way we consume digital. And social media has become a regular part of our daily lives—Australians spend more time social networking per month than any other country*' explains Brad. 'What this means is Australians are very receptive to digital. And Australians are certainly hungry for more, so the best approach is to make stuff and put it out there. That's the beauty of digital: you can make variations and test and learn, then readjust the strategy and republish—so long as the budget allows.'

Soap's ability to comprehend the way their audience access information allowed them to successfully run a multi-platformed campaign for Lynx deodorant. Brad explains, 'Lynx wanted to introduce the new body spray "Lynx Instinct" to teenage boys across Australia. So we approached them in their natural habitats—ranging from MySpace, Facebook and YouTube through to gaming, men's mags and cinemas—to send out the call on behalf of "Lynx Instinct". We created an integrated campaign centred around Primal Instinct, a multiplayer game that was as popular as it was addictive.'

Creating a 'primal' world where players could explore their caveman selves and rescue 'cave babes' from an impending ice age, the game encouraged social interaction. Players could join tribes and recruit friends, which helped to grow the audience.

The campaign was then supported and amplified across Soap's audience's favoured channels. Rich interactive media created impact and awareness. While some banners were also embedded with unique game codes that could be used to advantage when playing Primal Instinct. These banners were awarded Best Rich Media at the 2009 IAB Internet Awards.

A campaign profile was developed through MySpace and Bebo allowing fans to post comments and receive content such as wallpapers, icons and the iPhone app. 'We developed a Magic 8 Rock app, for the iPhone, giving the audience decisive prehistoric wisdom for use in the mating game,' says Brad.

FMCGs (fast-moving consumer goods) are goods that sell quickly and at low cost. They are supplied in the retail environment to meet the daily demands of customers.

Further promotion through PS3, Xbox live in-game advertising, print campaigns in Ralph and FHM magazines and a 15 second cinema spot promoting the game before the target audience's favourite movies cemented the success of the campaign.

Adding to the success was the creative recognition at the 2009 IAB Internet Awards, where the campaign was awarded 'Best Product Launch' and was the Grand Final winner at Creative Showcase 2009. It also won silver at the New York MIXX Awards.

(*SOURCE: HTTP://ROSSDAWSONBLOG.COM/WEBLOG/ARCHIVES/2010/06/LEADERS_IN_SOCI.HTML, ACCESSED 17 MARCH 2011)

Screenshots of the Lynx Primal Instinct campaign, the online game and iPhone app.

251

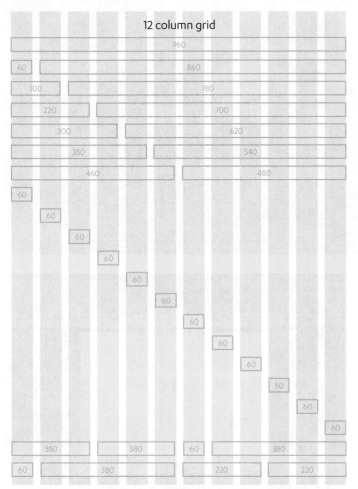

12 column grid

16 column grid

WEBSITE DESIGN SIZE
For websites that are aiming to be viewed on standard desktop computers and laptops with a resolution of 1024 × 768, a good size to design at is 960 pixels width, then as high as the site needs to be to display all the information.

↖ ↑ The 960 grid system is a 960 pixel wide grid used to assist in the designing and layout of websites.

Pixels are the units used to measure the resolution of a computer display.

SCREEN SIZES, GRIDS AND TYPOGRAPHY

Screen sizes, grids and typography are important factors to consider in digital design.

↓ Google's Chrome toolbar

SCREEN SIZES

Computer screens come in a range of sizes. Screen size, known as resolution, is measured in units called **pixels**. Each pixel is one square of the computer screen. Computer screens also come in a variety of screen ratios.

Ratio refers to the horizontal size in relation to the vertical size, the most common being 4:3 (4 units across to 3 units down) and 16:9 (16 units across and 9 units down).

One of the limitations of digital design is the screen resolution at which the audience will view the final outcome.

When designing for the screen, establish what screen resolution the design must target. With web design outcomes the smaller the resolution, the wider the reachable audience; conversely, the larger the screen resolution, the smaller the audience number that can view it.

A tool such as Google's browsersize (see http://browsersize. googlelabs.com) shows you what percentage of audience can view different resolutions.

The range of digital displays is changing rapidly and the range of resolutions and ratios is growing with it. With a standard 4:3 **aspect ratio** screen, designing for a 1024 × 768 pixel screen is a good starting point.

The resolution of the screen is often referred to as 'screen real estate'. What a designer needs to know is how much of this screen real estate is usable for design presentation?

The image above demonstrates that, even without any content, screen real estate is reduced by the toolbar of the browser (in this case, Chrome—the silver bit at the top of the screen). If the design is taller than 768 pixels, then it will have to allow for additional width for scrollbars and other elements of the browser Chrome. All these elements reduce useable screen real estate.

There are a variety of other devices that may be used to view a website, such as mobile phones, **netbooks**, televisions and other devices with a variety of resolutions.

Research into browser and screen statistics for the target audience will give some insight into which resolution is best for your design. Again, a tool such as Google's browsersize shows you what percentage of audience can view what resolution.

Grids

Grids are used to create a framework for your design. The screen is broken down into rows and columns. To give design elements as much flexibility as possible, it is good to have more columns rather than less. A good starting point is between 9 and 12 columns.

Begin with some initial sketches of ideas for the website design. Vertically, the design may be broken down into three main areas:

1. navigation
2. content
3. additional navigation or content.

Aspect ratio refers to the horizontal size in relation to the vertical size, the most common being 4:3 (4 units across to 3 units down, and 16:9, 16 units across and 9 units down).

A **netbook** is a small, low-powered laptop used for web browsing and email.

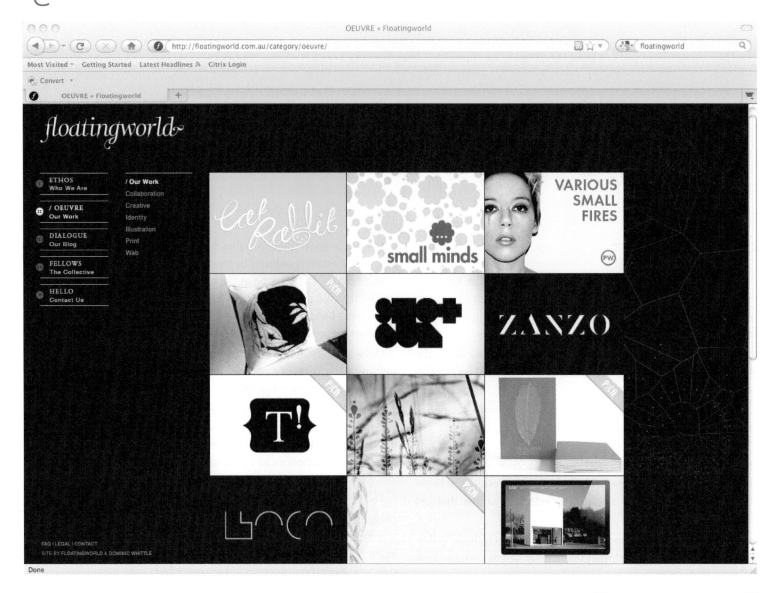

Having a grid that allows subdivision within these sections will allow a flexible layout for the design. Remember, a grid not only divides the screen into sections, but also allows gaps of space for the blocks of content to 'breathe' between columns. The gaps between these columns are called the **gutters**.

A grid can be used to develop the wireframes (see below) and more detailed sketches of the design, and to lay out the elements on the screen. A grid provides a strong structure for applying designs consistently to each screen.

GRID SYSTEMS

For some great examples and useful information for web design (as well as for print), read *Grid Systems in Graphic Design* by Josef Müller-Brockmann. It is the definitive word on using grid systems in graphic design.

A **gutter** is the space between columns of text or images.

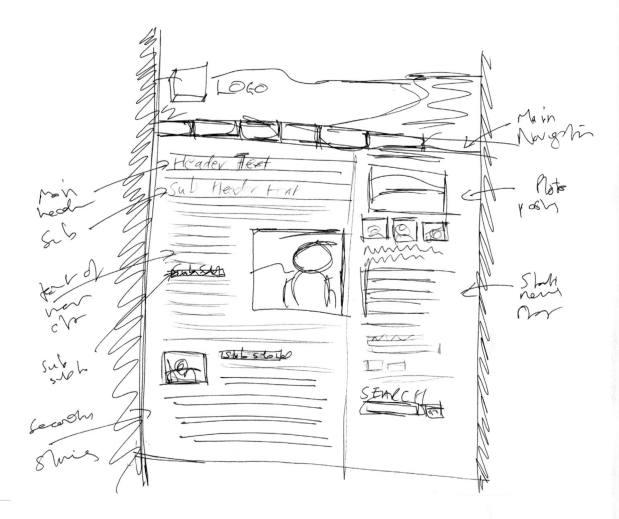

Within the sketch (handwritten labels):

LOGO

Main Navigation

Header Text

Sub Header Text

Main header

Sub

Photo posting

Start off main c/o

Short news bar

Sub sub h

SUB story

Secondary stories

SEARCH Text

← Floatingworld has used a stro
grid to display their portfolio. Wi
two narrow columns on the left
for text, the repeated rectangles
to the right create a harmonious
layout that allows different
projects to be presented equally

Designer **FLOATINGWORLD**

→ An example of a wireframe
for a website layout.

Designing layouts with wireframes

A **wireframe** is an outline of a website's layout. Wireframes are used so designers can concentrate on layout of design elements without getting too bogged down in details such as colour and font.

Wireframes are a great way to quickly create layout designs informed by the information organisation and ranking we discussed earlier in the chapter. They also allow you to apply some design principles to your website:

⊙ Use position and scale to separate groups of information.

⊙ Use proximity to group related categories or ranks of information close together.

⊙ Use contrast to define which areas of the layout will have high contrast, and which will have lower contrast.

⊙ Using knowledge of the grid system, examine how areas will align, and how many grid columns and rows each area will take up.

⊙ When building these wireframes, look at matching the information design categorisation and ranking with the visual design.

Using a wireframe ensures that a design is informed by a process rather than by pure intuition. The wireframe can be designed before the grid is set up, or can be placed within the grid to help with the relationship between the size and position of elements.

These flickr groups display a range of wireframe styles and approaches:

www.flickr.com/groups/ilovewireframes/pool

www.flickr.com/groups/uxsketch/pool

↓ The use of a strong grid
and visible type hierarchy aids
the clever typography used by
Image Mechanics to explain their
development process.

Designer **IMAGE MECHANICS**

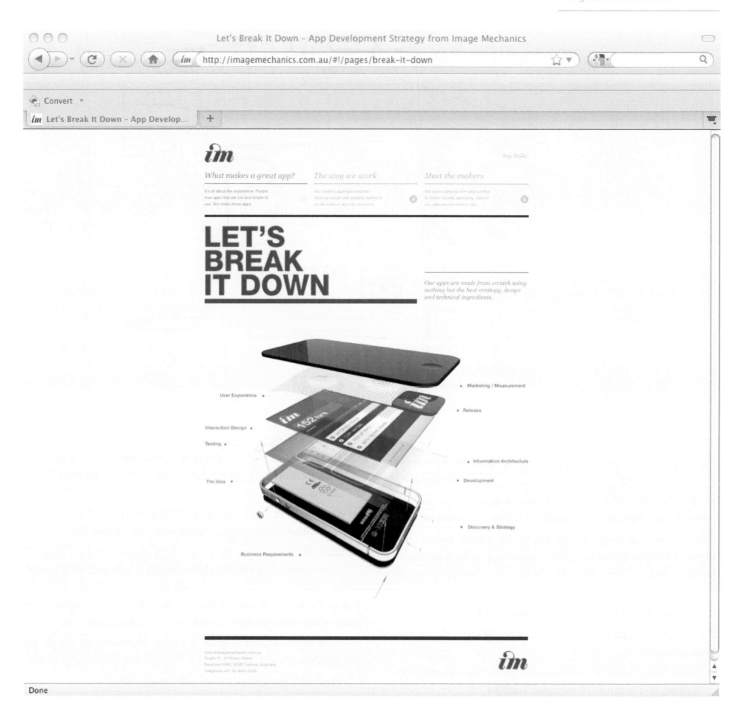

WEB TYPOGRAPHY

As discussed in Chapter 4, typography should always be considered when creating any design. Some considerations when formatting the type are audience, the requirements of the digital design outcome and the amount of information needing to be displayed.

Typographic design is informed by the information design tasks, the audience and the needs of the digital design outcome. The amount of information will affect the number of type sizes and styles required.

There are a number of type styles that may be required in any design, including:

- the body style, which is the general-purpose style for the text that will be read
- various heading styles for different ranks of headings
- styles for other text features, such as lists, quotes, links and sidebar items.

When choosing a type size, start with the body style size and work up from there. Look at the relationship between the size of the body copy and the highest level of information, such as the main headings. For example, if the main headings are twice as big as the body copy, how does that size relationship flow down to the other levels of information and headings? Use the **em** as a unit to establish this relationship once the body copy size has been defined.

These flickr groups display a range of typographic styles that relate to web design:

www.flickr.com/groups/nicewebtype/pool

www.flickr.com/groups/37996583675@N01/pool

Readability and legibility

Important aspects of web typography are legibility and readability. To ensure readability and legibility in their design, a designer needs to explore both the measure of the type and the colour of the type. Poor computer displays can also affect readability, though as computer displays have become more advanced and higher in quality, the issues relating to screen reading and prolonged screen viewing have become less important. It is worth noting, though, that not everyone has access to good quality computer displays.

The measure of type

The measure is the width of the block of type from the left margin to the right margin. This will be defined by the grid. If the measure is too long, the type will be hard to read. A long line of type causes the reader to lose orientation, as it becomes hard to see where one line ends and the next line begins. There is a long distance between the end of the line and the start of the next line, meaning the eye has to travel a greater distance across the page. If the measure is too short, the eye has to move back and forth quite quickly as it jumps from the end of one short line down to the beginning of the next, which becomes tiring on the eye.

A good guide is to use between 45 and 75 characters in a column width. The 66 character line is often viewed as ideal. Note that these character lengths include spaces between words, as well as punctuation and all other elements. If the body font is a 12 pixel font then 45 characters would give a block width of 540 pixels, whereas 60 characters in a block width would be 780 pixels. This demonstrates the interrelationship between the type and the grid.

The larger the type size set, the larger the **leading** needs to be to ensure readability. A good start for leading is 1.5 em. As an em is a proportional measure, the larger the type size the larger the leading will automatically be. For example, 12 point type would have 18 point leading (12 × 1.5 em), and 16 point type would have 24 point leading (16 × 1.5 em).

The units here are given as a rough guide. Ideal measurements would depend on the type of font chosen, the character kerning of the font and the default tracking of each font.

An **em** is a unit of type measurement that defines the proportion of the letter width and height in relation to the size of the current font. Originally, the unit came from the width of the capital 'M' in the typeface being used. Therefore, 1 em in a 16 point typeface is 16 points.

Leading is the space between lines of type.

RESOURCE ON TYPE

A great resource for type is Robert Bringhurst's *The Elements of Typographic Style*. An online version of the book, with its rules applied to web typography, can be found at: http://webtypography.net/toc.

The colour of type

Colour of type refers to the density of type in a particular block of type. This is also affected by the measure of the type: the heavier the type density, the darker the colour of the type; the more spread out the type, the lighter the colour of type. Both of these affect readability.

If type is too dense, it becomes hard to read. Adding leading will lighten the type and allow it to breathe and become more legible. If the leading is increased too much, the type becomes lighter to the point of illegibility. The distance between the lines becomes so great that the reader's eye cannot continue from one line to the next.

Leading between elements also affects proximity. Proximity is important, as groups of information that are associated are usually placed closer to each other. Giving too much leading between headers and content can cause readers to disconnect. Ensure associated content is designed to sit in close proximity, but with enough leading to remain readable.

THE WEB CAVEAT

While it is important to bear screen sizes, grids and typography in mind, the final control of how digital design outcomes are displayed through a web browser lies with the end user. The end user can alter type size by making it larger or smaller; they can change the colour; they can even have their own custom **style sheets**. They may be viewing the site in high-contrast mode so that all the colours are reversed out.

Keep this in mind when turning visual designs into html. Where possible, use ems as units for widths of elements, so that if font sizes are increased or decreased, the design will change size in relation to the type.

A web page will appear exactly as designed when displayed in modern web browsers, but when displayed in older browsers it will not. Minimise the impact of this on the end user by allowing the design to **degrade** gracefully where possible.

For greater control over the end display, it is possible to deliver the design via a number of plug-in technologies, such as Adobe Flash® or Microsoft's Silverlight®, but bear in mind that this might limit the devices on which your design can be displayed.

Colour of type refers to the density of a typographic layout.

A **style sheet** is a set of rules that define the presentation of a website.

Degrade describes the way a website's design changes in different, usually older, web browsers.

INFORMATION SORTING AND PRESENTATION

When designing for a digital environment, there are a variety of ways to present and sort information. The following examples are based on the paper 'Information interaction design: a unified field theory of design', by Nathan Shedroff. These guidelines could be used for a website, directory service and many other applications.

Taking the example of a cinema website, let's consider the number of ways that you can present information to an audience.

If a user of the website wants to select a movie and view session times, an alphabetical list of movies currently screening is a good way to do that. An alphabetical list is useful when the user knows exactly what they are looking for. If the user wants to check a variety of cinema locations, it may be useful to sort the film listings by location.

Locations are a natural way of organising data, where the importance lies in relation to other data—in this case, place and movies.

Another useful way for users to browse this cinema website would be by time. The user can select a day and time they wish to view a movie, and then see what movies are screening at that time. Time is great for organising information that follows a timeline.

One way to organise the movies would be to use categories such as genre. This way, the user could browse, for example, action movies that are currently screening. Categories are good for allowing similar types of things to be grouped together.

Another way to view the movies might be by reviewer ratings. A user might be more inclined to see a movie with a four-star rating than a movie with a one-star rating. This is a numeric way of sorting information. Numeric systems can be used to organise information; a movie rating system is one example.

The reviewer rating system could be described as an arbitrary (made-up) numeric; it could also be called a relative scale. Other more obscure examples of a relative scale include listing the movie by duration or price. The user could browse the movies by duration; or, they might wish to view any cheaper seats or session times that are available. Use of a relative scale enables organisation of things by amount or size.

Finally, there is the strangest way of sorting information: by chance. A good example of this might be a manager's special, or a monthly movie club recommendation. The movie could be chosen at random and displayed on the front of the application to draw the users into a movie they had not considered watching. Sorting information by chance can provide the users with pleasant surprises, and provide them with a bit of a challenge.

All these ways of sorting and presenting information are legitimate techniques when it comes to digital design. Another option is to combine these techniques by filtering information. This way, a user can apply a number of filters to the main movie list, so that the initial result might be for films from the action movie category; then they could filter to a specific day and time; finally they could refine the list based on the film's review rating.

EXERCISE
1. List as many different ways to sort information as you can think of.
2. Consider the movie website example. In what other ways could you sort information for this application?

MOTION GRAPHICS

Motion graphics is one of the fastest growing areas of interest for design students. Motion graphics is a combination of animated two-dimensional (2-D) and three-dimensional (3-D) graphic design elements with sounds, music and narration. Motion graphics work can be found in film and television titles, advertisements, websites and viral animations. Motion graphics combines traditional 2-D hand-drawn animation with computer generated 2-D and 3-D animations. Motion graphics is usually accompanied by music and the animations are set in time to the music. Websites like Motionographer (http://motionographer.com) feature a range of motion graphics, from student work to the latest commercials.

The level of production quality for commercials, program and film titles, TV station identity graphics (idents) and other motion graphic design outcomes has increased rapidly, as software such as Adobe After Effects® becomes more accessible. Motion graphics can be extremely appealing to digital design students, as it has few of the issues associated with the web. It's animation, and animation is fun. It requires no programming skills to implement, which is one of the drawbacks of web and game design. With increased channels for delivery, such as YouTube and Vimeo, work can be accessed anywhere in the world.

In this section, we will briefly look at some of the steps in the process of motion graphics production and explore some important elements that are often overlooked.

CONCEPT

Motion graphics design must begin with some kind of narrative or concept. The concept can be something very simple, but it needs to be there. A trap that some work falls into is to mimic a popular look and feel to create a folio piece. While this approach can show off good technical skills, it fails to display design skills such as **ideation**, conceptualising and process.

DEFINE THE BRIEF

Before starting the process, define the brief:

- Work out what the brief is asking you to do.
- Write this down as a 'return brief', outlining your understanding of the client's needs.

Using a return brief to document your understanding of the brief will help define what has to be done. Having this document approved by the client will ensure that both the client and the designer have the same understanding of the project and the desired outcomes.

IDEATION

Ideation is the process of coming up with ideas. There are a number of techniques that can be used to help the process, such as mind mapping, brainstorming and card shuffling. The ideas that are created should be tested against the return brief. Does the idea do what it needs to?

Mood boards

Using **mood boards** designers start to visualise the concept or idea. Mood boards are created by sourcing lots of relevant visual references and placing these on display boards. Mood boards may relate to styles, colours, typographic treatment or other themes within the concept.

Ideation is the process of generating ideas.

Mood boards may consist of images, text and samples of objects. Designers and others use mood boards to develop their design concepts and to communicate to other members of the design team.

STORYBOARDS

The next steps in the process are **storyboarding** and **scripting**. These may be done in any order, or concurrently. One thing to not worry about when making these initial storyboards is drawing skill. The idea is to firstly get the concept across using a **time-based medium**. There are a few techniques that can be employed for storyboarding, such as the use of rough stock images for shots, architectural models for people in scenes or elements from mood board as textures and patterns in the storyboard.

Create enough frames to document the motion graphics outcome accurately. It is a good idea to think about timing in the storyboard. Consider the following points.

- Which parts will happen quickly?
- Which parts will be slower?
- What is the pace of the animation, and how will elements move across the screen.
- What types of **easing in** will be used?
- What types of motion will be used; for example, naturalistic or mechanical?
- Will there be lighting? If so, where from?

The more clearly the idea is defined before production starts, the more time will be saved.

SOUND DESIGN

An important consideration at this stage is sound design. A common student mistake is to leave the sound design until the last stage of production. The audio track should really come first, so that the animation can work with the audio. Think about what background sounds may be needed, as well as sound effects (SFX), incidental music, and where the sound will be sourced from.

Apple Macintosh users have GarageBand®, which comes loaded with a number of free to use musical loops. If the Mac has Soundtrack Pro® installed, it comes with about 20 GB of free audio files that can be used. If not, there are plenty of royalty-free websites where audio files can be downloaded for student work.

It is better to clearly define what audio is needed before looking for it. Once the storyboard is complete, it will provide a breakdown of all the shots and animations involved. Then work can start on selecting the soundtrack.

Once the soundtrack is complete, an animatic can be started. An animatic is the process of scanning the storyboard and setting it out to the audio. This will give a rough idea of pace, where elements need to be faster or slower, which elements work well and which may need more work. An animatic can be as simple as a series of rough sketches to audio or as complex as scanned illustration and backgrounds in perfect timing to the soundtrack.

Refine the animatic through each step of the design process: ideate, conceptualise, realise, refine and evaluate. The animatic is a great milestone to review the work, before the labour intensive process of motion graphics production begins.

A **storyboard** is a series of illustrations or images created to demonstrate motion graphics. **Scripting** is the process of writing a script.

A **time-based medium** is a medium such as film, TV or video that relies on time to communicate its meaning.

Easing in is the use of acceleration and deceleration to make motion appear more naturalistic.

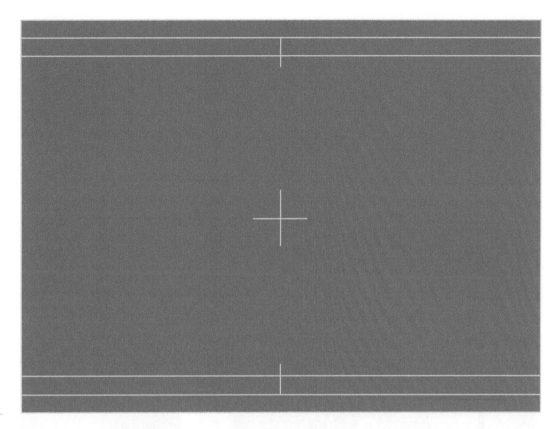

→ When producing videos and motion graphics you will see an action safe/title safe grid similar to this, within your chosen computer software.

← This seasonal promo for LifeStyle Food Channel animates Christmas baubles falling like snow, then forming the shapes of both words and objects.

Designer **XYZ NETWORKS**
Client **LIFESTYLE FOOD CHANNEL**

PRODUCTION CONSIDERATIONS

It is useful to ask a lot of questions about how the motion graphics outcome will be delivered to the audience. The answers to these questions will ensure that when the designer creates the graphics and other elements for the motion graphics production, they will all be in the correct size and format. Let's consider some of the questions that should be asked, and their relevance to production.

❯ What will the audience be viewing this on?

❯ What screen size is the final outcome?

There are a number of ratios, formats and sizes for screens. For example, standard definition has two size ratios—widescreen 16:9 aspect ratio and standard definition 4:3 aspect ratio.

There is the potential for a high-definition outcome. If creating high-definition content, there are a variety of sizes for the final product: 768i, 768p, 1080i and 1080p. (The 'i' in these measurements means **interlaced** and the 'p' means **progressive**.)

Interlaced refers to a field-based video display, where alternate lines form one sequence that is followed by the other lines in a second sequence.

A **progressive** video display is frame-based instead of field-based.

Alister Coyne

www.hairycow.com

Inspired by *Transworld Skateboarding* magazines, Alister Coyne set off for the world of graphic design with stars in his eyes. He soon found design wasn't a simple game of tic-tac-toe. 'My portfolio coming out of high school was ok; nowhere near strong enough to get into university. I was accepted into Brighton Bay Art & Design, which bridges the gap between high school and TAFE/university,' explains Alister. 'It allowed me to study graphic design at Swinburne University, where over a thousand people apply, competing for 60 places. I failed my first year. It wasn't until I was studying my Honours year working in-house at Swinburne's Multimedia Design Centre that I came into my own.'

Now based in Auckland, Alister is part of a freelance collective called The Pond that helps source work on his behalf. 'I design anything that appears on a screen, from websites, television graphics, iPhone apps, banners, ecommerce and brand guidelines. I'll also produce more traditional design work that covers branding, logotypes and the occasional print job.'

Having created work for notable clients like Adidas, Nike, Chupa Chups, Honda, SAAB, Toyota and Vodafone, these days Alister not only produces the concepts and design for his clients but strategy as well. 'Generally speaking, I come up with the visual direction of each project that works in the digital medium. Quite often there's work being produced by agencies in which digital is an afterthought, so my role has been trying to retrofit ideas that just don't suit the medium,' says Alister.

Alister started his career in Melbourne at Sputnik Agency before making his mark internationally, first in Edinburgh, where he worked in a small multimedia studio, then in London, where he began his freelance career. 'After the tiny market in Scotland I was suddenly creating work for an audience of 80 million people. The scale was staggering. Freelancing allowed me to develop key skills required to take on new projects, including negotiating wages and conditions. It also allowed me to travel whenever I liked, which suited my lifestyle.'

Returning via Melbourne for another stint at freelancing, Alister has now settled in Auckland. He has found working as an Australian designer in another country can sometimes require changing your design 'voice' to communicate. 'It shouldn't matter but in a sense it does. I've been working on a project recently for a rugby team based here in Auckland. Between a

LEFT | Website for Kim Crawford, Marlborough Sauvignon Blanc wines.

ABOVE | Toyota Believe. Desktop wallpaper for an integrated brand campaign.

Canadian, Englishman and an Australian we've been able to create a very local website. Really it comes down to research and collaboration with the right people. In London I created a website design that was displayed in five languages, which gives a sense of universality to the work. I do recall in Scotland I created my own tartan pattern to be used for a tourist website. It wasn't received warmly. If there are instances where local context is important, do your research!'

Still, Alister believes the success of a design relies not only in the design or concept, but in your belief that your concept is the best solution for the problem. However, he feels culture doesn't influence people's reaction to design more than interaction. 'In digital it's not so much a reaction to design, it's more a reaction over something that doesn't work. If your website, banner or application hinders the process of interaction, people will react badly, which is to be expected. A positive digital experience is a seamless experience.'

TOP | BNZ Whale Watch. TVC brand lockup for an integrated brand campaign.

ABOVE | ABC International 'My Pacific Story'. A blog following two presenters as they return to their home countries.

265

If the final outcome is for cinema, will it be a 2k or 4k format? Cinema formats can be 2k or 4k, which refers to the pixel size of the image (2000 pixels wide or 4000 pixels wide).

How will the final outcome be delivered?

Delivery could be via the web, on DVD (which allows for choice of PAL or NTSC) or broadcast. The audio format also relates to delivery format. Best practice would be to keep the audio quality as high as possible, then lower the quality for the delivery format.

Consider also the following:

- If the final outcome is for broadcast, then all colours need to be broadcast safe.
- All typography needs to be well within the title safe guidelines
- All the important action must be within the action safe guidelines.

These guides are viewable inside Adobe Photoshop® and After Effects®, as well as Apple Final Cut Pro®, so designers can check their work as they construct it.

When it comes to production, it's easier to break the work up into scenes as defined by the storyboard and animatic. If working with After Effects, break each scene into separate compositions. Place all these compositions into one main composition. It is possible to mix the finished scenes with the animatic to obtain a sense of the whole project.

The design principles mentioned earlier in the chapter are just as relevant in motion graphics as they are in other digital design. Ensure that what is being communicated isn't lost in a flurry of animation. Is the required information easily digestible by an audience? This applies not just to typography but also to the visual cues used to communicate ideas. This means considering the following:

- Do elements balance well on the screen?
- Does the movement of elements work within the concept?
- Is use of scale, colour and texture appropriate?

If re-creating naturalistic environments, your animation should use ease in and ease out, and your background and foreground elements should move in parallax. Are organic objects moving with enough bounce, stretch and squash? When creating a more cartoonish outcome, then these naturalistic elements may be extended to extremes to give a sense of playfulness or whimsy within the piece.

When creating something that is mechanical, or non-organic, turn off all easing and use straight motion with no motion blurring to give a mechanistic feel to the movement.

Explore the use of time to reveal and expand ideas and communicate the brief—it may be that visual gags unfold throughout the piece. Don't give the gag away too quickly. Also, if the viewer is tricked with a visual technique, be careful of using it too often, as it may become tired if overused; and when using metaphors within the design, make sure they are consistent and that any visual language set up is well thought out.

Remember that work that is derivative of a particular style or design movement needs to be using that style in response to the brief rather than as an exercise in replicating style. Check continually throughout the production process that the design decisions made are being true to the return brief, and that there is some kind of narrative, however tenuous it may be.

EXERCISE Watching a movie such as *Legend of the Guardians: The Owls of Ga'Hoole*, it is easy to see the influence of the 12 principles of animation. Watch the movie and list the scenes where the principles of animation are at work.

THE PRINCIPLES OF ANIMATION

When beginning an animation or motion graphics project, it is important to have sound knowledge of the principles that underpin animation. These principles can be used as a guide to assess the work that is being created. The first book to define the 12 principles of animation was *The Illusion of Life* by Frank Thomas and Ollie Johnston. This is a standard book for anyone wanting to work in the animation field. The information can also be applied to any form of motion graphics, and its guidelines on character designs also apply to computer game characters and commercials.

1. SQUASH AND STRETCH

This is usually demonstrated with a bouncing ball, and shows the deformation of the ball as it hits the ground, which is caused by the weight of the ball and gravity. This illusion of weight and volume can be used to give an organic feel to any animated object, from kinetic typography to 3-D animation. This is one of the most important elements to master as it can be used to convey realism in organic objects, and in the extreme to create highly comedic animations.

2. ANTICIPATION

Anticipation is used to prepare an audience for action that is about to happen. This is usually shown in an over-the-top way as a character winds up to do something dramatic, such as run, jump or punch. This preparation for action is a great way to create tension.

3. STAGING

Staging is the composition of shots to effectively describe and convey the narrative. This should be worked out in the storyboard, looking at issues such as: use of close-ups, medium or long shots; camera angles to be used; and how characters will appear in the frame.

This is not limited to character animation: it is important to all aspects of animation, especially in kinetic typography, where the audience has to read a large portion of moving text. In this case, the text needs to be framed and paced in a way that allows it to be easily read.

4. STRAIGHT AHEAD AND POSE-TO-POSE ANIMATION

Straight ahead animation is based on drawing one drawing after another to get from one action to the next. Pose-to-pose is more planned: initially, key pose drawings are created, with each drawing in between to be composed at a later stage. With the advent of computer animation and **tweening**, most animation is now pose-to-pose, with the animator setting key frames and the computer doing some of the tweening, to be checked over by the animator.

5. FOLLOW THROUGH AND OVERLAPPING ACTION

This is about movement, weight and realism. When the body moves, not everything moves at the same speed at once, and nothing stops all at once. Imagine someone starting to run: the torso moves, then the arms and legs catch up. Think about the movement of a runner with long hair: if they suddenly stop, their hair and clothes may keep moving forward for a short period of time.

This use of realism brings inanimate objects to life. The attention to detail of using follow through and overlap, combined with anticipation and stretch and squash, is what separates great computer animation from mediocre Saturday morning television fodder.

Tweening refers to the creation of 'in between' drawings that capture the stages between one key pose and the next.

← This animation combines video footage of an alley with CGI to create an eerie commercial of a genetically modified prawn-like character for MTV.

Designer **UMERIC**
Client **MTV**

6. SLOW-OUT AND SLOW-IN

This is also known as 'ease-out' and 'ease-in'. All objects need to accelerate to get to their travelling speed. With computer-based animation, we can remove all forms of easing to give a very unnatural movement. Adding easing to animation ensures that movements speed up and slow down more naturally.

7. ARCS

Most organic objects move in some kind of arc. Think about the movement of arms and legs: they swing in an arc. All aspects of an animal's motion move on this arc, from the movement of its eyes to the way its tail swings. Avoid using arcs to animate robots or mechanical devices, unless those devices have some elements of **anthropomorphism**.

8. SECONDARY ACTION

Secondary action supports the main action, and is used to bring characters to life. Imagine someone walking and having no movement apart from their legs: this would actually be pretty unnatural. In reality, there would be a swinging of the arms, and a swaying of the head and shoulders. These secondary actions support the main action—walking—and add greater character to the action.

9. TIMING

Timing is about making animation smooth and natural, or using extreme timing for comedic effect. A good understanding of timing comes from an understanding of the movement of people and animals. View frame-by-frame the movement of animals or humans. With computer-based animation, a good understanding of timing is just as important. One expensive but quick way to get a good understanding of human and animal movement is to use **motion capture**, and then assign the motion capture data to computer-based animations.

10. EXAGGERATION

Exaggeration is not limited to the extreme distortion of actions or characteristics, but also includes the subtle exaggeration of poses, movements and expressions. These subtle exaggerations, especially with comic and cartoon characters, create a sense of non-reality. They provide a clear contrast to actions and characteristics that are too closely based on reality.

11. SOLID DRAWING

Solid drawing is about creating interesting poses, with well-proportioned shapes and a clear sense of weight and form. Is each key frame an interesting composition, and would it work well on its own? The idea is to have well-drawn and constructed frames, that contain well-drawn characters with a sense of weight and shape.

12. APPEAL

Animated characters need to appeal to the audience. The design of the characters needs to be appealing to the eye. Avoid the use of symmetry in character design, as this tends to reduce the appeal.

While most of the principles of animation have been in use since the 1930s, they still have a great deal of relevance to any character design, animation or motion graphics project undertaken today. They can be used in conjunction with the principles of design to ensure the digital design outcomes are as effective as possible in communicating to the audience. They are also a way of measuring the design against a set of criteria, and provide a framework of guidelines for generating ideas.

Anthropomorphism is the attribution of human characteristics or behaviour to a god, animal or object.

Motion capture is the capture of motion data from a subject that is then applied to 3-D models.

DESIGN BRIEF: CREATE A WEBSITE TO PROMOTE A FAMOUS MOVIE DIRECTOR

 Create a promotional website for one of the following famous movie directors: Paul Verhoeven, Michael Bay, James Cameron, Sophia Coppola, Sergio Leone, Oliver Stone, John Woo, Martin Scorsese, Jane Campion, Kathryn Bigelow or George Lucas. It must carry across to the audience the feel of the chosen director and their movies.

The website must contain: a biography of the director, a list of films they have made, still images from movies they have made, music or audio from their films, a help section, and links to sites about their films. Most of this information can be found on www.imdb.com, and any other sources both online and offline.

Size

The website must work on a 1024 × 768 screen.

Format

All screens must be presented in a storyboard.

Research and collect

1. Research one of the movie directors.
2. Create a flowchart of the website sitemap.
3. Document the purpose of the site.
4. Document user and business goals for the website.
5. Collect content for the website from various online and offline resources.

Sketches and storyboard

1. Sketch at least five potential interface designs for the website as thumbnail sketches.
2. Draw a final comprehensive colour sketch of the main interface of the website—this is to be mounted on A3 board.
3. Document how your design relates to the chosen director.
4. Document how your design meets the principles of graphic design.

Create and author

1. Create screens based on your storyboard designs.
2. Create the website in keeping with storyboards designs, incorporating any interactions, animations and transitions.
3. Publish your finished site, with html files.

Items to be submitted

1. Visual diary containing your sketches.
2. Mounted final sketch of main interface.
3. Storyboard of your design.
4. Word document about your design.
5. Html files.

SUMMARY

Digital design is a constantly evolving and developing field, a forward-looking aspect of design that responds and adapts to new technologies and mediums. The designers that are most successful within the digital design field are those who can adapt quickly to these developments, but are also well-grounded in the traditions that digital design draws on, be it information design, film-making, animation, graphic design or sound design. Digital design allows for many specialisations, such as 3-D modelling and animating, web design, web programming, interface design, user experience design and the growing area of service design.

KEY TERMS

REFERENCES/WEBSITES

Austin, T 2007, *New media design*, Laurence King Publishing, London.

Bringhurst, R 2004, *The elements of typographic style*, H&M Publishers, Vancouver.

Muller-Brockmann, J 1996, *Grid systems in graphic design*, Niggli Verlag, Sulgen.

Shedroff, N, 1994, 'Information interaction design: a unified field theory of design', www.nathan.com/thoughts/unified

Thomas, F & Ollie, J 1995, *The illusion of life*, Hyperion Books, New York.

Information design

Edward Tufte (www.edwardtufte.com/tufte)

InfoDesign (www.informationdesign.org)

Jesse James Garrett (www.jjg.net/ia)

Nathan Shedroff (www.nathan.com/thoughts)

Principles of design

Design-lib.com (www.design-lib.com/graphic-design-principles-gd.php)

Digital Web Magazine (www.digital-web.com/articles/principles_of_design)

The Elements of Typographic Style Applied to the Web (http://webtypography.net/toc)

Grid systems

The Grid System (www.thegridsystem.org)

960 Grid System (http://960.gs)

Mark Boulton (www.markboulton.co.uk/journal/comments/five-simple-steps-to-designing-grid-systems-part-1)

Web design

A List Apart (www.alistapart.com)

Sitepoint (www.sitepoint.com)

Smashing Magazine (www.smashingmagazine.com)

Motion graphics

Creative Cow (www.creativecow.net)

Mograph (www.mograph.net/board/index.php?act=home)

Motionographer (http://motionographer.com)

The principles of animation

3D Ark (www.3dark.com/archives/animation/the_principles.html)

Animation Arena (www.animationarena.com/principles-of-animation.html)

Animation Toolworks (www.animationtoolworks.com/library/article9.html)

Siggraph (www.siggraph.org/education/materials/HyperGraph/animation/character_animation/principles/prin_trad_anim.htm)

Siggraph (www.siggraph.org/education/materials/HyperGraph/animation/character_animation/principles/lasseter_s94.htm)

chapter 8

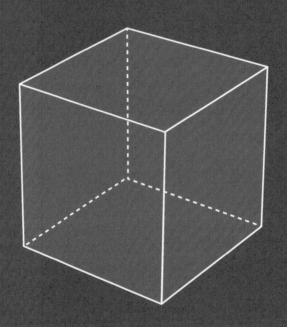

THREE-DIMENSIONAL DESIGN

INTRODUCTION

This chapter is not about 3-D animation: it is about packaging design, point of sale, environment design and wayfinding. These are all potentially three-dimensional and are often freestanding, meaning they can be viewed from many sides by a consumer. Consequently, they need a different approach than two-dimensional or digital interactive design. These designs also require a different knowledge of materials, because they may be exposed to the outdoors, they may be weight bearing or they may need to hold perishable products. Fortunately, technicians in this industry give designers a lot of support with regard to design and development processes, material selection and printing. So don't be afraid to tackle a three-dimensional project— it is a different way of looking at problems but it can be fun.

DEFINING EACH AREA

All areas of design require designers to develop original design concepts with particular consideration to utility, environmental concerns, commercial viability and aesthetics. After all, our job is about working to a brief to create the best possible end result. Designers need well-developed planning and organisational skills to complete a project to a high level and refine it after client feedback within the allocated time— sometimes repeatedly.

Graphic design is said to promote the language of image, text and symbols and this is most true in **wayfinding** or environmental graphics. The language of pictograms has been in high use over the past 50 years since Lance Wyman used pictograms extensively for wayfinding systems at the 1968 Mexico City Olympic Games and for the National Zoo in Washington. Many of the early sign systems drew influence from architecture, product design, interiors, colour theory, typography and symbol design.

Our clients expect each and every design to be innovative, original and relevant as well as practical, within budget and on time. In packaging and wayfinding design the basic design principles are customised to meet the objectives of each new brief. These principles not only define the structure but also the use of colour, imagery and typography to create the right sense of balance, tension, proportion and appeal.

Inevitably, although the structure and format are very different, a designer uses similar skills in creating a family of products and a wayfinding system. Packaging and wayfinding signage both have a strong primary purpose: to inform. If we didn't know where to go when driving or visiting someone in a hospital, or how much medication to take and when, or how long to cook our Basmati rice, our busy lives would be much more complicated.

→ Environmental directory signage at the district court of Western Australia.

Designer **TURNER DESIGN**
Client **MULTIPLEX CONSTRUCTIONS PTY LTD**

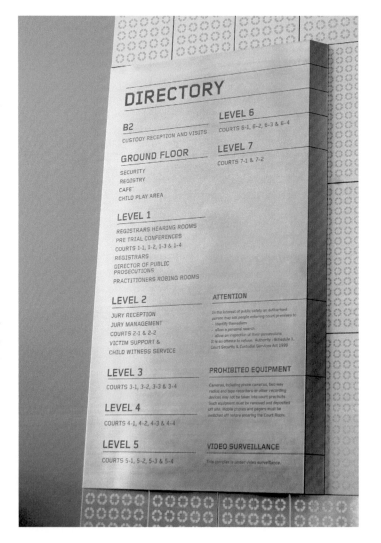

Wayfinding refers to systems that direct people or help them navigate space, either within structures, along streets or through a complex of buildings.

PACKAGING: TAKE ME HOME

Packaging imagery is vital: it enhances sales, it differentiates, it protects and it helps in the creation of a brand and in developing the personality of the pack. Consumers see a shape, a combination of colours, or recognise a particular brand and product styling. When you're rushing through the supermarket, chemist or cosmetics shop looking for a particular product, it's the shape, colour, size and general brand characteristics that you are looking for.

SUZIE HADDOCK

↑ Packaging can be highly functional as well as beautiful, as demonstrated by this decorative gift box.

Packaging's main role is not just for brand recognition—it's also about protecting and preserving the contents or produce. There are many positive benefits of packaging but these are forgotten as soon as the pack is emptied and it becomes throwaway rubbish. Although some packaging is so delightful that it becomes a collectable item, in most cases there are mainly negative images surrounding packaging.

Visibility of products can be increased with the use of 'point-of-sale' displays, such as:

- shelf edging, wobblers
- dummy packs (larger than life-size)
- display packs and stands
- mobiles
- posters
- banners
- digital displays and other specialised forms of sales promotion found near, on, or next to a checkout counter.

Encounters with packaging are an everyday experience—from the moment you get up in the morning and have your cereal with milk, or bread toasted with a spread, and then clean your teeth with toothpaste, you have engaged with some form of packaging in a pack, carton, jar or tube designed by a graphic designer.

A typical supermarket stocks about 30 000 to 40 000 fast-moving consumer goods (**FMCGs**), some with innovative packaging solutions, combining technological advances in materials and techniques with graphics designed to target **niche markets**. The supermarket has become the packaging design gallery of horrors and delights, and it is in this environment that competition for consumer attention is most intense.

FMCGs (fast-moving consumer goods) are goods that sell quickly and at low cost. They are supplied in the retail environment to meet the daily demands of customers.

A **niche market** is the smaller market on which a specific product with defined product features is focusing; e.g., the

sandal market is a niche within the shoe market.

Marketers rely on consumers quickly recognising products from a distance because of the colour, shape and other brand characteristics of a product. Point-of-sale displays such as these reinforce brand recognition and are generally placed in areas where consumers will impulse buy.

← *Designer* **NAUGHTYFISH**
Client **FORD FIESTA MOONLIGHT CINEMA**

↙ ↓ *Designer* **SAINSBURY POS DISPLAYS**

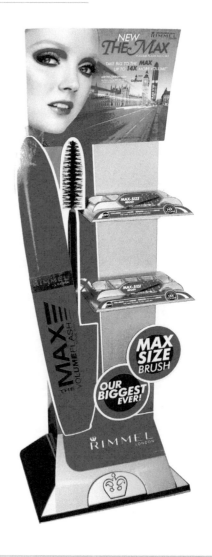

276

EXERCISE Go to a large chemist and see if you can identify a wobbler, a dummy pack, a mobile, a counter display pack and a poster.

Demographic, social and cultural trends, and translating these concepts into something visual we can understand, are key factors in the design process. Designers have to consider how a pack will sell on a shelf, in an advertisement, even on a screen, ensuring that the product brand characteristics are not lost in any of the mediums. Brand reinforcement is a powerful tool in maintaining the product at the front of consumers' minds. Shapes and materials bring their own character to the design and also their own advantages and disadvantages. Unique shapes are often **patented** to protect the branding attributes of the product.

The tactile nature of materials can have an impact on consumers' attitude to the product. Features such as embossing, surface textures, shapes and finishes will influence whether they will recall the product when they want to satisfy that need again. In the initial stages of design, it is important to think outside the square and consider all options. Later, you can reject designs that you have discovered will not be practical or cost-effective, or that could cause filling problems. But to begin with, keep an open mind.

→ Unique product shapes can be key aspects of brand recognition and are often patented by companies. Patents are often required for glass, plastic and other 'shaped' vessels but can also be awarded for unique opening and fastening systems.

SUZIE HADDOCK

Demographics are characteristics of a specific area of the population including age, gender and marital status.

A **patent** is a legal means of protecting a unique product, shape or process from use by anyone else.

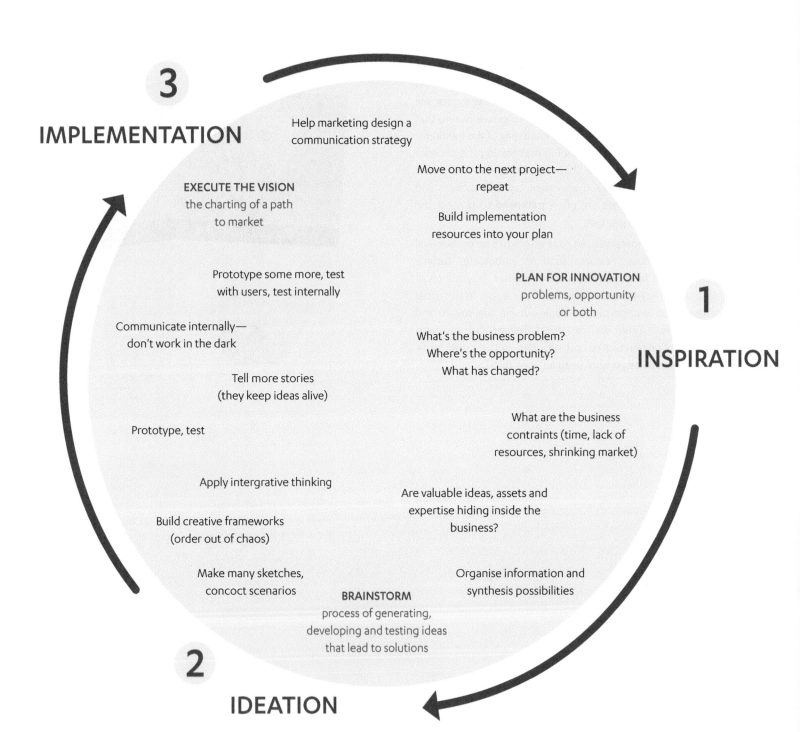

3

IMPLEMENTATION

Help marketing design a
communication strategy

Move onto the next project—
repeat

EXECUTE THE VISION
the charting of a path
to market

Build implementation
resources into your plan

PLAN FOR INNOVATION
problems, opportunity
or both

Prototype some more, test
with users, test internally

1

Communicate internally—
don't work in the dark

What's the business problem?
Where's the opportunity?
What has changed?

INSPIRATION

Tell more stories
(they keep ideas alive)

What are the business
contraints (time, lack of
resources, shrinking market)

Prototype, test

Apply intergrative thinking

Are valuable ideas, assets and
expertise hiding inside the
business?

Build creative frameworks
(order out of chaos)

Make many sketches,
concoct scenarios

Organise information and
synthesis possibilities

BRAINSTORM
process of generating,
developing and testing ideas
that lead to solutions

2

IDEATION

THE DESIGN PROCESS

The brief is the defining part of the design process. How has the client decided on what they think they need and have they considered all aspects of the product, the environment and the stakeholders? Material choices will be determined by the requirements of the product, and by the needs of your design. They may also be influenced by factors such as environmental concerns or exposure of the design to weather.

Research and analysis

Before design work starts, an in-depth understanding of the target audience or the **stakeholders** of the product is required. This involves researching the target audience's lifestyle, wants, desires and motivations. Knowing the target market allows the designer to predict their behaviour in relation to the product. Typically you need to know:

- brands they buy
- where they live (flat/house)
- what cars they drive
- what food they eat
- what fashions they follow
- what type of holidays they take
- what TV/magazines they view
- what drinks they prefer.

↓ Toiletries and beauty products with a unique style. The bold, colourful photography of fruit and flowers creates the brand identity.

Designer **ANNETTE HARCUS, HARCUS DESIGN**

← This three-step process is the start of creating a product that focuses on the client's brief.

Brown, T 2008, 'Design thinking', Harvard Business Review, June

Stakeholders are all the people (including groups, organisations and shareholders) who affect or can be affected by the design.

Large brands have whole teams of marketing and communications professionals who will have much of this audience information already. When working with these brands, you will be able to tap into their resources to get a good picture of their clients. If they don't have any information because they are trying to target a new product category, work with them to research new information.

You may also need to think about the **category drivers** for that product. What makes someone buy Product A? Is it hunger? To keep warm? To feel good?

Environmental checklist

Throughout the design process, think of the impact of your packaging design on the environment.

- Always use the minimum amount of material to perform the task capably.
- Use as few material types as possible to avoid recycling contamination.
- Consider where the materials are to be sourced.
- Use recycled materials wherever possible.
- Make the package as light as possible, which will use less energy getting it to market.
- Consider how the pack is to be used and disposed of.
- Most importantly, always consider the uncomplicated solution— there is no need to overcomplicate any design brief.

↓ More and more designers are being asked to design 'cradle-to-grave' packaging. This includes individual item packaging, transport packaging and point-of-sale packaging. These designers have created the total package for pharmaceutical products sold in convenience stores.

Designers **CLINTON DUNCAN, IVANA MARTINOVIC, CHRIS MACLEAN**
Client **REMEDIES HEALTHCARE**

All products have a generic set of **category drivers**. These drivers are the basic need states consumers use to guide their purchases. For example, if your product is vitamin water, your category driver is health or healthy living.

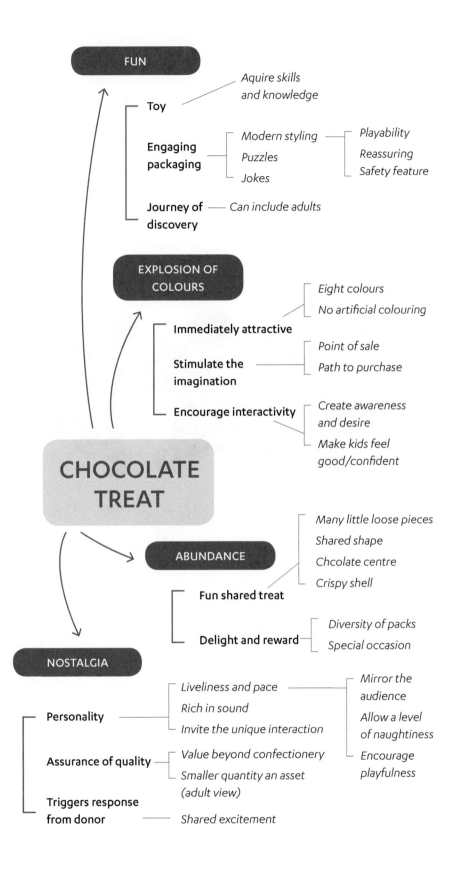

FUN

Toy —— *Aquire skills and knowledge*

Engaging packaging
- *Modern styling* —— *Playability*
- *Puzzles* —— *Reassuring*
- *Jokes* —— *Safety feature*

Journey of discovery —— *Can include adults*

EXPLOSION OF COLOURS

Immediately attractive
- *Eight colours*
- *No artificial colouring*

Stimulate the imagination
- *Point of sale*
- *Path to purchase*

Encourage interactivity
- *Create awareness and desire*
- *Make kids feel good/confident*

CHOCOLATE TREAT

ABUNDANCE

Fun shared treat
- *Many little loose pieces*
- *Shared shape*
- *Chcolate centre*
- *Crispy shell*

Delight and reward
- *Diversity of packs*
- *Special occasion*

NOSTALGIA

Personality
- *Liveliness and pace* —— *Mirror the audience*
- *Rich in sound*
- *Invite the unique interaction* —— *Allow a level of naughtiness*

Assurance of quality
- *Value beyond confectionery*
- *Smaller quantity an asset (adult view)* —— *Encourage playfulness*

Triggers response from donor —— *Shared excitement*

← This is an industry driver map or mind map for a non-specific chocolate confectionary product; it indicates how many other ideas, trends and resources in our environment can impact on your perceptions of a product.

281

CONCEPTS AND STRATEGIES

Once the research is complete, it's time to begin developing design concepts.

Mood boards

As we discovered in Chapter 2, ideas and themes are sometimes initially best expressed using a mood board. Mood boards usually consist of five different components—colour, texture, typeface, shape and theme—that hang together to give the client an idea of your proposed direction for the design. Mood boards can be presented to the client before work on the actual designs begins. They can help ensure that all stakeholders are on the right track and save a lot of time in the long run.

↑ Mood boards provide an initial look and feel for the concept of the product and help to identify the design approach to attract the target market.

EXERCISE

Think up a new concept milk drink aimed at teenagers. What colour will work best? What image would work best on the front of the package? What shape is the container? Draw sketches for three different ideas.

← A mock-up of a chocolate milk drink design and branding.

Designer **DAVID WONG**

→ Originally designed for the
Valentine's Day market, this pack
uses vampire references in the
form of a rose dripping blood.

Designer **NATHAN LAWES**

Initial concepts

Strange though it may seem, three-dimensional designers still sketch
out their ideas—whether it's with a pencil, fineliner or Wacom tablet.
The biggest hurdle is just getting the ideas down. The design of the
pack's shape is a major consideration, but graphics and branding
need to be considered from the outset. There is no need for highly
finished renderings—it's all about concepts at this stage.

Proposals

When at least three good ideas are formulated, it is time to move to
the next step.

When refining the design, mock-ups (or 'dummies') of the shape,
layout and format should be produced to test how the package
would feel when being handled. During the design process, constant
review against the design brief is essential and you should test each
design proposal against the specified objectives.

← The Canadian products pictured may have little relevance in Australia as they use totem imagery of salmon. The indigenous totem imagery is so well identified in Canada that the design needs no written external description. Mandatory information is included on a sticker on the reverse of the product.

PACKAGING DESIGN COMPONENTS

Imagery and cultural perception—symbols and icons

Colours, shapes and symbols are important aspects of packaging design. Symbols are used extensively as 'shorthand' to describe aspects of the product on what can be a small surface. Images, shapes and symbols can also cause packaging design to look out of date. A design that taps into the zeitgeist by utilising a trend of the moment—such as vampire imagery—will make the packaging look dated once the consumer no longer follows this trend.

Graphic devices

The perception of images varies in different cultures so it may be possible that a product sold in different parts of the world will need different colours and images on its pack (as well as the brand name in a different language). There is no limit to the techniques that can be used to produce illustrations, icons, symbols and characters but their styling will relate back to the decisions made on the initial mood boards or during the research process.

Photographs are often used on food packaging as serving suggestions or to ensure that the package creates appetite appeal. The attraction of any food packaging relies on sparking the senses. Our senses of smell, taste, sight and touch can all be stimulated by appealing photography and sometimes illustrations. Imagery must be designed to fit within the context of the layout and not the other way around: care must be taken when producing photography or illustrations.

Turner Design

www.turnerdesign.com.au

After studying graphic design at Curtin University of Technology, Western Australia, Neil Turner spent a year working for a PR consultancy before taking the leap and starting his own business, Turner Design, in 1978.

With a long legacy in the graphic design field, Neil focuses his substantial skills on projects that have a high level of interactivity with the audience. He works almost exclusively in brand, print, packaging, signage and web design. Renowned for their work with wine and beer design, Turner Design also create packaging solutions for cosmetics and food products.

When asked if there is such a thing as Australian packaging design, Neil explains, 'As most of my packaging experience is in the wine industry, I believe there is a recognisable Australian style in the approach of designers to the design of wine labels. This can be epitomised in the often whimsical, humorous and slightly irreverent values in the design as well as contemporary forms and typography. A brief tour of the wine section in any Tesco store in the UK will attest to that. In fact, all of the major wine producing countries of the world have a distinct design "language"—it's part of their design DNA.'

Developing a deeper understanding of each product and the audience is part of Turner Design's strategy when approaching each brief, making sure the final outcome is unique and true to the client. 'Every wine brand has a distinctive intrinsic character whether it be the location of the vineyard, its history, the meaning or image behind the brand name,' explains Neil. 'Careful consideration of these elements defines the design process and leads to a design solution with a unique "reason for being". It is the designer's role to discover these design values and interpret and develop them in a unique and compelling way.'

Examples of Turner Design's packaging and label design.
RIGHT | Limoncello bottle label and stylist packaging.

To produce a successful design outcome and quality, product collaboration is key, whether it is with typographers, illustrators and photographers (depending on the design direction), or with the client themselves. Neil and his team understand the benefit of collaboration and actively work with their clients.

'Any design process involves a close relationship between the client and designer working together in partnership. The client obviously knows more about his particular business than anyone else and it is the designer's role to understand that knowledge, interpret it and redefine it in a design sense.

I always like to respond quickly to the client with initial design concepts which helps ensure that both parties are clear on the desired direction. The client is included in all further design development stages so that he shares ownership of the outcomes. We also like to include the client in the production supervision so that they can appreciate the complete process.'

TOP LEFT AND BELOW | Indi Pilsner bottle labelling, transport packaging and cap design.

TOP RIGHT | Three solutions for one product that comes in variety of volumes.

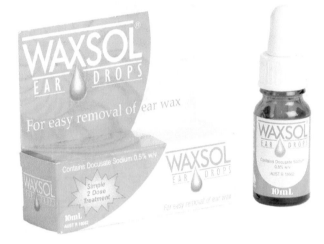

← The branding of this FMCG product appears on the lid as well as the primary display panel to ensure that consumers can easily identify the product for selection.

↓ The primary display panel on this product has the brand identity, the product descriptor, the net weight/volume and the active ingredient. The box has a **French lid** which extends the surface area to provide more 'on-shelf' presence.

Mandatory labelling requirements

Required elements on a package's label can include: brand mark, brand name, product name, ingredients (if a food product), net weight, nutritional information (if a food product), expiration, hazards, directions, dosage information (if a medicine), unique product code or **barcode**. These and other terms are defined in Table 8.1.

There are strict guidelines for nutritional information and ingredients copy on food packaging. Pharmaceutical goods need to be labelled with warnings such as 'Keep out of reach of children'. Label requirements include minimum sized type, colour specifications and positioning.

Unique product codes or barcodes are a very important component of pack design that communicates much more than just the price of an item. Modern logistics (movement of products) is tied to barcodes and allows for an instant assessment of how many of that product are in a shop and when they need to be ordered.

Primary display panel (PDP)

Brand identity and primary communication are usually on the front of a package or point of sale item and are necessary for product recall and identification in a busy supermarket environment.

The front panel is the most important aspect of a product's design. Often, this is the only part of a product that is easily visible and although all surfaces of the product must be designed well, it is the PDP (primary display panel) that must be the attention grabber. The four top attention grabbers are:

- colour
- physical structure or shape
- symbols and numbers
- product name (typography).

Together, these contribute to brand recognition.

A **barcode** is a code for a product within the market that is individualised to include information on size, colour, dispenser type, brand and price.

A **French lid** has an extended edge beyond the base of the box to increase the surface area of the packaging.

Inner packing refers to the materials or parts used in supporting, positioning or cushioning an item.

TABLE 8.1   PACKAGING ELEMENTS THAT MAY BE REQUIRED

Packaging element	Description
Product descriptor	Copy on a product's label that describes the product contents. Often used as a selling and marketing device along with an inviting, often in situ image of the product.
Ingredients copy	Mandatory information to help consumers identify ingredients they may be allergic to or wish to avoid.
Labels	Die-cut, often self-adhesive applications used to decorate or identify packages.
Net weight	Relates to the weight of the product less the weight of the container
Dosage information	Mandatory information for prescribed and unprescribed medicines that details dosage requirements.
Nutritional information	Mandatory information to be included on the label design; provides a breakdown of all nutritional information in the product.
Unique selling point	The characteristic(s) of the product or service that set it apart from all other products in that category.
Universal Product Code (UPC) or barcode	A printed code on containers and other forms of packaging that provides information about the product for purposes of inventory control and retail pricing.
Violator	A visual device that is used by marketers to draw attention to the product. Usually positioned in a prominent position on the primary display panel and contains a word such as 'new' or 'improved', or another type of special feature of the product or packaging.

Material choice

Material choices for some products are standard—cereal comes in cardboard boxes and plastic bags, tablets come in foil-sealed containers in boxes or plastic containers. This doesn't mean you can't design something new, but unless sales are going to make it worthwhile, few clients will agree to pay for unusual materials for no reason other than that the designer likes it that way!

Generally, material choice consists of plastics (in varieties such as breathing, non-breathing, polystyrene, biodegradable, rigid or flexible), glass, board (coated, unbleached, corrugated fibre board), metals (such as aluminium, steel or tinplate) and wood. There are also many new biodegradable materials used for **inner packing** of products.

From the many options, the designer needs to select the material that is most relevant to the product contents and the pack style. Regulations for some products are so strict that there is no choice of the container. With others it's just common sense—liquids can only be contained in water-resistant membranes and biscuits can't be in a container that breathes or they won't stay crisp.

EXERCISE   Go to a supermarket and gauge how many cereal brands there are. Many of these products are sub-products or subsidiary brands of the master or 'monolithic' brand. List all the brands of cereal that come under the monolithic brand of Kellogg's.

THE IMPORTANCE OF BRANDING AND BRAND POSITIONING

Branding is about perception—of your products, your service, your staff and the way you do business. Brands are the key to getting buyers to purchase a particular product every time, and they rely on **touchpoints**. For some companies, branding is about social status and convincing customers that they can afford a certain lifestyle or that they appreciate luxury. Other brands are built on reliability and trust.

Brands have the power to make consumers identify with a product or a service, and sometimes even to feel that they belong to something important. When you think of the Kraft, Kellogg's and Arnotts brands there are many words that come to mind. These could include, for example, 'trust' (that the product will always be fresh), 'confidence' (that it will always taste the same) and 'assurance' (that food products have been produced hygienically). When you think of the Oxfam brand, you know that when you buy one of their products you are supporting something worthwhile.

↑ The essentials range for Woolworths South Africa is centred on everyday items that represent true value for money without compromising standards.

Designer **FROST* DESIGN**
Client **WOOLWORTHS, SOUTH AFRICA**

Touchpoints are what the consumer visually identifies with the product.

The complexity of brands

Let's look at some of the terminology used to discuss the complexity of brands.

BRAND MANAGEMENT A complex multi-faceted and multi-disciplinary process that affects every aspect of the brand experience, name, identity, mark and communication strategy.

BRAND IDENTITY All the elements, including packaging and advertising, that make up the perception of the brand.

BRAND COMMUNICATION STRATEGY The strategy should take into consideration the design, marketing, communication and human interaction with the brand. Strategies may be short- or long-term and should include measurable goals.

BRAND EXPERIENCE Every contact that a customer has with a brand is a part of the brand experience. The brand experience can also affect the behaviour of the employees in the organisation and can create pride and motivate employees. A high level and continuously positive brand experience creates brand equity.

BRAND IDENTITY The perception of the brand, which can include the logo and all visual elements as well as packaging, signage and advertising.

BRAND MARK The symbol used to identify the product. It could be words, an image, or a combination of both.

BRAND NAME The word used to identify the product by consumers.

BRAND EQUITY The marketable value of the product due to the perception of its worth in the current market.

There is a great deal of social consciousness surrounding packaging. Because of the powerful marketing of brand leaders, own-brand products from supermarkets have a brand image of being less valuable. People may use these brands themselves but are often unwilling to offer them to guests. Often the cheaper own-brand product represents value-for-money, but the overall brand value is much less.

An own-brand product or the redesign of a single product from an existing range should not be designed as an individual item. It has to sit on the shelf as a member of a family of products, so it must retain something of the identity of the existing group. The product can look like part of a family using the brand name and the brand colour. It is anticipated that as own-brand or home-brand products become more popular in Australia, there will be an increase in the levels of perceived quality and more opportunities for designers to rebrand these products.

EXERCISE Think about a brand of computer, magazine or shoe and write down five words that express how you feel about that brand. Now think about Oxfam; if possible, visit one of their shops. Write down five words that express how you feel about Oxfam.

DESIGN REVIEWS AND PRESENTATIONS

Your final design and its presentation to the client are crucial to its acceptance and progression to final manufacture. Clients want to see the presentation of a range of solutions that demonstrate higher-order thinking, experimentation, exploration and analytical skills as well as convincing mock-ups that display not only technical competence but a convincing structural finish of the three-dimensional components of the project. There is nothing more satisfying and convincing than holding the almost-real model.

Final proposal

The final proposal should present a strong idea, displaying the branding with consideration of colours, shape and form. The client can then assess the proposal with the original brief and against the evidence found at the research stage. An assessment will be made as to whether the design process has produced a design that has potential for further development.

General guidelines

Keep in touch with suppliers all the way through the process to ensure that your design doesn't impede the practicality of the product. For example, check with printers that the paisley print of your design will come out on **paperboard** or sheet metal in five different colours in offset printing and that the price will be worth it.

Once the designer has decided on the shape and form of the package, the printer or carton maker creates a die. As discussed in Chapter 6, die-cutting is the use of sharp steel rules to cut material into desired shapes. A die, die form or cutter is a piece of wood that contains creasing and cutting rules that make up the form to die cut or score any given material. The creasing rules are blunt and the cutting rules are sharp. Die-cutting can be done on a flat-bed plate or rotary press. However, laser-cutters are becoming more common due to their accuracy. Dimensions for laser cutting are taken from the designer's Adobe InDesign® or Illustrator® file.

There are many package templates available commercially. You may have to create your own template through trial and error. Some printing companies will create the template for you, working out the type of closure needed to hold the weight of the product and ensure that the **grain** of the board is correct for the **scoring.**

Paperboard (or cardboard) is a material made from laminated layers of paper in sheets of 12 points or more.

Grain is the direction in which the fibres in paper line up.

Scoring refers to the process of making an impression or crease in a box blank to facilitate bending, folding or tearing.

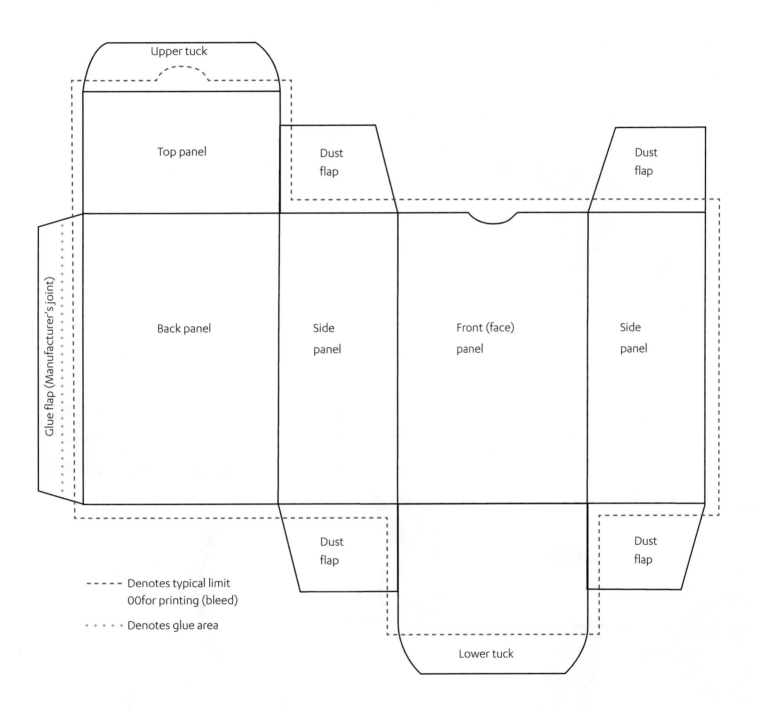

Upper tuck

Top panel

Dust flap

Dust flap

Glue flap (Manufacturer's joint)

Back panel

Side panel

Front (face) panel

Side panel

Dust flap

Dust flap

- - - - Denotes typical limit 00for printing (bleed)

· · · · · Denotes glue area

Lower tuck

EXERCISE   Photocopy the pictured template onto heavy paper (150+ gsm) at different sizes and fold into boxes.

293

UGHT
KE WATER
TAKES ITS
OWN SHAPE
IN THE
HOLLOWS OF
MY MIND

ENVIRONMENT DESIGN:
LEAD THE WAY

In this section, we consider environment design; specifically, the design of wayfinding and exhibition displays.

EARL CARTER

← ↑ The SA Water Headquarters in Adelaide. Frost* Design used large scale super graphics as a major feature on the building facade and foyer stair glazing.

Designer **FROST* DESIGN**
Client **SA WATER**

THE DESIGN PROCESS

Wayfinding systems and exhibition displays have a number of issues in common that must be considered during the design process. Both forms of design must generally be viewed from a distance by people on the move. Whether promotional or instructional, wayfinding and exhibition displays must often comply with a high-level system or format in order to work properly. For example, wayfinding systems can be as broad as a national highway signage protocol, or as narrow as signage for a block of suburban townhouses; either way, the signs need to be easily read by people of all ages, many nationalities and possibly people with physical disabilities that restrict their viewing capability.

Exhibition signage and displays may have fewer limitations than external wayfinding systems. They are often protected from the elements, and therefore materials are not subject to rain and sun damage. Large shopping centres contain good examples of signage and exhibition displays, combining complex signage systems with sophisticated window and merchandise displays. Whichever system is used, it is important to fit the signage or display with the way that people will interact with it.

The briefing

What are your client's goals and expectations? The client may not have investigated or have knowledge of every possibility in relation to the brief. But they usually know what their design problem is and they often know what they are trying to achieve. Make sure you have a clear understanding of their goals. At the same time, question everything: in a time of guerrilla and open-source marketing, clients and the public are beginning to understand that tradition has its limitations and that the competition between **aesthetic** subversion and economic collaboration can bring some interesting results. The most heinous crime is to produce boring design—inevitably it will disappoint the client, and poor and fruitless results are more than a waste of time for you.

Signage and wayfinding systems to consider include:

- street signage—signs stamped out of metal with lettering embossed or printed (or both)
- modular signage—a signage system that consists of pre-designed elementary units
- LED signs (light-emitting diodes technology)
- company identification—information on streets, outside and inside of buildings
- sign systems—design elements that aid orientation within the built environment
- external environment waymarkers—for example, systems that draw motorists to the location of stores or car parks.

Exhibition design may apply to:

- public exhibitions
- installation design
- conferences
- trade shows (display stands for events)
- temporary displays for business, museums, libraries and galleries.

Research and analysis

In the case of wayfinding systems, most of your research will relate to the site and any existing graphic design or architectural elements that you will need to consider. For instance, is the site against a coloured wall? The sky? Set into rock? These backdrops can all affect the structure of your design, and the colours and materials used.

Your research will need to consider a number of questions. For example, what existing information is there, including logos and mandatory requirements, for the site of the wayfinding system? (Existing logos will have parameters involving colour and typography that need to be considered.) Is there an existing style manual? Should the period of design that has influenced the building also influence the typeface used? Is the site constrained for a vertical (portrait) or horizontal (landscape) format?

You need to find out who the user will be. If there are multicultural implications to consider, pictograms can be extremely useful as a communication tool. How do people find your product? Is the product a directional device? In what direction will it face? Prioritising and summarising the research and creating a graphic, visual or text-based portfolio of information will allow you to focus and refine the information. In the analysis you will need to draw conclusions from the research material gathered, and be prepared to voice your professional opinion to your client.

Aesthetic is the philosophical theory of what is beautiful and pleasing in appearance.

CONCEPTS AND STRATEGIES

Once you have ascertained all the parameters for the problem, you can start to develop the concepts. Use brainstorming, and the other techniques for generating ideas discussed in Chapter 2, to find the best solution.

Sketches

Multiple sketches of your ideas are very important, as they convey to the client that you have investigated many different avenues of thought. Clients can't always understand a designer's sketches so make them clear and thorough. You may need to question whether other people understand your concept or message before you show it to your client.

Contextualise the ideas

Show the client the concept in context. Take a photo of the site where the sign, banner or wayfinding system would go, and then Photoshop your design into the image. Creating a photomontage of your ideas in situ is a great way to convince clients—but make sure that the proportions are correct. Don't make the sign, banner or system look bigger or smaller than is intended. The client may be very disappointed on delivery if it's different. Present a range of solutions to the client that demonstrate higher order thinking, experimentation, exploration and analytical skills.

↑ This panorama for the SA water headquarters in Adelaide stretches nearly 40 metres.

Designer **FROST* DESIGN**
Client **SA WATER**

Sophie Tatlow and Bruce Slorach, Deuce Design
www.deucedesign.com.au

Coming together from diverse design backgrounds, including fashion design and design director of Mambo, Bruce Slorach and Sophie Tatlow have created a unique design studio producing solutions for their varied and often illustrious clients.

Deuce Design specialises in signage, branding, strategy, research and copywriting and has completed more than fifty major signage projects, including interpretive, wayfinding and retail programs. The studio has a reputation for producing projects that are both contemporary and culturally significant, from graphics for public domain and environmental design to branding, print, web, fashion, fabric and lighting.

Collaboration with designers and architects across numerous disciplines plays a large part in Deuce's creative process. The studio endeavours to maintain a small team to nurture creativity and preserve integrity, securing the best client and team outcomes.

Some of the many wayfinding and environmental projects created by Deuce include: Bondi Beach coastal signage; Ballast Point Park, Balmain; interpretive and wayfinding signage for the Australian Railway Monument, Werris Creek,; and signage, strategy and interpretation for the former Water Police Park.

The design thinking behind much of the studio's solutions is that by providing good, clear wayfinding, you are inspiring confidence and hopefully calm to the intended audience. 'Good wayfinding is the science of information and considers access points in sequence, logistics, rational pathways and consistency of information. The nature of the information may not be emotional but the way it's conveyed graphically appeals to the emotions,' explains Sophie.

'Imagine driving down the street, visiting a museum or major art gallery without signs. We are regularly commissioned to do interpretive and wayfinding signage to guide and inform across all cultural landscapes. Good signage systems are essential for conveying messages, information and adding to the "sense of place".'

ABOVE LEFT AND OPPOSITE PAGE LEFT | Combining multiple methods for signage at the Former BP Site. Metal, printing and spray paint add to the user experience.

ABOVE RIGHT | Letterforms punched out of metal create an extra level of design when the sculptural signage casts a shadow at Ballast Point Park, Sydney.

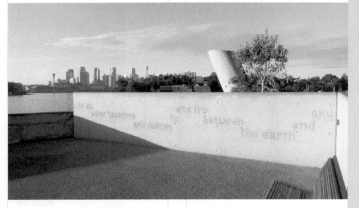

In some instances, combining a map with wayfinding systems means the viewer is able to quickly extract spatial information, which Sophie says is a powerful navigation aid. 'If there's a number of signs and a large area to cover, they're vital.'

With many wayfinding and signage installations needing to stand up to Australia's changing extremes of weather, Deuce must consider every material used to increase the lifecycle. 'We use vitreous enamel as often as we can because of its 20-year-plus lifespan, and it's beautiful and robust. If the client has the budget, we recommend vitreous enamel because of its resilience to the elements, and it's slightly tougher when it comes to vandalism. It's more expensive than other materials but you get what you pay for.'

The studio has designed many external systems from Bondi Beach to Balmain to Royal Randwick Racecourse. Vandalism is probably the greatest threat to external signage. 'It's very difficult to design a sign that is vandal-proof, if someone has the intention to destroy a sign; it's almost impossible to prevent them.'

ABOVE RIGHT | Words cleverly integrated into the cement walls at Ballast Point Park, Sydney.

DESIGN REVIEWS

It is a good idea to stop at this point and review all the different criteria that impact on the end product before the final design is completed. Use this review to make sure that the treatment of typography, symbols and the hierarchy of information are carefully considered.

Symbols as a unique design language

Some designers believe that symbols, like the alphabet, can be learned like any other language, through education and constant use. These designers have worked to establish a set of symbols that are meant to be learned over a period of time, based on iconography recognised through years of cultural tradition. These symbols are usually not the only primary design object in a scheme and are used with text, arrows and colour information.

Other designers feel too constrained by a rigid standard of symbols, shapes, sizes and positions. They feel that symbols can be used to mix a universal language into design work that incorporates landmarks and unique aspects of the site. These designers enhance the use of universal symbols by modifying them to meet specific project needs.

Guidelines for symbol use

Are there too many symbols? There is no optimum maximum or minimum number. The site of the signage and the limitations of the viewer should be guiding factors. For example, road signs should be kept to a minimum as drivers need to read them while in motion.

Are the symbols easy to remember? Generic services, activities and regulations are often already a part of an established system so it's best not to stray too far from these designs. Site-specific symbols are best when designed using familiar images; they are then easier to understand and remember. Try not to use arbitrary images—it helps if the symbol is readily identifiable so that users can not only remember the symbol but also describe it easily in words.

Can the user read the symbols? The visibility and readability of a symbol depends on a number of factors including form, size, viewing distance, lighting, colour and contrast. When a symbol is abstracted it may lose its clarity, and meaning will become blurred. Symbols should be used to communicate, not decorate, as meaningless decoration will confuse the user.

Do the symbols say the right thing in the right way? The goal is to communicate easily to the user. As with words, symbols can have many levels of meaning or they can direct, identify and inform with clarity. Clever designers who achieve a wayfinding system that visually expresses and supports the location, culture and history while communicating clearly to the user have crafted their design for maximum value and effectiveness.

← Courts and other public facilities are used by a large number of people. Signage that can be read by people at many levels, including those people who have a low proficiency in English, or people with a physical or visual disability, is an important component of the wayfinding system.

Designer **TURNER DESIGN**
Client **MULTIPLEX CONSTRUCTIONS PTY LTD**

Hierarchy of needs

It is important to ensure that the system responds to the hierarchy of needs and decisions. What is most important in terms of information? How will you communicate this? Work with your client to create the best solution. Though this may entail many meetings, it ensures that the end result is a true solution to the design problem. The final design should never be a surprise to the client. By working together you have the expertise, knowledge, experience and agreement to develop the process.

Identify key decision points

- Does the signage system need to be displayed outside?
- Is there an existing corporate identity or do you need to create one?
- Does the system need certain colours, type, photography, other company logos or to be a certain size?
- Will the light at this site affect the signage and its readability?
- Are there different cultural limitations on the project?
- Have you considered all potential users, including children (height implications), the elderly (sight and hearing implications), and people with vision or hearing-impairment, or physical disability (wheelchair access)?

Final design refinement

After you have agreed with your client on the approach to take, you will need to finalise your design. This involves final sketches of each and every element. You may also need to produce models, plans and elevations of the design. You will need to produce a draft schedule for client review and consult with suppliers (such as a printer, signage contractor or environmental architect) on budget and buildability of your designs.

You may need to submit your design to the local council or Heritage Council (for heritage listed buildings). These local government bodies make decisions on whether signage is appropriate and meets their requirements. There are also various safety regulations that must be considered. You may need to work with other designers who have already created a framework for any future designs. Previous creative input by interior designers, architects and entertainment designers should be respected. Collaborate where possible to achieve the best result for your client.

Production choices

New techniques and materials for environmental systems are being created continually. Trade shows are a great way to learn about new systems, materials and production methods. Collaborate with suppliers and manufacturers to find out what's available and how it can be used to your advantage. Visit trade shows in your state or visit trade magazine websites to keep up to date.

General guidelines

Most large projects require putting together tender documentation requesting quotes from suppliers or manufacturers. You will need to give the suppliers mock-ups and drawings that convey your design intent. These must be clear or the supplier may misinterpret specifications such as the dimensions, required materials or positioning, which will impact on the accuracy of the quote. Once you receive the tenders, select the best two, not the cheapest, and check with each of those suppliers to make sure that what they promise is achievable within the time period given by the client.

← ↑ Tactile alphabet signage at Sydney Park is designed to include children and carers of all abilities as well as encourage learning. A tight budget pushed the design team to create new and interesting responses to the brief.

Designer **FROST* DESIGN**
Client **CITY OF SYDNEY**

DESIGN EVALUATION AND PRODUCTION CHECKLIST

You can test your design in two different ways: by evaluating prototypes at different stages of the process, and by evaluating some key elements after installation.

Prototypes of signage will need to be created to communicate with the client and your suppliers; you can then seek feedback from external people (i.e. people outside of the project team) to test whether the prototypes are achieving desired outcomes. If they are not, you won't necessarily need to change the entire design approach, but you will need to adjust aspects of the signage.

Post-installation testing may seem like a waste of time, but it is necessary to constantly evaluate the success of the project, particularly as other environmental components change. For example, before installation, you may have found that the colour of the type needs to change because under certain light it can no longer be read; then post-installation, you may discover that the height of the signs is fine when there are no people in the exhibition, but when it is crowded the signs are obstructed and thus need to be moved.

Final design evaluation

In coming to a final evaluation of your finished design, ask yourself the following questions. Does your completed design:

- ❯ communicate the appropriate message to the user
- ❯ display conceptualisation, development and execution
- ❯ display technical competence in the execution of typography and branding components
- ❯ comply with the client's needs and the brief
- ❯ present the design solution to its best advantage?

Is your project:

- ❯ completed by the due date
- ❯ completed to a professionally satisfactory standard?

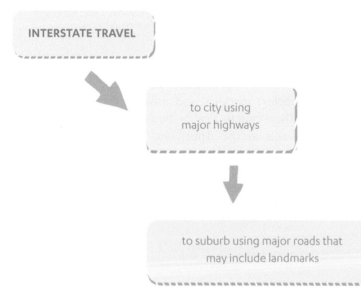

INTERSTATE TRAVEL

to city using
major highways

to suburb using major roads that
may include landmarks

to street using a complex
series of turns and instructions
that may include landmarks

to house using number and
perhaps house description

 EXERCISE Think about the hierarchy of needs in explaining to someone how to get to your home from another state (see the flowchart above). Reflect this concept in terms of a signage system. Could some details be communicated through symbols?

DESIGN BRIEF 1: DESIGN A BRAND

 Design and promote a product with attention to the identity/brand.

1. Identify the requirements of the brief.

2. Choose from one product range listed below and develop a timeline and five products or branding variations.

3. Develop a promotional strategy by producing a poster or other promotional item to introduce your new product to consumers.

4. Present your product range in a presentation box (could be a point-of-sale item).

Product choice (select either Revive or Renew)

Organic tea

Product name: REVIVE

    Organic Black Tea chai

    Organic Green Light Tea

    Organic Moroccan Mint Tea

    Organic Cape Rooibos Tea

Create a mock-up range of 20 g sachet designs, packet of 10 and packet of 100 (use different sizes of the template on page 293).

Cosmetic products

Product name: RENEW

    Jasmine Bath Oil

    Moroccan Rose Otto Bath Oil

    Seaweed and Sage Shower Wash

    Rosewood and Chamomile Soap

    Mayblossom Balancing Facial Wash—Combination

Create a mock-up range of bath oil, shower wash, soap and facial wash, keeping in mind the continuity of design across the range.

Consider

1. Where will these products be sold?

2. What primary and secondary information will you need to include on the packs—weight, ingredients, nutritional information, and so on?

3. What type of materials production techniques will you use?

DESIGN BRIEF 2: RESEARCH AND ANALYSIS

 Develop your fact-finding and report-writing skills.

Prepare a research report that expands your understanding of brand management. Focus on one large organisation that utilises brand management as a major function of its business processes and sight references to the selected company in your document. The selected organisation should advertise in print and to the wider public in other media (e.g. TV)—in other words be highly visible. Designers should ensure that the layout of the pages reflects the information in the report (see Chapter 5). Examples of companies include Kraft, Kellogg's, Dove, Apple.

Develop an understanding of brand management:

1. Research and analyse all points of contact with a brand.

2. Describe the brand experience.

3. Investigate the influence of advertising, design and media commentary.

4. Explain what triggers a consumer's reaction to brands.

5. Identify the expectations by the consumer behind the brand experience.

6. Identify the components of a brand management strategy including a logo, fonts, specified colours, symbols, sounds, ideas and personality.

DESIGN BRIEF 3: COMPLETE A SIGN OR WAYFINDING AUDIT

 Go to a large building, park or shopping complex and complete a wayfinding system audit. Sketch or photograph different aspects of the system and write down your findings.

1. Take into consideration the use of colours, logos, symbols, hierarchy within the system and numbering systems.

2. Assess whether the system highlights the culture of the site or is unrelated to the other built/architectural aspects. Does the system extend the brand experience in a positive way?

3. Document your first experience in the environment.

4. If you are analysing a wayfinding system, take yourself on a journey and judge if you can easily understand the designer's code or system.

5. Does the system anticipate change by allowing flexibility?

Collate all your information and images into a document that is a complete analysis.

SUMMARY

Designers use the same design process to create three-dimensional designs as a digital design or a paper-based product. The difference with three-dimensional design is that consideration must be given to the view of the medium from different angles, in different lights and landscapes, and by people with different needs. There is strict legislation governing food and pharmaceutical packaging and in some circumstances wayfinding systems can be strictly controlled by local councils and other legislative bodies. To some designers these controls can be a nuisance while others find them a challenge.

Whether or not you enjoy the challenge of three-dimensional design, there is no doubt that the ability to design in three dimensions will add to your repertoire of design capabilities when applying for a position in a design studio.

KEY TERMS

REFERENCES / WEBSITES

Berger, CM 2005, *Wayfinding: designing and implementing graphic navigational systems*, Rotovision, Mies, Switzerland.

Denison, E 2006, *More packaging prototypes*, Rotovision, Mies, Switzerland.

Fawcett-Tang, R 2008, *Mapping graphic navigational systems*, Rotovision, Mies, Switzerland.

Gordon, SK 2005, *Packaging makeovers: graphic design for market change*, Rockport Publishers, Minneapolis, MN.

Hampshire, M & Stephenson, K 2007, *Packaging: design successful packaging for specific customer groups*, Rotovision, Mies, Switzerland.

Klimchuk, MR & Krasovec, SA 2006, *Packaging design: successful branding from concept to shelf*, John Wiley and Sons Inc, Hoboken.

Olins, W 2008, *The brand handbook*, Thames and Hudson, London.

Terstiege, G (ed) 2009, *Three D: graphic spaces*, Birkhauser, Basel.

Demo Design (*www.demodesign.com.au*)

chapter 9

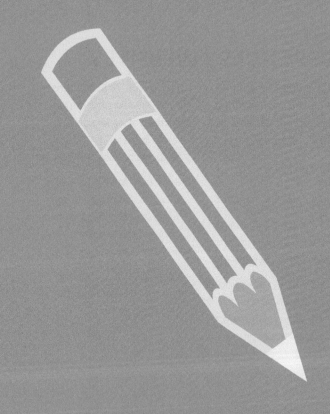

STUDYING AND BEYOND

09

INTRODUCTION

So far in this book we have looked at the design side of being a graphic designer; in this chapter, we introduce the other aspect of working as a designer—the business side. The business side of working as a graphic designer is no less important than the design side: it plays a crucial role in getting work, behaving professionally and getting paid.

→ You need to gather your best
work to capture a design studio's
attention.

Designer **BRENT WOODS**

THE BUSINESS SIDE OF DESIGN

Many graphic design students focus heavily on producing a portfolio of their work. Once the portfolio is complete, there is often only a vague idea about how it should be used to promote the designer and secure them a job in a design studio or work from clients. In this chapter we will discuss 'designing' the portfolio so that it can be a used as a true marketing tool. The bulk of the chapter, however, is about what happens next. We discuss working at the lower levels of the design industry and how designers are expected to behave ethically.

Many designers prefer to work for themselves. It has been estimated that up to half of all designers will only ever work for themselves as the 'hired gun' called a freelancer. Others will work for a studio before eventually setting up a studio of their own. The second half of this chapter deals with issues associated with working for yourself, from working out how much to charge to setting up a business. You may feel that you only want to work as an employee of a design studio; however, even if this is the case, understanding a little of the business side of design will help you progress to more senior positions within a design business.

You will notice that the language and terms used in this chapter are more business-related than design-related. Do not be intimidated by these new concepts: as mentioned in the section on portfolios overleaf, the theme of this chapter can be approached as a design problem. The language used and outcomes may be different—financial success as opposed to creative success—but the approach is essentially the same.

Establishing a successful design business involves the following steps:

- develop your brief—in this context, a 'business plan'
- do your research—talk to experts, lawyers, accountants, experienced designers
- develop your solution—this includes working out cost structures and a business structure
- implement your design—register your business and start trading
- review—revisit regularly your business plan and systems for tracking business health.

You can see now that the problem-solving skills so necessary in design work actually serve the designer well in setting up a business. In fact, business experts are starting to realise this: they are studying the way designers think and operate in order to develop new models for the way all businesses might be run.

So, fear not and read on.

DESIGN PORTFOLIOS

Before creating your own design portfolio, ask yourself a few questions: What sort of portfolio should I create? How will prospective employers and clients view my work? Will I be with them when they view my work or will it have to stand on its own without any verbal input?

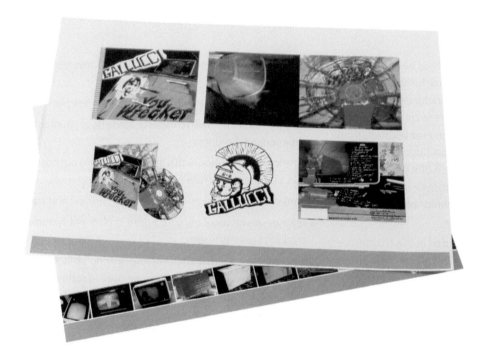

SUZIE HADDOCK

Some designers believe that with a high level of competition in the industry, being the best isn't enough— you have to leave a lasting impression by providing a portfolio that is different and surprising. To do this you have to make sure that you are showing your portfolio to the right person, which means someone who is senior enough to make a decision. You should also be clear on your intent with the portfolio and able to articulate why you made every decision—such as choice of colour, type, layout and grid.

You need to plan how you will achieve your goal. If you want to work in a particular studio, will you call by phone first? Email your contact and send a follow-up email in a couple of weeks? Find out if they take on work experience participants or interns? Turn up at the studio and leave an example of your work? Which strategy will work best?

↖ *Not all portfolios are contained in black presentation folders. In fact, most designers try to avoid this style of display. Instead they create a portfolio that shows their style and individuality. This portfolio consists of separate A3 cards that are interchangeable, depending on the client.*

EXERCISE

CREATE A DIGITAL PORTFOLIO
Number of pieces: approximately 10 of your best work. Use standard screen dimensions when choosing page size. Remember that images need not have greater resolution than 72 dpi. Include your name and contact details in the portfolio so that interested people can contact you.

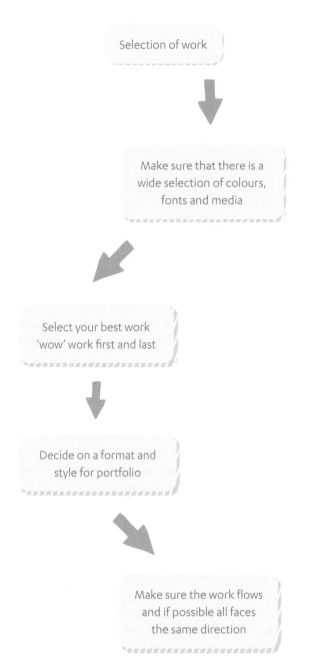

Selection of work

↓

Make sure that there is a
wide selection of colours,
fonts and media

↙

Select your best work
'wow' work first and last

↓

Decide on a format and
style for portfolio

↘

Make sure the work flows
and if possible all faces
the same direction

↑ The flow of work in a portfolio and the look of the portfolio says a lot about the creator. Having dog-eared corners or dirty fingerprints indicates a lack of care or no eye for detail. Showing your best work at the front creates interest in the viewer. Always finish with a great piece to leave a lasting impression.

Set yourself a brief to fulfil the needs of this portfolio, outlining what are you trying to achieve and who your target market is. Run through the design process to make sure that you stay on track.

Because clients are always looking for solutions to their problems, a prospective employer will want to know how you devised a solution to a specific problem. Problems come in the form of design briefs or assessment exercises and your solution to these problems manifests itself in completed projects. Your solution will indicate to the client or employer how you decided to solve the problem. They will want to know what process you used, so provide a succinct caption with each project in your portfolio and be ready to explain your thinking during the interview. They will judge how well the solution works by analysing your idea and the finished result of the project.

PORTFOLIO DESIGN

Your portfolio is a reflection of your personality and your skills—it is your communication tool. Studios want to employ designers who are clean and tidy, but most of all who have good layout skills and innovative ideas.

It is a good idea to get someone who can give you a constructive and objective opinion on the work to look over your portfolio. Make sure the pieces you choose provide a broad spectrum of examples of your work, but don't hesitate to put in more than one of any medium. Employers will want to know that a junior designer hasn't just fluked a good end result and that he or she can create great design projects consistently.

If you have completed projects with a group of people, be prepared to explain to a prospective employer your role in the group. This is very important as commercial jobs are rarely completed by just one person. An ability to work with a group to complete a successful project shows that you have learnt how to negotiate. Good design outcomes often require strong negotiation skills, and the ability to communicate your ideas or to accept that someone else's ideas may be better.

Guidelines: you can create a portfolio with a navigation bar and lots of pages or use one long page that can be scrolled to see work. Consider the format of the pages, the size of the type, the flow of imagery and the resolution of all images. Your portfolio should begin and end with the best examples of your work.

Try to differentiate between your favourite pieces and the projects that really answered the brief. Talk through how you collaborated with the client to come up with the best solution to their individual business problem.

Don't forget that the portfolio itself is an example of your work. This is why we suggest you write yourself a brief. Treat it like a real design job. It is a piece of communication worthy of all your design skills and should be at least as good as the work you are presenting.

You should also consider a portfolio website. This is a very useful tool for print designers and is absolutely essential for interactive media designers. Portfolio websites have a number of advantages:

- They are easily accessible and prospective clients and employers can view them at any time. Many of both groups use Google to find designers so make sure the site is registered with this search engine.
- More material can be included on a website than in the other forms of portfolio.
- Once set up, they are very cheap to maintain and keep up-to-date.

Interactive media designers, particularly web designers should have no trouble setting up a portfolio website, but print designers may have more difficulty. However, there are many low-cost package options, such as blogs, that can be used. The important thing is that your site incorporates a **content management system** that allows it to be easily updated.

MARKETING YOURSELF

What is the purpose of the portfolio? Put simply, it is to market yourself. Many designers find this very difficult to do, but it is essential to getting a job with an existing firm or to winning new clients.

In Australia, it is generally not considered good form for graphic designers to advertise. Designers usually get work by **referral** ('word-of-mouth') and by **cold calling**. The portfolio is essential in each of these approaches, leading, if successful, to an employer or client looking at your work and talking to you directly.

The process of winning jobs or clients is hard work and should not be treated flippantly. There are many other designers out there and it is up to you to demonstrate why you should be given a job over another designer. Put real effort into designing your portfolio (hardcopy, digital and website). Doing this will help you to understand what makes you unique as a designer. This is essential to winning work.

If you are approached for design work, research the employer or client before meeting with them, and don't be late. If you are cold calling, again, do your research. Find out as much as you can about each prospect before you approach them, as this is the only way you will be able to find out what they might need of you.

Marketing yourself is a career-long task and you will receive many more knock-backs than wins. This is part of being a designer in the commercial world. Winning new work will always remain a deeply satisfying experience, as it is a true validation of you, the designer. Approach each new employer or client as an exciting new journey.

A **content management system (CMS)** is a restricted-access part of a website that allows the content of the site to be updated without accessing the basic structure of the site.

A **referral** is when an employer or client is told about a designer by a third party and approaches them directly. This is also known as 'word-of-mouth'.

↑ Promotional pieces that have been designed as course work can be used for self-promotion when contacting studios.

Design **ST GEORGE COLLEGE, SYDNEY INSTITUTE, TAFE NSW DESIGN STUDENTS**

A CUSTOMISABLE PORTFOLIO
As you complete the process of creating a portfolio, aim to have several customisable versions. You will able to select from a larger body of your work to finetune a portfolio depending on the prospective employer or client you are talking to. This may seem like a lot of unnecessary work but it is not. It is the right way to proceed.

Cold calling is when a designer (after researching them) contacts an employer or client who doesn't know that designer and arranges an interview to show their work.

Frost* Design

www.frostdesign.com.au

From Vince Frost's arrival in Australia in 2003, when he was partnered with Gary Emery, to his current much-lauded Frost* Design agency, Vince's passion for design and his adventurous spirit have given him a reputation as one of the most playful creative directors today. Having built Frost* Design in both Sydney and London, Vince has a thorough understanding of studio dynamics and the importance of hiring the right person for the job. Here, he imparts some of the knowledge he has gained over the years.

Frost* Design is the realisation of a long-held dream, and has a diverse and talented team of 30–35 people. In Australia, the business covers print, branding, environmental, multimedia, motion, broadcast and much more for iconic Australian clients such as the Sydney Opera House, Sydney Dance Company, Qantas and the Australian Institute of Architects, along with many international clients.

With such a prestigious portfolio and inspiring hunger for design, Frost* Design receives hundreds of applications from both Australian and international design graduates each week. Vince says the calibre of applications varies and they do try to review them all. However, he is most attracted to applicants who go the extra mile, whose work is presented well and is unique in the sea of PDF portfolios that flood his inbox. Vince says, 'You can tell the thinkers by the expression of their work when they are confident in their abilities.' Applicants are let down by their impersonal approach, mass emails and generic letters.

Arrogance is the number one no-no when approaching a potential employer. 'You need to understand that you will never stop learning, you have your entire life in front of you so take your time. You don't have to have all the answers right now, but that doesn't mean you should lack ambition,' says Vince.

Once you do have your foot in the door, it is important to work within the creative team. To be indispensable you need to be fluent in all the tools of the trade. As Vince puts it, 'you need to be a very useful pair of hands', which means being able to use InDesign®, Photoshop®, Illustrator®, 3-D programs and so on. Being able to pitch in and work quickly to deadlines is integral.

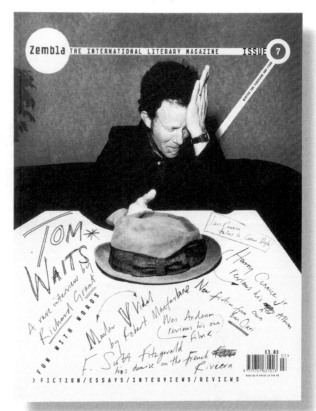

FROST* DESIGN

FROST* DESIGN

FROST* DESIGN

FROST* DESIGN

Vince also feels that drawing is a valuable skill to bring to studio work: being able to sketch out design concepts and understand perspective allows you to visualise your ideas quickly.

Equally essential skills for recent graduates are accuracy, doing things well and learning the standard of design produced in the studio, as well as communication. Graphic design juniors will often need to communicate with senior designers, account mangers and, on occasion, clients. This means they need to be articulate and confident.

Vince believes that energy brought to the studio by young people is vital—they are a positive and valuable element—and he encourages them to ask questions, learn and, most of all, get excited about design and the work they are creating. Vince provides an induction process for junior designers, which includes pairing them with a senior member of the team in order to provide mentoring to aid the integration of studio and work life.

Approaching potential employers and settling into studio work are two challenges that a recent graduate will face; although it will be a trial, it is important to remember to never lose the hunger to learn, or the passion for design.

OPPOSITE PAGE | Covers of *Zembla* magazine, published five times a year and designed and art directed by Frost* Design.

ABOVE | Cover and internal spread for the book *The Last Magazine*, published by Rizzoli International Publications.
BELOW | Promotional brochure for Central Park urban village development.

FROST* DESIGN

THE REAL WORLD OF COMMERCIAL DESIGN

When starting out in the world of commercial design, the process of approaching potential clients and employers can be difficult. However, a well-developed portfolio with supporting promotional material will help aspiring designers to make their first contact. The most important point to remember is: make sure you are contacting studios who create work in your field of knowledge. That is, don't contact a company that specialises in print design if you hate producing print-ready design projects.

WORK EXPERIENCE

If you are seeking a work experience placement, be clear about your availability and what you hope to achieve. It is likely that you will have to compromise, but if you can communicate your goals, then the employer will know whether the work experience program can be managed. It is highly recommended that students get work experience early in their design course if possible. Working in a studio on real projects helps to put information gained at a tertiary level into context.

Work experience is not paid and, depending on your level of experience, you will generally be given fairly menial jobs. This could include anything from getting coffee for the rest of the staff in the studio to deep etching 40 Photoshop files. The more enthusiasm and effort you put into the work, the more studio managers will be able to assess your potential and give you the opportunity to work on larger and more important projects. Work experience could last a week or six months—that is an agreement that you make with the studio. Many designers start out in studios this way.

INTERNSHIPS

Many large design studios now offer internships that enable students to sample the studio environment. Some internships are paid and some are voluntary. Internships are usually based on a set period of time after which the best interns may be asked to continue with the studio. Try to find out what the studio hopes to achieve from the internship—if they are creating positions to give students a taste of the industry but they have no intention of hiring anyone at the end of the internship period, you should be made aware of this.

Although there may not be the promise of a position at the end of the internship, these placements can still be a valuable experience. Make sure that you get a letter of reference and an agreed contact who will speak to any future employers. The design industry is a thriving community and networks of people talk across the country—word travels about good young designers.

It is important to work quickly and provide quality work and acknowledge that everyone in a design team brings different experiences, skills, knowledge and abilities to the studio.

YOUR FIRST FREELANCE JOB

Your first freelance jobs will probably come in the form of friends' business cards and flyers. Every job gives you experience, but free jobs are usually more difficult than paid jobs because your 'client' may want to make endless changes as they are not being charged. It is difficult to freelance on big projects if you haven't had any studio experience, mainly because charging clients for work is an art in itself and understanding how long a specific design job is going to take can be difficult to judge for an inexperienced designer.

Always discuss payment at the first meeting or in a follow-up email straight after the first meeting. You might think that discussing payment is difficult with someone you don't know, but it can get harder the longer you leave it. Misunderstandings are the greatest

Freelance work involves working for different companies at different times rather than being permanently employed by one company.

On the image:

A
FLOWER
FOR
THE
PEOPLE
A
BOUQUET
TO
THE
CITY

Live in Central Park and enjoy an entirely fresh take on the inner-city. Here, past and future entwine to provide a rich experience of urban village life. Come home to an urban village where a green ethos delivers the exhilarating sensation of being surrounded by nature in the midst of a global city.

CLIENT MEETINGS
Make sure when you go to see your client for the first time that you take a pen and paper and you arrive five minutes before the scheduled meeting time. Take your portfolio, ensuring that its contents reflect the sort of work that the client is looking for.

↗ Working in an established studio can give you the opportunity to work with clients and on projects you may not experience as a fledgling freelance designer.

Designer **FROST* DESIGN**
Client **FRASERS PROPERTY**

cause of conflict in business relationships, so make sure all communication is clear and concise. See the section 'Getting paid', below, for more on the business and money side of design.

Establish a professional business relationship by following up all discussions with a confirmation email or phone call. Text messages can be used to confirm meeting times and places, but most business communication is still done by email.

Make sure that you have an email address that is simple and businesslike. Keep your funny email address for your friends.

↓ Each year Hero Print creates a
promotional kit to send to clients.

Designer
HERO PRINT

SO YOU WANT TO WORK IN A LARGE DESIGN STUDIO?

When you work for a studio you can expect to:

· be treated with respect

· have your creative input respected commensurate with your skill level

· be able to ask for help and gain knowledge from more senior designers

· receive an employment contract

· be paid a fair wage regularly (including superannuation) for the hours you work.

In return, you would be expected to:

· work for a certain number of hours per day

· abide by the terms of your employment contract

· respect your coworkers commensurate with their level within the company

· contribute positively to the success of the studio by working hard and being involved with any social aspects of the studio

· actively improve your skills and knowledge of design.

THE DESIGN STUDIO

Design studios tend to be structured in one of two ways. The first is where the owner becomes a manager and delegates everything to his or her employees. The second is where the designer runs the studio and completes all of the administrative work. The second can become difficult if the studio takes on many employers as working with staff gets more and more complicated.

Some studios foster a relaxed, open and fun atmosphere while others are more studious and formal. Quite often the atmosphere is reflected in the type of work, the purpose of the projects and the clients of the design studio. If you have to concentrate intently with no noise to create good design, then a more relaxed studio may not be right for you.

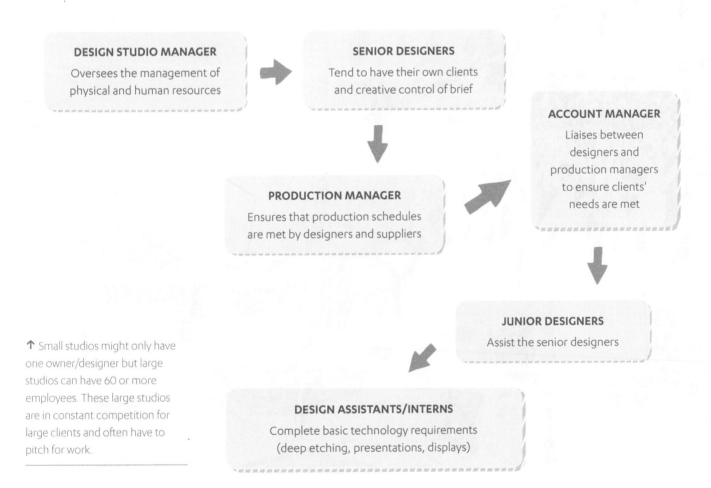

DESIGN STUDIO MANAGER
Oversees the management of physical and human resources

SENIOR DESIGNERS
Tend to have their own clients and creative control of brief

ACCOUNT MANAGER
Liaises between designers and production managers to ensure clients' needs are met

PRODUCTION MANAGER
Ensures that production schedules are met by designers and suppliers

JUNIOR DESIGNERS
Assist the senior designers

DESIGN ASSISTANTS/INTERNS
Complete basic technology requirements (deep etching, presentations, displays)

↑ Small studios might only have one owner/designer but large studios can have 60 or more employees. These large studios are in constant competition for large clients and often have to pitch for work.

→ ↓ Custom graphics adorn the
studio walls of Melbourne-based
design company Canyon

A **free pitch** is when a client
approaches a number of design
firms and asks them to provide
detailed solutions to a brief. The
client then selects what they
feel to be the best solution. The
winning firm/designer gets to
complete the job, the others go
away hungry.

ETHICS

Behaving ethically is always important.
In the main, it is just about being honest.

ETHICS AND THE DESIGNER

Setting up a studio can be expensive, so there is a strong temptation to use pirated or illegally downloaded software (and fonts). A properly financed design studio (including that of a freelancer) should not have to consider this option. If it is necessary to go down this path, then questions should be asked about how financially viable the studio actually is. If there is a belief in the studio that it is all right to do this, then questions might also be asked about what other unethical behaviours are occurring.

Ethical behaviour for the designer means not stealing the design work of others. This does not mean that you should avoid looking at the work of others for fear of copying inadvertently. Just be honest with yourself: if you find yourself copying too closely, question whether you have the right solution. It is very rare that a design solution for one problem actually solves another exactly as well. Behaving ethically also means giving credit where credit is due by acknowledging when others have contributed to work, including other designers, photographers and so on.

Ethical behaviour also means charging a fair price for the work you are doing.

Unethical behaviour will eventually be found out, and it will be talked about among others in the design industry. Behaving unethically is a guaranteed way of ruining a reputation.

FREE PITCHING AND CROWD SOURCING

We have to assume that clients will behave ethically, and of course the vast majority do. They will hire a designer to do a job for an agreed some of money, and if the job is delivered as expected they will pay. However, there are two client-driven behaviours that you should avoid, as they involve you doing work for free: these are **free pitching** and **crowd sourcing**.

In both free pitching and crowd sourcing, the client has asked the designer to work for nothing. Work done for nothing is unlikely to be highly valued by the client. If the designer wins the job, often they can't charge directly for the work done. This means they have to recoup the costs by overcharging on other work or, worse still, they are forced to overcharge other clients. It is clear that free pitching and crowd sourcing can force the designer into a position of behaving unethically.

By free pitching or becoming involved in crowd sourcing, not only is the designer devaluing their own work, they are effectively devaluing the work of every other designer too. For this reason in particular, the Australian Graphic Design Association (www.agda.com.au) is strenuously opposed to these activities.

Crowd sourcing is when a client put a job on the internet (there are a number of dedicated sites) and allows anyone to submit a solution. The client then selects what they feel to be the best solution. The winning firm/designer gets to complete the job, the others go away hungry.

FONT LICENSING
When designers purchase fonts, they are actually only purchasing a licence to use them. They do not actually own the font. The licence may be to use that font on a certain number of computers and/or print devices. Designers cannot claim them as their own, sell them for a profit or even give them to a client.

FREE PITCH COPYRIGHT
Usually unsuccessful winners of free pitches, crowd sourcing and design competitions retain ownership of their work, meaning they can use it for another job. However, increasingly this is not the case, with additional conditions demanding the designer hand over ownership of the work as well. This is truly working for nothing and shows a profound disrespect for design.

DESIGN COMPETITIONS

Design competitions are another method whereby clients get designers to work without payment. In fact, the designer often needs to pay to submit work. Design competitions are usually associated with very high profile jobs, with an exhibition of short-listed entries. There may be considerable kudos in being on the short list, and the design work will be seen by many people. Nevertheless, a designer needs to consider carefully whether the amount of work required and the unbillable cost to produce it will translate into enough work from other clients.

COPYRIGHT AND INTELLECTUAL PROPERTY

Copyright and intellectual property (IP) are two different things. Copyright determines who has the right to use and reproduce a design. Intellectual property, on the other hand, has to do with the actual ideas, the creativity, that have gone into the design. Both come into existence automatically as soon as a design exists; however, copyright cannot be registered, it can only be assigned to a person or organisation. IP can be registered and is theoretically much easier to protect by law.

Copyright ownership for designers can be complicated. If the design was created for any government or even semi-government body, then copyright is automatically assigned to that body. If a design was created for a private individual or company, the copyright generally stays with the designer (or the designer's employer if the design firm they work for was commissioned to do the design). However, the designer may only have copyright over parts of the work. If there is text involved, then the author of the text may retain copyright of the text, while a photographer may retain copyright over any images used (if they were not specifically commissioned for the job). Many clients may insist that copyright be assigned to them; in such cases, designers have to decide if they will allow this (it may cost them the job) and how much extra they will charge for the reassignment. Assignment of copyright should be determined in writing before a designer starts on a job—it should outline exactly what is being assigned, when the transfer is to occur (usually at the end of a job) and for how long (it may be indefinitely, or for a number of years).

IP as a concept sounds simple: you had an idea, it is yours to own or sell. Actually, it is more complex than that. The designer must be able to demonstrate that the idea is truly original, which can be challenging. For example, for an MP3 player, the external visual design may be able to be registered for IP while the internal functions may not, because they are not sufficiently original. Another example might the Qantas logo, where the shape of the kangaroo might be sufficiently original to register for IP, as might the word Qantas, being a unique spelling. The letterforms are probably sufficiently customised to be registered as well, but the actual letters Q A N T A S cannot be registered. It is possible to tell when a design has been registered because it will have an ® or a TM symbol™ next to it.

EXERCISE Go to the websites for AGDA and The Australian Copyright Council (see tip box above). Download and read the documents mentioned. Write a summary on the articles. What information is given? How does it effect you as a designer?

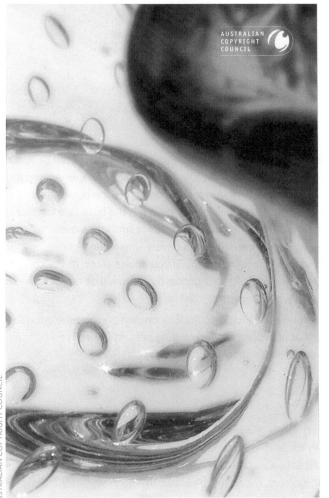

Graphic designers & copyright

B131v01

DESIGN COPYRIGHT

It is a myth that a designer can take an existing design, change it by some low percentage (like 10 per cent) and then assert copyright over the modified design. If you are asked by a client to modify an existing design, ascertain who owns copyright and get permission to do so. If it is refused then you will need to have a discussion with your client.

BROCHURES ON COPYRIGHT

The Australian Graphic Design Association (AGDA, www.agda.com.au) has a very good brochure on the subject entitled *Protect Your Creative*. The Australian Copyright Council (www.copyright.org.au) also has a couple of information sheets about copyright entitled *Ownership of Copyright* (Info sheet G58) and *Owners of Copyright: How to Find* (Info sheet G51).

 For further reading on copyright and intellectual property in Australia, see the Australian Copyright Council's publication, *Graphic Designers & Copyright: a Practical Guide* by Libby Baulch.

↑ Logos, both graphic marks (like the kangaroo here) and word marks ('QANTAS') are the most common items to register as trademarks. Even so, only portions of the actual design may be able to be registered.

One of the reasons we all become designers, rather than artists, is that we have decided we would like to get a regular stable income from being creative. The key to this is the contract between the designer and client.

If you are working as an employee for a design studio much of what follows may seem irrelevant. However, it is always a good idea to keep informed of general trends in salary for designers of your experience. It can help with salary negotiation and indicate when it might be time to move on to another design firm.

This chapter includes information about setting up a business. To do so in Australia and New Zealand there are certain legal requirements to be met and failure to comply can have serious consequences for the business owner. The authors wish to point out that they are not legally trained and the information provided is to be used as a general indication of what is needed, and no more.

If you are intending to start your own business we strongly recommend that you seek proper legal and business advice from trained professionals.

DETERMINING YOUR HOURLY RATE

Before you can get paid you need to work out how much to charge. This is determined by your experience, what other designers are getting and the prevailing economic conditions. It should increase over time, but may need to dip now and then. To determine your rate, you need to do research: AGDA is a good place to start, as are your colleagues.

There are, in fact, two rates you need to work out. The first is the actual rate for designing, which will vary depending on whether you are doing conceptualisation or straight layout work. This is the **base rate** that you use to calculate the charge-out rate. The **charge-out rate** is the rate you use to calculate your quotes and should be about 3½ times your base rate. Why this figure? It represents one times the base rate for the actual design; plus one times the base rate for the **overheads** of the business; plus one times the base rate for profit; and, finally, a half times the base rate for small time over-runs and so that you don't have to itemise every single print, photocopy, or phone call you made for the job. If you do not allow for the costs of overheads and profit in your quotes then you will go out of business very quickly.

Your hourly rate should not include one-off purchases relating to a job such as photography, copywriting or fonts (even if you do them all yourself)—they should be treated separately.

THE CONTRACT

Contract law is a complex area, so beware. Contracts are legally binding for both parties. If a designer promises to have something completed by a certain date, in a certain form, and then does not fulfil that agreement, they could be breaking a contract and therefore be liable for damages.

Emails, receipts, order forms, letters and faxes, which are classed as examples of written materials, may all create an express contract between a designer and the client. An express contract clearly contains the terms the parties have agreed upon and can be achieved through documents, the spoken word or both. Avoid relying heavily on spoken agreements and confirm any spoken agreements in writing.

The **base rate** is the rate for actual design work (conceptualisation or layout). It is used to calculate the charge-out rate and need not be disclosed to the client.

The **charge-out rate** is rate that includes designing, overheads, profit, etc. It is 3½ times the base rate and is used to calculate the cost of design to the client.

DESIGN PROPOSAL, QUOTE AND INVOICE

The three main documents that form the basis of the contract between client and designer are the initial proposal, the quote and the invoice.

The design proposal

This is in fact the written expression of the design brief. It contains:

- a cover letter briefly introducing the proposal (and thanking the client contact for meeting with the designer—start building a positive relationship early by being polite)
- a brief outline of who you understand the client to be
- an outline of what you understand the needs of the client to be and what they hope to achieve with the design they are asking you to do
- an outline of the scope of work—that is, roughly what design work is involved in total
- a very rough indication of cost involved (this may also refer to the client's desired budget—you can ask what it is)
- an indication of how long it will take (don't forget to consider your other work commitments).

The purpose of the proposal is to make sure you and the client understand the job and have agreement on what is involved before you start designing. Don't be disappointed if the first version of the proposal is not completely right; for complex jobs the proposal may require several revisions before both sides agree. It is certainly a lot more efficient, and cheaper, to get the proposal right before you start working.

BUSINESS COMMUNICATIONS

Under Australian law, any piece of written communication that involves money and/or contractual arrangements must display an Australian Business Number (ABN). It is wise to incorporate this number into the design of your business stationery and email signature.

In some circumstances, invoices must also include the words 'Tax Invoice' as well as the ABN and these should appear at or near the top of the page.

It is vital to investigate the legal obligations of your particular business structure.

Overheads are the costs of running a business beyond the design work done for specific clients. It includes things like rent, insurance, phones, electricity and any non-design staff (accountants, for example).

→ Each designer has their own workspace in the the open plan studio for 3 Deep Design. This creates a sense of privacy within a communal environment.

3 DEEP DESIGN

QUOTE VERSUS ESTIMATE OF FEES AND CHARGES
Because of the fluid nature of the design process, and that during the progress of a job to completion there may be many changes to the brief, many design firms prefer to send an estimate of fees and charges instead of a quote, which is often perceived as being more fixed and unalterable. Apart from the name and title of the document, there is no difference in how you prepare them.

The quote

Once the proposal (and therefore, the brief) has been agreed on, you can prepare a quote. This provides accurate costings of the job including **bought-in services** such as printing, photography and copywriting.

The quote comprises:

- ❯ a cover letter pointing out any key points you want to make, especially in relation to the client's stated budget
- ❯ a reasonably detailed breakdown of costings—you might break down the design fees into concepts, layout and implementation, and then provide a separate cost for each of the bought-in services
- ❯ a clear expression of how many concepts and rounds of revisions are included in the fee
- ❯ a clear statement that changes to specifications (the brief) may change the costs and re-quoting may be required
- ❯ your **Terms and Conditions of Trade**.

Bought-in services

These are any services that a designer or design firm does not actually perform in-house. They may also include non-time based costs that are done in-house. Note, all bought-in services should have a **mark-up** attached to them of between 15 and 30 per cent.

Bought-in services are any services that a designer does not perform in-house, or any non-time-based in-house costs.

Terms and Conditions of Trade (T&Cs) are the conditions under which a designer trades, including payment terms and any confidentiality, copyright or contract issues.

Mark-up is a percentage above the amount a supplier charges a designer for bought-in services, which is then charged to the client to cover certain costs.

Mark-up

This is a percentage above the amount the supplier charges the designer for the product or service. The designer charges it (to the client) because:

- it covers the cost of briefing and managing the bought-in service
- the client is relying on the designer's good credit with that supplier, rather than setting up their own credit relationship with them
- the client may only pay weeks after the designer has paid the supplier, meaning a financial cost in terms of lost interest
- it acts as a kind of insurance against bad debt—if the client fails to pay, the designer still has to pay the supplier if the work was completed to the agreed specifications
- it is part of ensuring that a design business remains profitable.

Terms and Conditions of Trade (T&Cs)

The T&Cs document includes the conditions under which a designer trades, including:

- a statement of confidentiality—of the quote and the work to be done until completed
- payment terms, usually within 7, 14 or 30 days (and what will happen if the client does not pay on time, like charging interest and use of collection agencies)
- that a mark-up on bought-in services applies, and how much
- a statement about copyright
- a statement about re-use
- what has to happen if the project is to be terminated early (i.e, if the contract is broken)
- a statement relating to force majeure (i.e., what happens if a disaster occurs that is beyond the designer's control, such as a building fire destroying work).

The invoice

At the beginning of the project, a designer issues a quote to the client, which includes all the different components of the project. During the project, the client has been notified of any changes to the timing and cost of the work. This means that the client will not be surprised when the final invoice is sent.

To invoice, break a job into all the different components in the same way that they appeared in the quote. This ensures the client can clearly see that they are being invoiced for the work that they have agreed to. Include also:

- your payment terms
- your preferred payment method—cheque, direct deposit, credit card, etc.

Depending on the size of the job you may, in fact issue more than one invoice—for large or long-running jobs. The contract only terminates when the very last invoice has been paid in full.

↑ AGDA often holds seminars
inviting guest speakers to educate
and inspire their members, not
only on design-related topics but
also on business matters.

Australian Graphic Design Association (AGDA)

www.agda.com.au

The Australian Graphic Design Association (AGDA) is a national organisation for professional graphic designers. When first established in 1988, AGDA's main aim was to ensure that a design dialogue was developed that would improve design thinking and practice between designers across seven states and territories in Australia. More than twenty years later, AGDA's charter to 'Advance your design future' continues to serve that vision for members of the design industry, while embracing the values of integrity, unity, visibility, respect and creativity.

AGDA operates through a National Council and seven State and Territory Chapters and is managed by a National Office and the AGDA Executive Director, Rita Siow.

Rita Siow explains the role of AGDA for designers in Australia: 'AGDA's goal is the establishment of fair and productive working relationships between graphic designers and their clients. We do this by providing designers with the tools and information to take control of their professional lives. We also work on increasing awareness of the value and importance of graphic design in business, education and culture through an interrelated program of state, national and international activities many of which promote and advocate to the wider public, corporate and government communities.'

However, AGDA is not only an organisation for professionals. They also focus on design students by stationing members on education and training advisory boards and providing guest lecturers to schools and tertiary institutions, as well as supporting students and recent graduates by offering networking opportunities, research scholarships and industry mentorships. A majority of AGDA events are also offered to students free of charge or at heavily discounted rates.

'The annual AGDA mentor programs match students and professional designers, whilst the AGDA-Gordon Andrews Scholarship is a cash stipend awarded yearly to the successful student applicant interested in gaining specialised knowledge, skills or experience in graphic design through a research study,' says Rita.

'AGDA recognises the best students' work at the graduate shows, and also in the AGDA Student Awards category of the AGDA Biennial Awards program, whereby outstanding creative generated by design institutions, staff and students in their

FAR LEFT | South Australian AGDA exhibition, in collaboration with Ikea 'SALA: Find out what happened to Benjamin!'
LEFT | Guest speaker at an AGDA event.

RIGHT | AGDA exhibition, National Biennial Awards, New York.
BELOW | Mark Gowing 'Labelled' series, winner of the 2010 AGDA Pinnacle Award for poster design.
BOTTOM | AGDA's education policy publication, created to better inform educational institutions, policy makers and students of AGDA's position and ethos on graphic design training and education in Australia.

  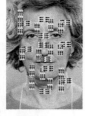 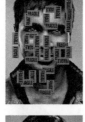

educational projects are acknowledged at the industry's premier event.'

When asked how belonging to AGDA helps the graphic design professional, Rita had the following to say: 'AGDA offers members the opportunity to grow their design expertise by providing information-rich seminars, workshops, conferences and showcasing best practice, innovation and sustainability via the AGDA Awards competition and exhibition program.

'Staying connected and engaged is a huge benefit. AGDA maintains a great website with a "find a designer" directory, professional practice notes and weekly updates; produces various publications including Awards compendiums and a quarterly members' newsletter, *Agenda*; and develops special member discount and partner programs with allied suppliers and organisations.

'AGDA conducts the largest industry salary survey, which is made available free to members—an invaluable tool when negotiating or setting wages.

'Professional associations can be an amazing resource, but as the saying goes, "you get out what you put in". Those who are willing to come along to events, get involved and make connections often get the most out of their professional associations. AGDA is the sum of its parts and we encourage you to get involved today!'

↓ Communal workstations like this one at Studio Round can aid communication and nurture group creativity.

LEGAL ADVICE
For those wanting to start out on their own, an option for legal advice is the Arts Law Centre of Australia (www.artslaw.com.au). They specialise in the law of the arts industry, which design is at the edge of, and the initial few consultations are usually free.

STUDIO ROUND

SETTING UP A BUSINESS IN AUSTRALIA

Running a design business, like any other business, requires well-considered decisions to ensure that regulations and legislation are followed and that a sustainable business is created.

AVOIDING FAILURE

The harsh reality is that more than three quarters of all new businesses in Australia fail within the first five years of operation. They fail for three main reasons: insufficient capital (money), disputes between the business owners and poor management.

Capital

It is important to have enough start-up capital. Starting a business of any sort needs money, and often there are quite a few initial costs that have to be paid for before you can start earning. It can take up to a year for a business to be earning enough to cover its running costs and wages. Allow for this—try to estimate how much you will need based on an assumption that you will earn nothing for a year (of course you will earn something; but this approach will give you some leeway). Do not assume you can get a bank loan, as banks need proof of successful trading over several years before they will give a business a loan.

Disputes

Going into business with a partner requires a great deal of trust, honesty and communication. The relationship is as intense as a marriage (in fact it is a kind of financial marriage); however, stress over money can have a corrosive effect on any relationship. In the excitement of starting a business with a friend, it is still necessary to sit down and actually write a business contract. This contract is called a **Heads of Agreement**.

Management

It is important to manage employees (if you have them), clients and the finances of a business properly. Do not be afraid to admit weaknesses in any of these areas. You may need to employ someone to manage these areas—a bookkeeper for day-to-day finances, an account services specialist for clients, for example—or learn the skills yourself.

It may cost a bit but getting good advice from lawyers and accountants is also a very good way to avoid failure. Try to find specialists who already have some design clients, as every industry has its own quirks requiring specialist knowledge.

THE BUSINESS PLAN

A critical step in setting up a business is forming the business plan. This plan should be reasonably detailed but flexible enough to adapt to changing circumstances. It should be revisited and revised every year. The business plan should include:

- A TWO- TO THREE-YEAR PLAN Where do you want the business to be in two to three years? Be as detailed as you can.
- A FIVE-YEAR PLAN Where do you want the business to be in five years? This can be less detailed.
- A LONG-TERM PLAN What is the ultimate goal of your business? This can be a very general indication.

A **Heads of Agreement** is a contract between the owners of a business. It outlines the differing roles and responsibilities of each owner; the financial stakes of each owner; what happens should more capital be needed; and, most importantly, what happens if the business fails, if the owners have a disagreement, or if one or more owners want to leave the business.

As you develop your business plan, consider the following:

1. BUSINESS STRATEGY PLAN Strategic growth of business, marketing direction, cash flow budgeting (an ongoing process evolving as business develops).

2. INSURANCE COVER This is a vital part of disaster-proofing a business. You can insure both equipment and income.

3. ACCOUNTING SOFTWARE/MANAGEMENT TOOLS These are vital for tax obligations and essential for proper job and workflow management. Having these tools in place will make items 4–6 much easier to achieve.

4. PROCEDURES AND SYSTEMS Efficient office management, time management, invoicing and effective control over office and administrative operations.

5. PROPOSAL LETTER/QUOTES Proposal letters and quotes are a vital part of your business that must be developed with care. See the section on 'Design proposal, quote and invoice', above.

6. BUDGETING PROCESS Establish and maintain an effective budgeting process. Keep track of the accuracy of your process by recording actual time spent on projects, and then cross-checking actual times with budgeted times. Keep track of fee structures and timing of instalments, and match revenue to actual time spent at each stage.

7. KEY PERFORMANCE INDICATORS (KPIS) AND BENCHMARKS Use KPIs and benchmarks for ongoing analysis. This enables you to check quickly on a weekly, fortnightly and monthly basis the health of the company before problems arise and to predict future viability.

8. EMPLOYMENT LETTERS You will need to get legal advice to draft employment contracts for any staff.

9. POLICIES ON DEVELOPMENT OF BUSINESS Develop policies that detail how you want to go about growing your business, including how much time needs to be devoted to it. Staff need to be kept aware of any policies relevant to them.

10. MARKETING PLAN A marketing plan will cover how to target niche markets, and what types of clients to attract/accept.

3 DEEP DESIGN

↑ Design studios are often highly creative environments filled with artistic inspiration, as illustrated here with 3 Deep Design's life-sized horse lamp by Moooi.

11. **QUESTION YOURSELF** Consider the following: Why am I here? What am I trying to achieve on personal, business and financial levels? Do I want business to grow?

12. **PROJECTIONS** Consider items 1, 10 and 11. Cover these objectives by projecting staff, marketing and financial requirements.

13. **REVISIT KEY SYSTEMS REGULARLY** Look for weaknesses, quoting, time recording, billing, marketing, expense approval, recruitment/payroll. Reporting systems need to be good enough to provide KPIs.

14. **DEVELOP A PLAN B** You will need a plan B, to counter the failure of any part of your business. This should include insurance, and a well-financed and documented succession plan.

15. **STRUCTURE** Are your current operating and investing structures appropriate on tax, risk and wealth-creation levels? Protect personal assets from business error. The next section will cover this in more detail.

↑ Graphic design professionals can keep in touch with the latest developments in Australian graphic design by attending industry events such as Top 7×7—Future Focus, a lecture offered as part of the Design Institute of Australia's iconic Top 10×10 series. At this event, speakers from seven different areas of graphic design presented their top seven future industry trends and predictions.

designer **LANDOR ASSOCIATES**

BUSINESS STRUCTURES

If you decide to set up a design studio, or even if you intend to work as a freelancer, you will need to understand business structures. Business structures include sole trader businesses, partnerships and companies.

A **sole trader** is usually an individual carrying on a business on their own. Sole trader businesses can still employ staff, but the owner/sole trader is responsible for all debts incurred by the business. **Partnerships** can be as many as 200 people (large law firms and accountants) or as few as two people. Partners are jointly responsible for all debts. If one partner has debts in the name of the business, and can't pay them, the other partner will be jointly liable. It costs very little to register a partnership or a sole trader, but in both cases owners have liability for all debts.

Companies, on the other hand, cost much more to set up but have the benefit of being a separate entity to the owner. Table 9.1 lists the advantages and disadvantages of the three business structures.

TABLE 9.1 **BUSINESS STRUCTURES**

Business structure	Advantages	Disadvantages
Sole trader	Formation is simple	Management problems
	Trader retains control	Limited expertise
	Trader retains all profits	Limited capital
	Tax benefits with small profits	Unlimited liability
	Dissolution is simple	Limited existence
		Tax problems with large profits
Partnership	Ease of formation	Unlimited liability
	Diversity of management	Limits on size/expansion
	Flexibility in business	Limits on capital
	Sharing profits and losses	Liability for actions of partners acting within authority
		No separate existence
Company	Separate legal entity	High establishment costs
	May conduct business in own name	High compliance costs
	May hold property in own name	Loss of control/takeover threat
	Limited liability	
	Fundraising capacity	
	Taxation advantages	

BASED ON BARRON, M L 2009, *FUNDAMENTALS OF BUSINESS LAW*, 6TH EDN, MCGRAW-HILL AUSTRALIA, SYDNEY, PP. 112, 114, 125.

A **sole trader** is an individual carrying on a business on their own.

A **partnership** is a business of between two and 200 people where each partner is jointly responsible for all debts.

A **company** is a business that is legally recognised as a separate entity from its owners.

EM&JON DESIGN

REGISTERING YOUR BUSINESS

Setting up a business to sell your graphic design services requires you to not only learn how to deal with clients and understand the complexities of running a design studio, but also to learn what legislation is applicable. Regulatory compliance issues on starting a business include compulsory registrations, accurate record keeping, business licences and local government approvals.

Core areas of legislation applicable to most businesses include:

- ❯ civil liability and other mandatory insurances: particularly relevant if someone comes onto your property and injures themselves (you are at risk)
- ❯ revenue, including income tax, superannuation and state taxes
- ❯ employment, antidiscrimination and privacy
- ❯ fair trading, Trade Practices Acts and consumer protection
- ❯ contract law.

We recommend that all graphic designers aiming to set up a design practice read the ACCC publication *Small business guide to trade practices compliance programs.*

↑ Not all design studios are large or employ many designers. For example this is the small but efficient studio of Em&Jon Design, the designers of this book.

Business name

Most businesses must register their business names in every state and territory in which they intend to operate. *The Business Names Act 1962* is legislation that has been written to ensure that customers know who runs and owns the business that they are dealing with, and to protect the public from being misled by the use of similar business names. The Australian Securities & Investments Commission (ASIC) keeps the details of all current company and business names on the National Names Index.

Businesses do not have to register their business name if the business operates under the surname and first name of the owner. In some states, such as New South Wales, you do not have to register and display a business name if your business trades only via the internet. Before spending money on business cards, brochures or stationery, check that your business name does not infringe on any trademarks. The owner of a trademark has exclusive use and can legally enforce their ownership.

The business name must be displayed at each place where the business is carried out. The owner of the business name must notify the consumer affairs agency of any changes in ownership and change of address.

Basic business tax registrations: the ABN, the TFN and the GST

A **tax file number (TFN)** is a unique once only identification for each taxpayer. It is a confidential tax identification number. If you operate as a sole trader, you may use your own TFN for both business and personal Australian Tax Office dealings. If you plan to have a partnership, you must apply for a separate TFN. A new TFN must be applied for and issued if the partnership membership changes. A company must apply for a separate TFN.

Whether you operate as a sole trader, partnership or company, you need to apply for an **Australian Business Number (ABN)**, which is essential to register for GST purposes. The Australian Business Register is a central collection system for identity information about businesses with an ABN. The ABN must be displayed on all business documents, particularly invoices; otherwise other businesses must withhold 46.5 per cent from any payment owed to you or your business.

The **goods and services tax (GST)** is a broad tax of 10 per cent applied to most goods and services within Australia. If you plan to have annual sales of $75 000 or more then you must register for GST (it costs nothing to register and you can register even if your annual sales are below the stated threshold). You cannot charge GST if you are not registered. The GST regulations require business owners to add an additional 10 per cent to the cost of their products or services. The collected GST is returned to government approximately every three months, depending on the business's annual revenue.

If you are registered for GST, you must include the GST amount in quotes, estimates of fees and invoices. If you don't, clients will not have to pay you GST, but you will still have to pay GST to the government.

Council approval

Local councils can determine how a business is conducted in its jurisdiction. Zoning, planning and environmental controls are enforced by councils and may include the granting of development approvals for the use of premises. The council will consider whether the business complies with fire safety, health, building, factory and shop legislation.

A **tax file number (TFN)** is a unique identification number allocated to a taxpayer.

An **Australian Business Number (ABN)** is an identification number required to operate a business. Sole traders, partnerships and companies must all have an ABN.

The **goods and services tax (GST)** is a broad tax of 10 per cent applied to most goods and services within Australia.

THE DESIGN DIALOGUE

With the advent of desktop publishing, graphic design has become something that everyone thinks they can do. This has meant that good design is simultaneously more accessible and more hidden.

Design has become a term that most Australians in the twenty-first century understand. It has become accessible through amazing architecture, designer home wares, designer jeans and designer stationery. Everyone seems to be creating something designed! While the proliferation of design is a good thing, at the same time there are so many people 'designing' that many small and medium businesses have a lowered perception of the importance of good design.

However, as this book has hopefully illustrated, the difference between the use of a typeface, a colour, or a layout can change the way the customer looks at a product, picks up a magazine, or decides to trust a company. Well-considered, analysed and researched graphic design can really make a difference to a company. It is this analysis that drives graphic designers to question the ethics and motives of companies and to question the social impact of their practice.

The book entitled *How to be a Graphic Designer Without Losing Your Soul* by Adrian Shaughnessy (2005) captured many designer's imaginations. The author asked designers to stop and reflect on their design practice. Membership of the industry body, the Australian Graphic Design Association (AGDA), creates a number of opportunities each year to get together with other designers and share experiences. AGDA is active in each state, inviting national and international experts to speak to members on specific topics, and allows substantial membership discounts for students.

Many Australian-produced books and conferences now allow graphic designers the stimulus and opportunity to reflect. *Open Manifesto*, created and edited by Kevin Finn, approaches graphic designers from all over the world to submit their thoughts and words for publication. The annual Semi-permanent conference draws crowds of more than 2000 to hear designers, illustrators, animators and photographers discuss their passion for their craft. This continued dialogue is very important to maintain the integrity of what we do—inspiring Australian graphic design.

STUDIO ROUND

↑ Reference libraries are very important in most design studios and can take up quite a large amount of space, as seen here at Studio Round.

DESIGN BRIEF: CREATE A PROMOTIONAL PIECE

 Create a promotional pack to send to a design studio or agency.

Prepare a number of documents that showcase your work.
You will need:

- a multi-paged portfolio in both print and digital format (pdf), with matching business card
- a letter of introduction
- a CD-ROM or DVD depending on software formats (for interactive media) with a label and a website.

Note: The documents you create will contain your work, but the documents themselves are also your work. Give them all the attention that you think they need. You will be assessed by employers on the portfolio design as well as the content.

Choosing what to include

- Choose your strongest work, not your favourite work.
- Choose work that shows a variety of skill but is weighted towards the area of design you actually want to work in.
- If you have done some paid/commissioned work, include the strongest of these.
- Your final selection should showcase 10–15 pieces only.

Organising the work

Tell the story of each piece of work, by including a very short description of the project brief.

Tell the story of you the designer. Open with some strong pieces, then include pieces showing breadth of skill in the middle, and finish with the strongest pieces in your preferred area.

Tips for layout

Apply everything you have learnt about design to these documents to create strong, exciting and dynamic layouts.

Each document in the pack should be both part of a set, but individually tailored to the purpose and requirements of the varying formats.

Multi-page documents (both printed and electronic) work as both single pages and as a unified series. Consider how the individual pages look and how they work in relation to each other.

For the printed portfolio, you are not limited by things like screen sizes so give yourself space for your work to 'talk'; make it no smaller than A3. Avoid generic binding methods and plastic sleeves.

SUMMARY

Most, if not all, designers become designers because they want to earn a living doing something creative. Unfortunately, this process is not as simple as doing the study, hanging up their 'shingle', showing the portfolio around and waiting for the work and money to roll in.

Graphic design is a service industry that requires designers to work within a business context. They interact with clients on a business-to-business (as well as personal) level and they interact with other service providers in a similar manner. They need to understand how to manage their financial affairs as well as they manage their creative affairs. There are numerous reasons for this, starting with presenting an additional level of professionalism to clients, through to legal and tax obligations associated with running a business correctly, down to ensuring the designer gets the money they are owed for the work they have done.

KEY TERMS

REFERENCES / WEBSITES

Australian Competition & Consumer Commission (ACCC) 2006, *Small business guide to trade practices compliance programs*.

Barron, M L 2009, *Fundamentals of business law*, 6th edn, McGraw-Hill Education Australia, Sydney.

Baulch, L 2008, *Graphic designers and copyright: a practical guide*, Australian Copyright Council, Sydney.

Cole, S 2005, *Dialogue: relationships in graphic design*, V & A Publications, London.

Dabner, D 2004, *Graphic design school: the principles and practices of graphic design*, Thames and Hudson, London.

Finn, K 2008, *Open manifesto*, (www.openmanifesto.net)

Hara, K 2008, *Designing design*, Lars Müller Publishers, Switzerland.

Heller, S & Fernandes, T 2006, *Becoming a graphic designer: a guide to careers in design*, 3rd edn, John Wiley and Sons, Hoboken.

Mito Design 2006, *10% design portfolio*, Index book SL C, Barcelona.

Shaughnessy, A 2005, *How to be a graphic designer, without losing your soul*, Laurence King Publishing, London.

Shell, RL 2003, *Management of professionals*, 2nd edn, Marcel Dekker Inc, New York.

Australian Graphic Design Association (www.agda.com.au)

Australian Copyright Council (www.copyright.org.au)

Australian Securities & Investments Commission (www.asic.gov.au)

Arts Law Centre of Australia (www.artslaw.com.au)

'ADSHELL' the brand name of the advertising shells around bus and tram stops. A digital adshell is enabled to display digital content or allow user interactions.

DIGITAL DESIGN OUTCOME a design outcome delivered digitally, such as a website, video, animation, application, DVD or CD-ROM.

AESTHETIC the philosophical theory of what is beautiful and pleasing in appearance.

ANTHROPOMORPHISM the attribution of human characteristics or behaviour to a god, animal or object.

ASPECT RATIO to the horizontal size in relation to the vertical size, the most common being 4:3 (4 units across to 3 units down, and 16:9, 16 units across and 9 units down).

ASYMMETRICAL BALANCE typically off-centre and created with mismatched elements.

AUSTRALIAN BUSINESS NUMBER (ABN) an identification number required to operate a business. Sole traders, partnerships and companies must all apply for an ABN.

BARCODE a code for a product within the market that is individualised to include information on size, colour, dispenser type, brand and price.

BASE RATE the hourly rate for actual design work (conceptualisation or layout). It is used to calculate the charge-out rate and need not be disclosed to the client.

BASELINE an invisible line on which all the letters in a line of type sit.

BASELINE GRID an invisible grid that allows the baseline of type (lines of text) to line up from column to column and page to page.

BESPOKE an object that is made to order. The term is often used to describe unique, highly customised pieces that have a great deal of direction from the client. It can refer to 2-D or 3-D pieces.

BINDING required to gather pages into a book or booklet.

BLEED the area of an image that extends past the trim lines, so that there is no white space between an image and the edge of the page.

BLEED OFF THE PAGE when images, type or blocks of colour are printed right to the very edge of the page.

BODY COPY (or body text) the main portion of text in a document or design. It contains the information being communicated.

BOUGHT-IN SERVICES services that a designer does not perform in-house, or any non-time-based in-house costs.

BULK how thick a paper 'feels'.

CARD SORTING a simple technique where a group of users are guided to create categories for information listed on cards or notes.

CATEGORY DRIVERS the basic need states consumers use to guide their purchases. All products have a generic set of category drivers. For example, if your product is vitamin water, your category driver is health or healthy living.

CELLOGLAZE a thin plastic coating bonding to the surface of paper after printing. It is good at protecting the printed surface.

CENTRED TEXT a column of text that has all lines arranged around an imaginary line down the centre. Both left- and right-hand edges of the lines are uneven.

CHARACTER SET all the elements of a typeface, including letters, numerals, punctuation and all the other accents required for setting type.

CHARGE-OUT RATE the hourly rate that includes designing, overheads, profit, etc. It is 3½ times the base rate and is used to calculate the cost of design to the client.

CHOKES constricted inner edges of an area of ink.

COLD CALLING when a designer contacts an employer or client (after researching them) who doesn't know that designer and arranges an interview to show their work.

COLOUR MODEL an orderly system for creating a whole range of colours from a small set of primary colours.

COLOUR OF TYPE refers to the density of a typographic layout.

COLOUR SEPARATIONS the result of separating coloured artwork into single colours; this is necessary because printing operates with inks of fixed colour that are laid down one at a time. The colours of artwork are separated into up to six base colours.

COLOUR THEORY and forecasting relates to trends and factors that influence the choice of specific colours for mood, voice and the intention of a design. It applies specifically to fashion, but can also be applied to consumer behaviour.

COMPANY a business that is legally recognised as a separate entity from its owners.

CONTENT MANAGEMENT SYSTEM (CMS) a restricted-access part of a website that allows the content of the site to be updated without accessing the basic structure of the site.

CONVERT TO OUTLINES turning the typeface from an editable form into an image.

CROWD SOURCING when a client put a job on the internet (there are a number of dedicated sites) and allows anyone to submit a solution. The client then selects what they feel to be the best solution. The winning firm/designer gets to complete the job, the others go away hungry.

CULTURE the set of shared attitudes, values, goals and practices that characterise the society in which we live.

DEGRADE describes the way a website's design changes in different, usually older, web browsers.

DEMOGRAPHICS characteristics of a specific area of the population including age, gender and marital status.

DESIGN COLLATERAL all the components that make up the promotions for a company, product or service. This could include brochures, business cards, letterheads, fliers and advertisements.

DIE-CUTTING the use of a sharp-bladed die (cutting tool) to cut shaped holes in paper.

DISPLAY FACE a typeface designed for headings. They tend to be eye-catching and not necessarily suited for use at small point sizes.

DPI (dots per inch)—a measure of image resolution.

DYNAMIC SYMMETRY the relationship between positive and negative space, and form and counter form.

EASING IN the use of acceleration and deceleration to make motion appear more naturalistic.

EM a unit of type measurement that defines the proportion of the letter width and height in relation to the size of the current font. Originally, the unit came from the width of the capital 'M' in the typeface being used. Therefore, 1 em in a 16 point typeface is 16 points.

EMBELLISHMENTS the effects and processes that are not printed but can be applied to a printing job.

EMBOSSING a process of creating a raised surface in paper that matches parts of the printed artwork. If it intentionally does not match printed elements, it is called a blind emboss.

EQUITY the various qualities of a product or service and the total experience that is communicated to the customer adds equity (real value) to the company logo. This is often referred to as brand equity.

FINISHING any final steps of a printing job required to prepare it for delivery.

FLUSH (or **RANGED LEFT**), **RAGGED RIGHT** text is arranged in a column that has a neat left-hand edge and an uneven right-hand edge.

FLUSH (or **RANGED**) **RIGHT**, **RAGGED LEFT** text is arranged in a column that has a neat right-hand edge and an uneven left-hand edge.

FMCGS (fast-moving consumer goods) goods that sell quickly and at low cost. They are supplied in the retail environment to meet the daily demands of customers.

FOILING the application of thin, originally metal, foils onto printed artwork. It creates a totally opaque and often high-gloss surface effect.

FONT (or fount) the character set of a typeface at a particular point size. These days, 'font' is often also used to mean 'typeface'.

FOOTER the publication title, chapter head or other information that runs at the bottom of every page in a book.

FOUR-COLOUR PROCESS can be abbreviated to '4cp'. It is also commonly called CMYK, which stands for cyan, magenta, yellow, and K = black (originally black ink was just for keylines, which are the boundary lines separating coloured areas of printing on a printed page).

FREE PITCH when a client approaches a number of design firms and asks them to provide detailed solutions to a brief. The client then selects what they feel to be the best solution. The winning firm/designer gets to complete the job, the others go away hungry.

FREELANCE WORK involves working for different companies at different times rather than being permanently employed by one company.

FRENCH LID an extended edge beyond the base of the box to increase the surface area of the packaging.

GAMUT a subset of colours that can be accurately represented in a given circumstance, such as within a given colour space or by a certain output device.

GOODS AND SERVICES TAX (GST) a broad tax of 10 per cent applied to most goods and services within Australia.

GUTTER the space between columns of text or images.

HALFTONE SCREENS applied in areas where the ink has been printed as a series of fine dots, creating shades of tone.

HEADER the publication title, chapter head or other information that runs at the top of every page of a book.

HEADING a line of type in a larger font that introduces a body of text, for example a headline in a newspaper, or a chapter title in a book.

HEADS OF AGREEMENT a contract between the owners of a business. It outlines the differing roles and responsibilities of each owner; the financial stakes of each owner; what happens should more capital be needed; and, most importantly, what happens if the business fails, if the owners have a disagreement, or if one or more owners want to leave the business.

HUE another word for colour.

IDEATION the process of generating ideas.

HEADER TAGS there are six header tags in html that define the importance of the header text, from <h1>, being the most important, down to <h6>.

INNER PACKING refers to the materials or parts used in supporting, positioning, or cushioning an item.

INTANGIBLE less defined, or immeasurable. Intangible qualities can be combined to give a fuller understanding of that which is being designed or examined.

INTERACTIVE DIGITAL MEDIA electronic media in which the user participates. Examples include websites, interactive television, social media and advertising kiosks.

INTERLACED a field-based video display, where alternate lines form one sequence that is followed by the other lines in a second sequence.

ITERATIVE DESIGN PROCESS involves repeating a set of instructions a set number of times or until a desired result is achieved.

JUSTIFIED TEXT is arranged in a column that has all lines of equal length.

KERNING a method used to add space between letters to give a visually equal space between them.

KEYLINES lines used to indicate placement of images as well as special printing requirements, e.g. die lines and fold marks. They generally do not print.

KIOSK a computer terminal designed to retrieve specific information.

LASER CUTTING the use of a laser to cut shaped holes in paper.

LAYOUT the general appearance of the design of a printed or digital page. It covers the management of form and space that creates the relationship between images and text.

LEADING the space between lines of type.

LOGO a design or symbol that forms the visual focus for a company's corporate identity. Most commonly a logo is either symbolic (using shapes, figures or abstract forms) or type based, in which case it is referred to as logotype or wordmark.

LOWER CASE (little letters, for example 'a', 'b', 'c'), also known as minuscules, are the letter shapes based originally on handwriting. The name comes from the positioning of the trays of metal type when hand-setting type.

MARGIN the space with no text around an image, a column of text or the edge of the page.

MARKET SEGMENT a group within the broader market that has similar wants and needs, or similar behaviour towards products and services.

MARK-UP a percentage above the amount a supplier charges a designer for bought-in services, which is then charged to the client to cover certain costs.

MASTHEAD the title of a newspaper, magazine or website, located at the top of the front page or in the top section of a website.

MEDIA PLATFORMS examples of media platforms include print, screen interactive, social media, games, apps, web, advertising, radio and TV.

MOCK-UP a print- or screen-based 'rough' version of a proposed design, used when seeking approval for production.

MONTAGE the process and result of making a composite image by collating and joining a number of other images either digitally or by hand.

MOOD BOARDS may consist of images, text and samples of objects. Designers and others use mood boards to develop their design concepts and to communicate to other members of the design team.

MOTION CAPTURE the capture of motion data from a subject that is then applied to 3-D models.

MOTION TRACKING the ability to track a user's motion with a camera.

MOVEABLE TYPE individual letters within a language able to be combined to form words and sentences to be printed.

MULTIMEDIA a combination of different media (often including digital and interactive media) and can include video, still images, audio and text.

NEGATIVE SPACE the form created by the space between and around other shapes

NETBOOK a small, low-powered laptop used for web browsing and email.

NICHE MARKET the smaller market on which a specific product with defined product features is focusing; e.g. the sandal market is a niche within the shoe market.

OFFSET PRINTING (or offset lithography) a printing method in which ink is transferred from a plate to a smooth rubber 'blanket' roller that transfers the image to paperboard.

ORPHAN the opening line of a paragraph that is separated from the rest of the paragraph at the bottom of the previous page.

OVERHEADS the costs of running a business beyond the design work done for specific clients. It includes things like rent, insurance, phones, electricity and any non-design staff (accountants, for example).

PAPER TYPES the two main types are coated, which has a chalk coating and can be gloss (shiny), satin (semi-shiny) or matt (dull); and uncoated, which has a dull surface.

PAPERBOARD (or cardboard) a material made from laminated layers of paper in sheets of 12 points or more.

PARTNERSHIP a business of between two and 200 people where each partner is jointly responsible for all debts.

PATENT a legal means of protecting a unique product, shape or process from use by anyone else.

PDA (personal digital assistant) handheld devices used to view digital content, e.g. iPads, and smartphones such as BlackBerries and iPhones.

PERSPECTIVE a person's particular attitude and point of view.

PHOTO-ETHNOGRAPHIC STUDIES the scientific description of individual cultures, in this case through photography.

PIXELS the units used to measure the resolution of a computer display.

POINT SIZE the measure of the size of type. There are approximately 72 points to the inch (2.5cm).

PRE-PRESS refers to the work required to prepare for printing client-approved artwork. It includes final artwork preparation, checking, proofing and printing plates.

PRIMARY RESEARCH original research undertaken by an organisation or individual.

PRINT AREA the area of a page that is within the margins. Print area is usually defined in books and magazines so that pages retain consistency throughout the publication.

PRODUSER a non-professional producer/end user who creates their own design, such as a mash-up animation for YouTube or social media.

PROGRESSIVE VIDEO DISPLAY frame-based instead of field-based.

PROJECT SCOPE the work that needs to be accomplished to deliver a product, service or result with the specified features and functions.

PROTOTYPE a 3-D, 'close-to-finished' version of a proposed design for research or user testing.

PUBLICATION a magazine, newspaper, catalogue, brochure or book. Typically, a publication is a multi-page document that is offset printed and bound.

REFERRAL when an employer or client is told about a designer by a third party and approaches them directly. This is also known as 'word-of-mouth'.

REGISTRATION the process by which the inks are printed in the right place in relation to each other. When this occurs, they are said to be in register. When they are not in the right place, they are out of register.

RIP (raster image processor) the software that converts electronic artwork into printable files suitable for output onto printing plates.

SANS SERIF FACE a typeface without serifs. These typefaces tend to have low contrast between horizontal and vertical strokes.

SCREEN ANGLE the method by which the orientation of the dots in halftone screens is varied to ensure colour fidelity of the separations in multicolour printing.

SCRIPTING the process of writing a script.

SECONDARY RESEARCH the collection and review of existing data or findings from sources such as magazines, newspapers, journals, the internet, podcasts, radio or television.

SERIF FACE a typeface with serifs, which are small extensions to the sides of the letterforms.

SHADES created by adding various amounts of black to any colour.

SHARE WIDGET a user interface element that allows users to share content on various social media websites.

SHOWTHROUGH when something printed on one side of the paper shows through to the other side.

SITE MAP a visual representation of the navigational links within a website.

SLUG an area that is printed but does not appear on the final document as it is outside the trim area. It is used to send instructions to the printer and contains file names, printer's colour bars, and trim and register marks.

SOLE TRADER an individual carrying on a business on their own.

SOLID INK ink that has been printed in a continuous even layer of 100 per cent strength.

SPOT COLOUR ink that is used in offset printing to produce a solid non-CMYK colour using one plate.

SPREADS outer edges of an area of ink that have been enlarged by a tiny amount.

STAKEHOLDERS all the people (including groups, organisations and shareholders) who affect or can be affected by the design.

STORYBOARD a series of illustrations or images created to demonstrate motion graphics.

STYLE SHEET (digital) a set of rules that define the presentation of a website.

STYLE SHEET (print) defines a consistent approach to the size, font, spacing and colour of different type within a document. Style sheets can be set up in most publishing software programs and are a great timesaver when changes need to be made across a large document.

SYMMETRICAL BALANCE a mirror image balance, with the same or very similar parts facing each other on either side of an axis.

TANGIBLE finite, quantifiable and measurable.

TAX FILE NUMBER (TFN) a unique identification number allocated to a taxpayer.

TERMS AND CONDITIONS OF TRADE (T&CS) the conditions under which a designer trades, including payment terms and any confidentiality, copyright or contract issues.

TEXT BLOCK a shape created in a software program to hold text, which can carry over multiple pages or sections of a publication.

TEXT FONT/FACE a typeface designed specifically for typesetting body text. Letterforms are usually clear, distinct and optimised for reading at small point sizes.

THEME can be used to determine symbolic relationships, the premise of a story or the use of a visual metaphor.

TICKERS originally electronic machines that printed data onto strips of paper. The most common use was for news or stock market reports. These days, tickers appear on television screens as well as websites.

TIME-BASED MEDIUM a medium such as film, TV or video that relies on time to communicate its meaning.

TINTS created by adding various amounts of white to any colour.

TONE the particular quality of brightness or depth of a tint or shade of a colour.

TOOTH how rough a paper feels.

TOUCHPOINTS what the consumer visually identifies with the product.

TRAPPING the use of spreads and chokes to aid registration.

TREND FORECASTING the concept of collecting information and attempting to spot a pattern, or trend, in the information. This is often used in fashion to assist in creating new looks many seasons in advance.

TRIANGULATION the cross-examination of a particular subject using two or more research methods.

TRIM LINES (or crop marks) lines or marks that indicate to the printer where the edge of a page should be trimmed.

TRIM SIZE the final size of a publication. It should be communicated to the designer as part of initial specifications.

TRIMMING the process of cutting a printed sheet to a smaller size, including the final size required by the client.

TVC stands for television commercial.

TWEENING in animation, the creation of 'in between' drawings that capture the stages between one key pose and the next.

TYPE or **TYPEFACE** refers to a particular design of the letterforms of a character set.

TYPEFACE FAMILY (also known as a font family) a group of a number of variants of a typeface. Variants include different type styles (roman, italic, thin to heavy), type weights (light to dark) and type width (condensed to extended).

UNSATURATED COLOURS dull, muted colours.

UPPER CASE (capital letters, for example 'A', 'B', 'C'), also known as majuscules, are the letter shapes based originally on stone carving.

VARNISH a clear liquid that can be applied to printing for effect or to stabilise the printed surface. If it is printed at the same time as the ink it is called a wet-trap varnish; if printed in a separate pass on dry ink it is a dry-trap varnish. A thick high-gloss version that dries under UV lights is called a UV varnish.

VISUAL ANTHROPOLOGY a subfield of cultural anthropology. It is the study of visual representation, which includes performance, museums, art and mass media.

WAYFINDING systems that direct people or help them navigate space, either within structures, along streets or through a complex of buildings.

WEB ANALYTICS the measurement of number of hits for a website, traffic through web pages, user habits or web locations.

WEB BROWSER (or internet browser) an application that can retrieve and present information on the world wide web.

WEIGHT the heaviness of a paper due to the amount of fibre and/or coating it has.

WHITE SPACE the space on a page containing no images or text. It provides a counterpoint to the information-rich portions of a page.

WIDGET a component of a user interface that operates in a particular way.

WIDOW a short line at the end of a paragraph.

WIREFRAME an outline of a website's layout.

INDEX